WASHOE COUNTY LIBRARY

3 1235 03781 7801

P9-AFA-349

GJELINA

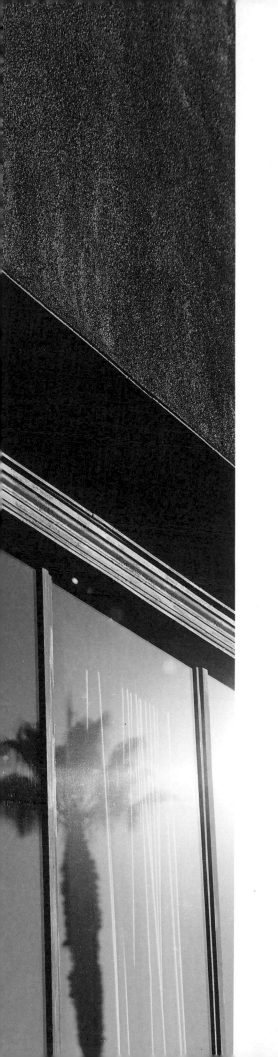

GJELINA
COOKING FROM
VENICE, CALIFORNIA

Travis Lett

Photographs by
Michael Graydon and Nikole Herriott

CHRONICLE BOOKS
SAN FRANCISCO

Text copyright © 2015 by Travis Lett.
Photographs copyright © 2015 by Michael Graydon
and Nikole Herriott.

All rights reserved. No part of this book may be
reproduced in any form without written permission
from the publisher.

Library of Congress Cataloging-in-Publication Data
available.

ISBN 978-1-4521-2809-2

Manufactured in China

Designed by Alice Chau

Prop styling by Amy Wilson
Food styling by Judith Babis, Travis Lett, and
Nikole Herriott

Chronicle books and gifts are available at
special quantity discounts to corporations,
professional associations, literacy programs,
and other organizations. For details and
discount information, please contact our
premiums department at corporatesales@
chroniclebooks.com or at 1-800-759-0190.

10 9 8 7 6 5 4

Chronicle Books LLC
680 Second Street
San Francisco, California 94107
www.chroniclebooks.com

IN MEMORIAM
LYLA LOUISE LETT
JUNE 25, 1942–MARCH 27, 2010

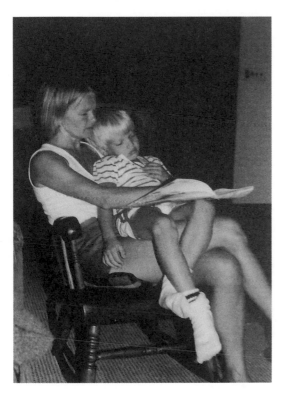

My mother represented all that is good in this world. A constant source of positivity and encouragement, she was the hardest-working, most-dedicated mother I have ever known. Among other acts, she made nutrition, environmentalism, animal activism, and sustainability her life's work and instilled a high value of them in me early on. Common colds were treated with umeboshi plum and bancha tea in our house, not Sudafed. Right or wrong, the idea of health and what we ate were not conversations that were mutually exclusive, so naturally I grew up looking at food as medicine and diet being an overall statement of health and a person's belief system. People thought my mother was out of her mind for driving ninety minutes to the closest farmers' market in western New Jersey. Brown rice went into the pressure cooker and onto the stove early in the day to be ready for dinner, and seasonal vegetable–based cooking was all I knew. I can still hear the sound of the stove clicking on as she started working on the night's fare, only moments after coming through the door from her first-grade teaching gig at the local public school. My gratitude for the love and wisdom she imparted is immeasurable.

CONTENTS

CHAPTER THREE
PIZZAS & TOASTS 102

CHAPTER FOUR
VEGETABLES 134

CHAPTER FIVE
PASTA **194**

CHAPTER SIX
SOUPS, STEWS & GRAINS **220**

CHAPTER SEVEN
FISH **250**

CHAPTER EIGHT
MEAT 286

CHAPTER NINE
DESSERT 320

INDEX 346

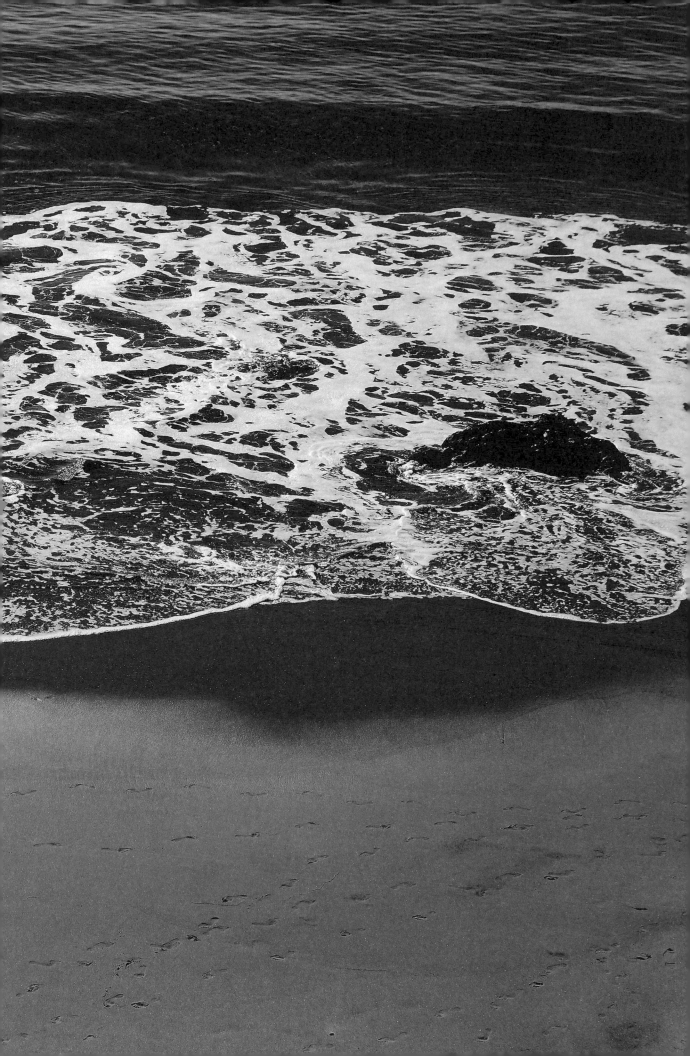

INTRODUCTION

The way we are eating is broadly changing. We now understand that our food system is a reflection of our culture, one that in some cases is in desperate need of continued progress. There is a large-scale rollback of some of the practices we have become comfortable with in the last couple decades. Cooks, teachers, health-care workers, political representatives, and even large organizations are accepting that their ideas of how people should be fed and how we should care for our lands are increasingly out of sync with the changing conversation. I believe that anyone digging in their heels to protect the old mentality is in for a surprise.

I am an optimist. I have to be. More than anything I feel grateful to be alive right now and to be participating in and witnessing a new revolution.

These recipes are a reflection of the changing dialogue about what we eat. People just want to know that someone cares at some point in the process of creating food, that someone is concerned with the big picture. It's not too much to ask.

My job is to participate in the conversation about food, and, whenever possible, manifest change in the decisions we make at Gjelina. More people at all levels of the food supply system are diligently working on improving it. Busy, thoughtful people want to know that someone is making this change a priority and demanding that it be the new standard of operation. This is still a work in progress, but the situation has improved remarkably since I first started working in kitchens.

From the beginning, we wanted Gjelina to feel like it had always been there. We wanted it to be the ideal neighborhood joint that you could rely on being open, somewhere you could count on the food, people, and environment having a certain honesty to them. I wanted Gjelina to have a real utility, to be of tangible substance in people's lives. I wanted the restaurant to offer something that didn't demand too much attention but at the same time had the ability to inspire if you paused and truly looked. It's an aspiration that we take seriously, but with a sense of humor at the same time. We have an eyes-wide-open, childlike curiosity, and a constant desire to learn and improve. We feel irreverant toward the world of critics and awards, but an absolute passion for the craft. We feel a sense of connection to a greater cause and dare to think we are making a difference, all the while with admiration for others who are furthering the cause. This is the chord I am always trying to strike and the work that has real meaning to me as a chef.

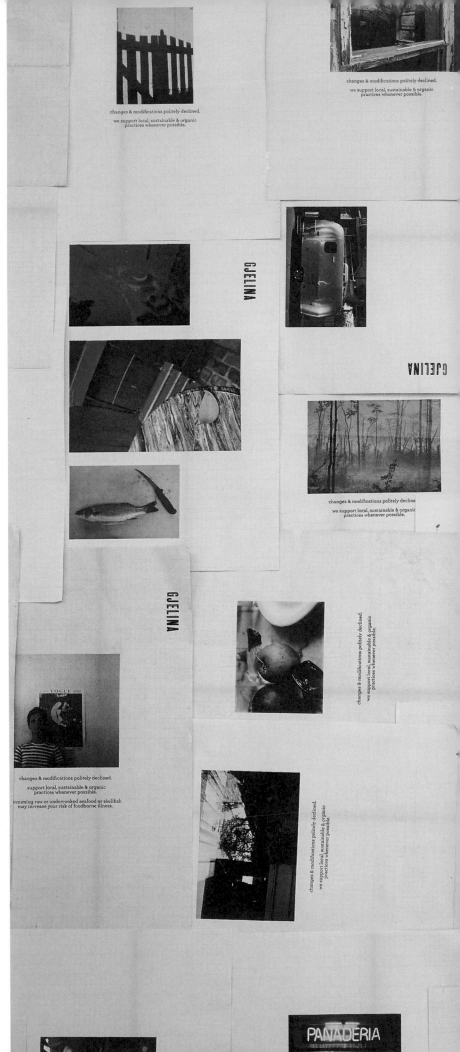

changes & modifications politely declined.

due to the current drought, water will be served upon request only

consuming raw or undercooked seafood or shellfish may increase your risk of foodborne illness.

changes & modifications politely declined.

due to the current drought, water will be served upon request only

consuming raw or undercooked seafood or shellfish may increase your risk of foodborne illness.

GJELINA

changes & modifications politely declined.

we support local, sustainable & organic practices whenever possible.

consuming raw or undercooked seafood or shellfish may increase your risk of foodborne illness.

practices whenever possible.

cha
w

GJELINA

changes & modifications politely declined. we support local, sustainable & organic practices whenever possible.

modifications politely declined.

rt local, sustainable & organic tices whenever possible.

GJELINA

The ingredients themselves are unique expressions of art—more so than anything I could manipulate them into. I am blown away every day by the sheer diversity and quality of the product I have access to in California. The ingredients reveal themselves slowly over time and require sensitivity to fully understand and get the most out of.

As a cook, I apply only the minimal amount of process so that those who eat my food can experience what is intrinsically nearly perfect. This is not to say this job is easy or unimportant. I give a considerable amount of thought to the task of cooking. Coercing of ingredients into distant versions of themselves is clever work, but more often than not it is subtractive. As a cook, I try not to stand in the way of what is beautiful and delicious. I try to capture the fleeting moment when well-cultivated ingredients are at their peak. I have always struggled to balance my desire to bring personality and to leave well enough alone.

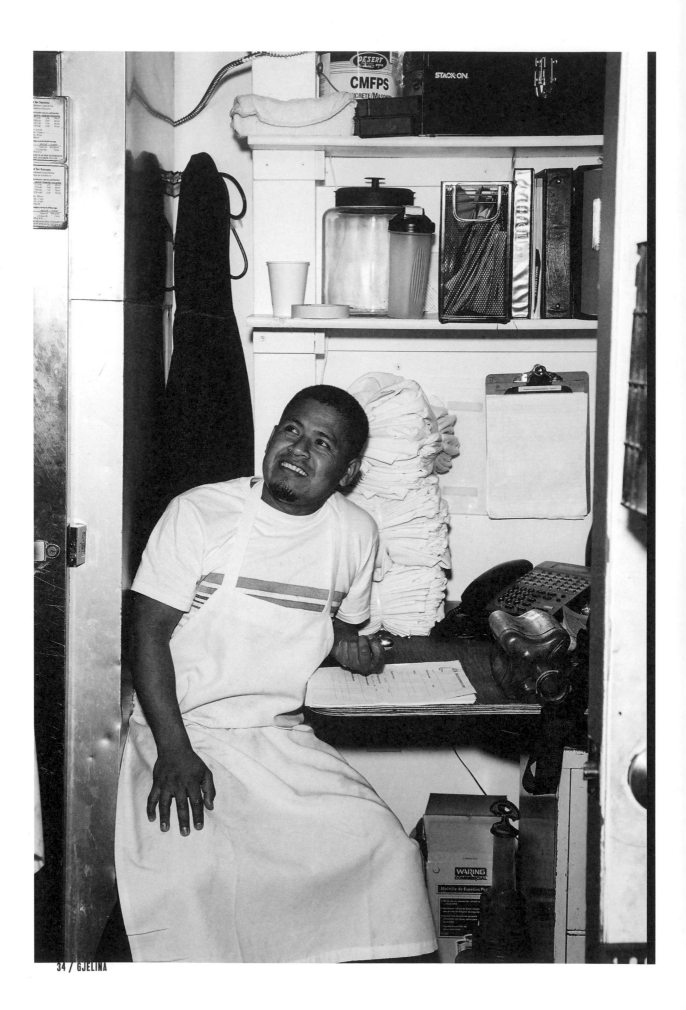

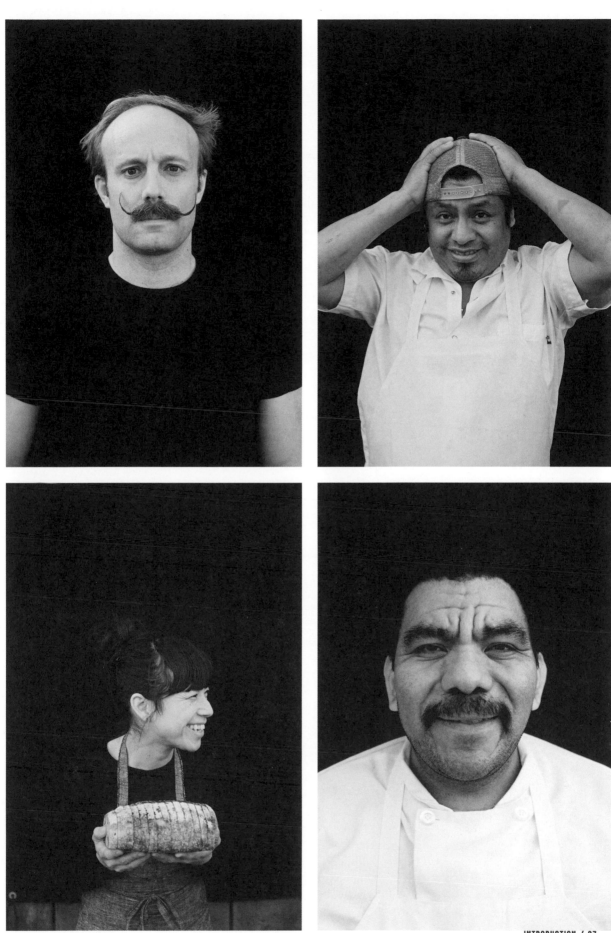

The real strength of Gjelina lies with the beautiful humans that I've been so fortunate to surround myself with from day one. The passion, integrity, sense of humor, creativity, and dedication to excellence permeates every level of the company. The sheer beauty of these folks blows me away every day, and drives me to continue pushing the work forward. We like to think that there is no particular job that is more or less important than another. Running the restaurant is a symphony of efforts that is staged, executed, broken down, and reset every day. By now there are a couple hundred of us, and it takes a high level of cooperation on a daily basis to pull it off, which I find extraordinary. I owe the success of the project to each and every one of them, past and present. I have tremendous gratitude to them for all the positive experiences they helped to create.

CHAPTER ONE
CONDIMENTS & PICKLES

At Gjelina we need to turn out a high volume of exciting food, without laboring too much over each plate. Having an arsenal of herb-laced, vinegar-spiked, spicy, sour, and sweet salsas, pestos, aiolis, and herb emulsions on hand makes it easy for us to add flavor to a dish quickly and without much fuss. We aim to keep the spirit of the food relaxed, not too showy, while giving the dish enough contrast to sustain interest. In my world, if food requires an explanation of either what it is or on how to eat it, it is, quite frankly, too complicated or clever.

We use the condiments in this chapter in a variety of ways, much like an artist building a collage, borrowing elements from one dish to make interesting new combinations in another. We might moisten a steak sandwich with some chimichurri at lunch and then, at dinner, use it to dress baby turnips roasted with their tops. I love salsa verde laced with anchovies on roasted sunchokes just as much as I love the briny herb-laced anchovy flavor on grilled beef. I use it to accent barely charred grilled squid, too.

As you prepare these recipes, you may find that you have leftovers. I suggest you get creative about how to use them. If nothing else, a lot of these condiments are delicious to eat smeared on grilled bread, in a sandwich, or to garnish fried eggs.

Vinegar and other acids will oxidize the herbs and dull their bright flavors, so add just before using. If you intend to serve a condiment with more than one meal, store whatever you're not using before you add the acidic ingredients and then add them when you are ready for the second meal.

Any of the herb emulsions made with olive oil will hold well for at least a couple of days and up to a week in the refrigerator. I like to store them in small glass jars, which I constantly reuse, but you can use anything that forms a good seal. Pour a little olive oil on top of the condiment to help preserve it before sealing the jar.

CALIFORNIA ZA'ATAR

MAKES 1¼ CUPS [250 G] / This blend of herbs submerged in olive oil makes a condiment that can be used to dip flatbread in, or to serve with grilled chicken, lamb, or roasted vegetables. Za'atar gives a sandwich a decidedly Middle Eastern vibe. The sumac is optional, but it adds a distinct tangy flavor.

¼ cup [30 g] sesame seeds
1 garlic clove
¼ cup [10 g] dried thyme
¼ cup [10 g] dried oregano

1 tsp finely grated lemon zest
2 tsp ground sumac (optional)
1 cup [240 ml] extra-virgin olive oil
Kosher salt

In a small, dry frying pan over medium heat, toast the sesame seeds just until fragrant and beginning to brown, about 3 minutes. Set aside and let cool.

Using a Microplane grater, grate the garlic into a small bowl and add the thyme, oregano, toasted sesame seeds, lemon zest, sumac (if using), and olive oil. Stir to combine and season with salt.

Store in an airtight container in the refrigerator for up to 1 week.

SOFFRITO

MAKES 2¼ CUPS [545 G] / Soffrito seems to be a broadly used and somewhat misleading concept for many. For us, it is simply a base of flavoring that we make ahead of time, so we can quickly build flavors in sautéed dishes that don't require long cooking times, such as Snap Peas & Tendrils with Prosciutto, Soffrito & Mint (page 141). The vegetables can vary but we generally just use celery, carrot, and onion, which allow us to add garlic or chiles later, when called for.

The idea is to cook the vegetables in olive oil until they become very soft and almost homogenous. The oil takes on the deep flavors of the vegetables as they give up their juices and begin to caramelize. Taste it as you cook it; depending on what flavor profile you prefer, you can vary the doneness of the soffrito accordingly. This blonde soffrito will darken when added to dishes before cooking is complete.

1 cup [240 ml] extra-virgin olive oil
1 yellow onion, finely chopped
1 celery rib, finely chopped

1 carrot, finely chopped
1 tsp kosher salt

In a medium frying pan over medium heat, warm the olive oil until hot but not smoking. Add the onion, celery, and carrot. Cook, stirring occasionally, until the onion and celery are translucent, 5 to 8 minutes. Taste and season with salt. Transfer to an airtight container, and make sure the vegetables are completely submerged in the oil.

Store in the refrigerator for up to 1 week.

CARROT TOP PISTOU

MAKES 1 CUP [200 G] / I'm not sure what qualifies this as a pistou, other than that we fancy the name, which is French for "pesto." This pistou is a logical and delicious accent for roasted carrots and lends a lively note to other root vegetables, too. I enjoy using the carrot tops when the greens are young and vibrant.

2 Tbsp pepitas (raw hulled pumpkin seeds)
¼ tsp coriander seeds
½ cup [20 g] young carrot tops
½ cup [15 g] fresh flat-leaf parsley leaves
½ shallot, minced
Zest of 1 orange

Zest of 1 lemon, plus juice of ½ lemon
2 garlic cloves
1 cup [240 ml] extra-virgin olive oil
Kosher salt
2 Tbsp freshly grated Pecorino Romano cheese
1 Tbsp balsamic vinegar

In a small, dry frying pan over medium heat, toast the pepitas just until fragrant and beginning to brown, 3 to 5 minutes. Remove from the pan and set aside.

In the same pan, toast the coriander seeds over medium heat just until fragrant and beginning to brown, 3 to 5 minutes. Remove from the heat and let cool before grinding to a fine powder in a spice grinder or with a mortar and pestle.

Fill a large bowl with cold water, and swish the carrot tops around to loosen the dirt. Repeat until the tops are clean. Remove them from the water and pat dry or spin them dry in a salad spinner. Chop the carrot tops and parsley finely.

In a medium bowl, combine the carrot tops and parsley with the shallot, orange zest, lemon zest, and toasted coriander seeds. Using a Microplane grater, grate the garlic into the mixture, and stir in the olive oil. Taste and season with salt. Allow to stand at room temperature for about 30 minutes.

Store in an airtight container in the refrigerator for up to 1 week. Add the Pecorino, toasted pepitas, vinegar, and lemon juice to the carrot-top mixture just before serving.

MINT-POMEGRANATE PESTO

MAKES 1½ CUPS [300 G] / This versatile pesto is good on all sorts of dishes. We like it on strongly flavored cuts of lamb, such as braised neck and shank; on duck; and even on chicken. It pairs well, too, with sweet-fleshed roasted fall vegetables, such as kabocha squash and parsnips. Pomegranate molasses can be found in Middle Eastern markets. It brings a little sweetness to the pesto and balances the acidity. Add the lime juice just before serving to keep it from discoloring the mint.

1 cup [30 g] chopped fresh mint
⅓ cup [55 g] pomegranate seeds
1 Tbsp minced shallot
1 cup [240 ml] extra-virgin olive oil
1 Tbsp pomegranate molasses

2 Tbsp freshly grated Parmesan cheese
1 tsp finely grated lime zest, plus 1 Tbsp fresh lime juice
1 garlic clove
Kosher salt

In a small bowl, combine the mint, pomegranate seeds, shallot, olive oil, pomegranate molasses, Parmesan, and lime zest. Using a Microplane grater, grate the garlic into the mixture, stir to combine, and season with salt. Allow to stand at room temperature for about 30 minutes.

Store in an airtight container in the refrigerator for up to 2 days. Bring to room temperature, and stir in the lime juice just before serving.

MINT-PISTACHIO PESTO

MAKES 1¾ CUPS [320 G] / A bit more delicate than the robust Mint-Pomegrante Pesto (above) this pesto nevertheless delivers layers of salt and citrus, and the distinctive flavor of pistachio. We use it to bring an extra hit of green flavor to spring vegetables, fish, and shellfish.

2 cups [60 g] chopped fresh mint leaves
1 cup [240 ml] extra-virgin olive oil
1 tsp finely grated lemon zest
1 Tbsp finely grated Pecorino Romano cheese

¼ cup [30 g] pistachios, toasted
1 small garlic clove
Kosher salt
Freshly ground black pepper

In a small bowl, combine the mint, olive oil, lemon zest, and Pecorino. Coarsely chop the pistachios and stir into the mixture. Using a Microplane grater, grate the garlic into the mixture. Stir to combine, and season with salt and pepper.

Store in a airtight container in the refrigerator for up to 1 week.

JALAPEÑO-GINGER-MINT PESTO

MAKES 1 CUP [200 G] / This spicy, mint-centric pesto is delicious on strong-flavored fish, such as sardines and mackerel.

3 jalapeño chiles, partially seeded and minced
1 cup [30 g] chopped fresh mint
2 Tbsp honey
1 cup [240 ml] extra-virgin olive oil

One ½-in [12-mm] piece fresh ginger
1 garlic clove
Kosher salt
Juice of 2 limes

In a small bowl, combine the jalapeños, mint, honey, and olive oil. Using a Microplane grater, grate the ginger and garlic into the mixture, stir to combine, and season with salt. Allow to stand at room temperature about 30 minutes.

Store in an airtight container in the refrigerator for up to 3 days. The pesto will discolor slightly, but it will still be delicious. Bring to room temperature, and stir in the lime juice just before serving.

BROCCOLI RABE PESTO

MAKES ABOUT 2 CUPS [420 G] / I love broccoli rabe and I'm always looking for excuses to use it. This pesto is delicious as a pasta sauce, and it makes an excellent garnish for grilled meats (especially lamb).

2 Tbsp pine nuts
½ bunch broccoli rabe, trimmed and roughly chopped
1⅓ cups [40 g] chopped fresh mint
1½ cups [360 ml] extra-virgin olive oil
2 cloves Garlic Confit (page 64), chopped

2 Tbsp freshly grated Pecorino Romano cheese
Pinch of crushed red pepper flakes
Kosher salt
Freshly ground black pepper

In a small, dry frying pan over medium heat, toast the pine nuts just until fragrant and beginning to brown, 3 to 5 minutes. Set aside and let cool.

In a food processor, combine the toasted pine nuts, broccoli rabe, mint, olive oil, garlic confit, Pecorino, and red pepper flakes. Process to make a coarse-textured but well-combined sauce (you should be able to see little pieces of pine nuts and broccoli rabe) and season with salt and pepper.

Store in an airtight container in the refrigerator for up to 3 days.

CHARMOULA

MAKES 1¼ CUPS [260 G] / This Moroccan-inspired condiment has been widely interpreted. Our version is more of a spiced cilantro pesto. It's great on whole grilled fish, and we dollop it into soups and stews as well.

1 tsp coriander seeds
½ tsp cumin seeds
1½ cups [45 g] chopped fresh cilantro
½ cup [15 g] chopped fresh flat-leaf parsley
½ Preserved Lemon (page 73), rind only, chopped
1 tsp smoked paprika
Pinch of crushed red pepper flakes

¾ cup [180 ml] extra-virgin olive oil
1 tsp honey
1 garlic clove
Kosher salt
Freshly ground black pepper
2 Tbsp white wine vinegar

In a small, dry frying pan over medium heat, toast the coriander seeds and cumin seeds just until fragrant and beginning to brown, about 3 minutes. Remove from the heat and let cool before grinding to a powder in a spice grinder or with a mortar and pestle.

In a medium bowl, combine the toasted and ground coriander and cumin with the cilantro, parsley, preserved lemon, paprika, red pepper flakes, olive oil, and honey. Using a Microplane grater, grate the garlic into the mixture, stir to combine, and season with salt and pepper. Allow to stand at room temperature for about 20 minutes.

Store in an airtight container in the refrigerator for up to 2 days. Bring to room temperature, and stir in the vinegar just before serving.

HORSERADISH GREMOLATA

MAKES ¾ CUP [65 G] / We use this gremolata to add sharp, acidic notes to braises and stews, varying the ingredients, depending what's going on with the rest of the dish. Sometimes I like the simplest variation with just olive oil, parsley, and lemon zest. More often than not I go for this version, which adds grated fresh horseradish and oily bread crumbs to the mix. Please don't substitute prepared horseradish here. Fresh horseradish is far more mellow and aromatic, and has a delicate texture when grated with a Microplane.

½ cup [15 g] chopped fresh flat-leaf parsley
One 3-in [7.5-cm] piece fresh horseradish root, peeled and finely grated
Zest of 1 lemon

2 Tbsp extra-virgin olive oil
1 handful Garlic Croutons (see page 80), fully cooled
Flaky sea salt

In a small bowl, combine the parsley, horseradish, lemon zest, and olive oil.

Place the croutons on a work surface and, using a rolling pin or a chef's knife, crush into coarse crumbs. Add the bread crumbs to the mixture, stir to combine, and season with salt. This is best made just before using.

PARSLEY SALSA VERDE

MAKES 1 CUP [210 G] / An important condiment in our kitchen, this salsa verde is one we use all year-round. It brings a lovely herbaceous briny note to things like grilled squid, grilled eggplant, and wood-roasted sunchokes. We even like it as a garnish for steak. As for most herb-based sauces, it's a good idea to make the base ahead of time and then spike it with vinegar just before using to avoid oxidation.

¾ cup [20 g] chopped fresh flat-leaf parsley
10 anchovy fillets, rinsed and chopped
1 Tbsp capers, rinsed and chopped
1 tsp finely grated lemon zest
Pinch of crushed red pepper flakes

1 garlic clove
⅔ cup [160 ml] extra-virgin olive oil
Kosher salt
1 Tbsp red wine vinegar

In a small bowl, combine the parsley, anchovies, capers, lemon zest, and red pepper flakes. Using a Microplane grater, grate the garlic into the mixture, add the olive oil, stir to combine, and season with salt. Allow to stand at room temperature for about 20 minutes.

Store in an airtight container in the refrigerator for up to 3 days. Bring to room temperature, and stir in the vinegar just before serving.

Substitute basil for half the chopped parsley to make basil salsa verde, which is especially good on grilled eggplant (see page 178).

CHIMICHURRI

MAKES 1½ CUPS [315 G] / Though it's similar to salsa verde, this herb emulsion has a decidedly different flavor, thanks to oregano and smoked paprika. We also include cilantro—I love its floral quality, especially with grilled beef. For a more authentic version, use 1½ bunches of parsley and omit the cilantro.

1 bunch fresh cilantro, stemmed and chopped
½ bunch fresh flat-leaf parsley, stemmed and chopped
1 Tbsp dried oregano
1 tsp smoked paprika
½ shallot, minced

½ cup [120 ml] extra-virgin olive oil
Kosher salt
Freshly ground black pepper
1 Tbsp red wine vinegar

In a medium bowl, combine the cilantro, parsley, oregano, paprika, shallot, and olive oil and stir. Allow to stand at room temperature for about 20 minutes.

Store in an airtight container in the refrigerator for up to 3 days. Bring to room temperature, season with salt and pepper, and stir in the vinegar just before serving.

HARISSA

MAKES ¾ CUP [180 G] / This is another North African condiment with many regional variations. Ours is essentially a dried chile–based sauce with North African spices. The caraway gives it a distinctive and addictive flavor.

12 dried guajillo chiles
2 dried cayenne chiles
½ tsp cumin seeds
¼ tsp caraway seeds
2 Tbsp extra-virgin olive oil

2 Tbsp red wine vinegar
4 garlic cloves, coarsely chopped
½ Preserved Lemon (page 73), rind only, minced
Kosher salt

In a small saucepan over high heat, combine all the dried chiles with enough water to cover. Bring to a boil, partially cover the pan, and continue boiling until about three-fourths of the water has evaporated and the chiles are beginning to soften, about 30 minutes. Allow the chiles to cool in the water.

In a small, dry frying pan over medium heat, toast the cumin seeds and caraway seeds just until fragrant and beginning to brown, about 3 minutes. Remove from the heat and let cool before grinding to a powder in a spice grinder or with a mortar and pestle.

Combine the olive oil and vinegar in a small bowl or cup.

In a food processor, purée the cooled chiles and their cooking liquid until smooth. Add the garlic, preserved lemon, and ground cumin and caraway to the blender and, with the motor running, pour in the olive oil–vinegar in a slow, steady stream until the sauce has the consistency of a loose paste. Season with salt.

Store in an airtight container in the refrigerator for up to 1 week. Bring to room temperature before using.

GREEN HARISSA

MAKES 1½ CUPS [330 G] / I love this stuff. It's a riff on Mexican salsa verde, but with North African spicing. Although it's good on almost any grilled vegetable or fish, it's even better with chicken.

¼ tsp cumin seeds

¼ tsp coriander seeds

2 Tbsp extra-virgin olive oil

5 tomatillos, husked and halved

3 jalapeño chiles, roughly chopped

2 shallots, roughly chopped

2 garlic cloves, sliced

Kosher salt

Freshly ground black pepper

½ cup [15 g] chopped fresh cilantro

½ cup [15 g] chopped fresh flat-leaf parsley

1 Tbsp white wine vinegar

2 Tbsp fresh lime juice

In a small, dry frying pan over medium heat, toast the cumin seeds and coriander seeds just until fragrant and beginning to brown, about 3 minutes. Remove from the heat and let cool before grinding to a powder in a spice grinder or with a mortar and pestle.

In the same frying pan over medium-high heat, warm the olive oil until hot but not smoking. Add the tomatillos, jalapeños, shallots, and garlic to the pan and cook until the shallots are translucent and the jalapeños are tender, 6 to 8 minutes. Season with salt and pepper. Remove from the heat and let cool for about 10 minutes.

In a food processor, purée the cooled tomatillo mixture with the cilantro, parsley, and ground cumin and coriander until smooth.

Store in an airtight container in the refrigerator for up to 1 day. Bring to room temperature, add the vinegar and lime juice, taste, and adjust the seasoning just before using.

BAGNA CAUDA

MAKES ½ CUP [120 ML] / This blend of anchovies, garlic, and olive oil tastes amazing on almost anything. Though it is traditionally served as a warm dip, we tend to use it as a dressing and pour it over grilled or roasted vegetables. I especially like it with grilled broccoli rabe, grilled red romaine, and roasted cauliflower, cardoons, and sunchokes. It is quite impressive to grill an array of summer vegetables like zucchini, squash, leeks, asparagus, peppers, and tomatoes, and serve them drenched with warm bagna cauda on a huge platter, along with some grilled bread.

¼ cup [60 ml] extra-virgin olive oil
20 garlic cloves, chopped
30 whole salt-packed anchovies,
halved lengthwise, boned, and rinsed

½ tsp crushed red pepper flakes
2 tsp red wine vinegar

In a small saucepan over medium-low heat, warm the olive oil until hot but not smoking. Add the garlic and cook until translucent, about 5 minutes. Add the anchovies, smashing them into the olive oil with the back of a spoon, and cook until softened and light brown in color, about 3 minutes. Remove from the heat and stir in the red pepper flakes and the vinegar.

Store in an airtight container in the refrigerator for up to 5 days. Warm over low heat before serving.

MOJO DE AJO

MAKES ABOUT 2 CUPS [480 ML] / This simple sauce of garlic caramelized in olive oil with lots of fresh citrus goes well with a wide range of ingredients. We use it as a marinade and as a glaze to brush on vegetables, meat, or fish as they cook.

½ cup [120 ml] extra-virgin olive oil
30 garlic cloves, peeled
½ cup [120 ml] fresh lime juice
½ cup [120 ml] fresh orange juice

1 tsp dried oregano
½ tsp crushed red pepper flakes
Kosher salt

Preheat the oven to 350°F [180°C].

In a small cast-iron or other type of ovenproof pan, combine the olive oil and garlic, making sure that the garlic is completely submerged. Place in the oven and cook until the garlic is very soft and golden brown, about 45 minutes. Stir in the lime juice and orange juice and return to the oven until slightly thickened, about 15 minutes longer. Remove from the oven and let cool slightly.

With a fork, smash the garlic to make a rough paste. Stir in the oregano and red pepper flakes. Taste and season with salt. The sauce will not emulsify; it will be very oily, and must be stirred before use.

Store in an airtight container in the refrigerator for up to 1 month. Bring to room temperature before using.

SPICED YOGURT

MAKES 2 CUPS [480 ML] / This is a lovely, cooling counterpoint to soups and stews, especially the spicy ones. I also like to use it to add richness to vegetables like beets, squash, potatoes, okra, green beans, and cauliflower. Thinned with a bit more water, this stuff makes an amazing dressing, especially for heartier salads with more substantial ingredients.

¼ tsp coriander seeds

¼ tsp cumin seeds

1 cup [240 ml] Greek-style yogurt

2 Tbsp chopped fresh cilantro

1 Tbsp chopped fresh mint

2 Tbsp extra-virgin olive oil

2 tsp white wine vinegar

Juice of ½ lemon

Kosher salt

3 Tbsp water, or as needed

In a small, dry frying pan over medium heat, toast the coriander seeds and cumin seeds just until fragrant and beginning to brown, about 3 minutes. Remove from the heat and let cool before grinding to a powder in a spice grinder or with a mortar and pestle.

In a food processor, combine the yogurt with the ground coriander and cumin, cilantro, and mint. Process until the herbs are broken down and the yogurt is tinted green, about 5 seconds. Add the olive oil, vinegar, and lemon juice and pulse just until incorporated. Taste and season with salt. Stir in the water, a little bit at a time, stopping when the yogurt is still thick but thin enough to drizzle from a spoon.

Over time, the lemon juice can cause the yogurt to break and lose its creamy texture, so make just a small amount and use it right away.

BUTTERMILK CRÈME FRAÎCHE

MAKES 4 CUPS [960 ML] / When our guests ask me for a recipe and find out that it calls for homemade crème fraîche, they're often hesitant, imagining that making crème fraîche is a complicated process. The reality is that it's very easy to make, but simply requires a few days of waiting to pull off. The plus side is that crème fraîche keeps well in the refrigerator and can be used to enrich pasta dishes, risotto, soups, vegetables—anything you want to bring a little richness to. Whip it gently to serve over desserts, slightly sweetened or not, in place of standard whipped cream.

4 cups [960 ml] heavy cream

1 Tbsp buttermilk

In a 1-qt [1-L] jar, combine the cream and buttermilk. Partially cover and let stand in a warm spot (about 78°F [28°C]) until the cream tastes slightly sour and has thickened to a puddinglike consistency, 24 hours to 3 days.

Store in an airtight container in the refrigerator for up to 2 weeks.

AIOLI

There are few dishes that don't benefit from the addition of this simple, garlic-enriched mayonnaise. Traditionally served with fish, aioli is also delicious slathered on a sandwich or stirred into a soup or stew. Thin it a bit with a little additional lemon juice or vinegar, and it becomes a salad dressing, one I particularly like with spring vegetables such as baby artichokes, asparagus, and fava beans, though it's just as mind-blowing alongside super-ripe tomatoes, grilled eggplant, and peppers.

Just as aioli goes with almost everything, almost anything can go into aioli. We make many variations of it in our kitchen. Horseradish, mustard, and roasted garlic are especially good mixed into aioli intended for use in a sandwich.

Making aioli with a mortar and pestle is an honorable act and really does yield a great result, but don't feel like you're cheating if you make yours in a food processor. We do it all the time.

BASIC AIOLI

MAKES ABOUT 1¼ CUPS [200 G] / As much as I love olive oil, I've found that aioli made with only olive oil has too strong a flavor. We use a 4:1 ratio of grapeseed oil to olive oil. I've also found that gently incorporating the olive oil at the end helps assure a rich aioli with fruity olive tones and no bitter oxidized flavors.

1 garlic clove, roughly chopped
Kosher salt
1 egg yolk
2 tsp fresh lemon juice

¾ cup [180 ml] grapeseed oil
¼ cup [60 ml] extra-virgin olive oil
3 Tbsp ice water, as needed

With a mortar and pestle, combine the garlic with a little salt and smash to make a rough paste. Add the egg yolk and use the pestle to incorporate it into the garlic. Add the lemon juice, and then, very slowly, pour in the grapeseed oil, mixing all the while. Once the grapeseed oil has been fully incorporated, drizzle in the olive oil while continuing to stir. At this point you should have a very thick aioli that is rich in color. Taste and season with salt. Stir in the ice water, 1 tsp at a time, adding only as much as you need for the desired consistency. (I like my aioli a bit on the loose side for a sauce on fish or meats, and somewhat thicker for sandwich spreads or a dip for *frites*.)

Store in an airtight container in the refrigerator for up to 3 days.

To make a flavored aioli, add fresh herbs, freshly grated horseradish, or paprika at the end, and taste to check for seasoning. Roughly chop denser ingredients, such as olives or smoked tomatoes, and add them with the garlic at the beginning of the process to make sure they are broken down and well incorporated into the sauce.

BLACK OLIVE & ANCHOVY AIOLI

MAKES 1½ CUPS [250 G] / I was introduced to this bold aioli, stained purple by olives and anchovies, in the south of France, where it was part of an elegant crudités platter. Up to that point, my idea of crudités was limited to the raw carrot, celery, and cucumber sticks set out with store-bought ranch dressing and served at birthday parties and bar mitzvahs. It was revelatory for me, a young cook, to see a dish I'd considered so bleak turned into something so sophisticated.

6 black olives, such as Gaeta or kalamata, pitted and finely chopped

4 whole salt-packed anchovies, halved lengthwise, boned, rinsed, and finely chopped

1 recipe Basic Aioli (facing page)

2 Tbsp chopped fresh flat-leaf parsley

1 tsp balsamic vinegar

With a mortar and pestle, combine the olives and anchovies and smash to make a rough paste. Gradually add the basic aioli and continue to mix until well combined. Stir in the parsley and vinegar.

Store in an airtight container in the refrigerator for up to 3 days.

PIMENTON AIOLI

MAKES 1¼ CUPS [200 G] / This paprika-laced aioli is used for garnishing any kind of fish stew, panfried sweetbreads, and grilled squid and octopus. It's delicious stuff. Use a good-quality smoked paprika from Spain or Hungary.

1 recipe Basic Aioli (facing page)

2 tsp pimenton

In a small bowl, whisk the basic aioli and the pimenton until well combined. Allow to stand at room temperature for about 20 minutes so that the pimenton can bloom and give the aioli a rusty hue.

Store in an airtight container in the refrigerator for up to 3 days.

SMOKED ALMOND AIOLI

MAKES ABOUT 1¼ CUPS [200 G] / This is amazing stuff if you happen to have smoked almonds on hand. The fattiness of the almonds lends this sauce an extra-luxurious flavor and texture that pairs well with meaty fish, such as grilled tuna or sturgeon.

2 Tbsp smoked almonds

1 recipe Basic Aioli (facing page)

With a mortar and pestle, crush the almonds to make a rough paste. Stir in the baisc aioli. Allow to stand at room temperature for about 20 minutes to allow the smoky flavor to bloom.

Store in an airtight container in the refrigerator for up to 3 days.

ROMESCO

MAKES 2 CUPS [420 G] / The almonds connect this condiment to its roots in Catalonia, where it's used as a sauce for fish and chicken. This romesco is our go-to dipping sauce for *frites*, as well as a garnish for roasted asparagus. I find its uses unlimited.

¼ cup [30 g] almonds

¼ cup [30 g] hazelnuts

4 red bell peppers

1½ lb [680 g] Roma tomatoes

¼ cup [7 g] chopped fresh flat-leaf parsley

2 cloves Garlic Confit (page 64)

½ cup [120 ml] extra-virgin olive oil

3 Tbsp red wine vinegar

Kosher salt

Freshly ground black pepper

Preheat the oven to 350°F [180°C].

On a rimmed baking sheet, spread out the almonds and hazelnuts in an even layer. Toast until lightly browned and aromatic, 10 to 12 minutes. Remove from the oven and let cool.

Increase the oven temperature to 450°F [230°C].

Place the bell peppers and tomatoes on a rimmed baking sheet and roast, turning occasionally, until charred on all sides and starting to soften. Alternatively, you can use a grill or a grill pan. Transfer the vegetables to a bowl, cover with a kitchen towel, and allow them to steam. When cool enough to handle, slip off the skins with a towel and remove the seeds.

In a food processor, combine the cooled almonds and hazelnuts, roasted vegetables, parsley, garlic confit, and olive oil. Process to make a coarse sauce with some chunks remaining. Add the vinegar and season with salt and pepper.

Store in an airtight container in the refrigerator for up to 1 week. Bring to room temperature before serving.

POMODORO SAUCE

MAKE ABOUT 6½ CUPS [1.5 L] / For our basic tomato sauce we use very ripe Early Girl tomatoes with lots of olive oil, sea salt, and basil. For me, there is no better tomato sauce, especially when tomatoes are in peak season. In the off season we use canned San Marzano tomatoes. These are generally imported from Italy, but you can also buy San Marzanos grown in California. I find that adding onion, garlic, carrot, or anything else to tomato sauce only gets in the way. The only acceptable addition in our kitchen is a small pinch or two of sugar when we are not in tomato season and the natural sugar levels of the tomatoes are lower.

8 lb [3.6 kg] tomatoes, such as Early Girl
or San Marzano, quartered

½ cup [120 ml] extra-virgin olive oil

3 Tbsp flaky sea salt

½ cup [15 g] basil leaves

1 to 2 tsp sugar (optional)

In a large stockpot over low heat, combine the tomatoes, olive oil, and salt. Cook, stirring occasionally, until the tomatoes have lost most of their acidity and the sauce begins to sweeten and thicken slightly, about 30 minutes. You want it thick enough to coat a spoon, but not too dense or pasty. Add the basil and taste; if the sauce seems too acidic, add the sugar, 1 tsp at a time, until the flavor is well balanced. Pass the sauce through a food mill and let cool completely.

Store in an airtight container in the refrigerator for up to 1 week, or in the freezer for up to 3 months.

SMOKY TOMATO BUTTER

MAKES ABOUT 2 CUPS [600 G] / Windrose Farms, in Paso Robles, provides us with amazing smoked tomatoes, which we use in this compound butter. We slather it on cuts of beef such as hanger and flatiron steaks. Smoked tomatoes can be tough to find, so we have substituted our Tomato Confit instead; but if you happen to get your hands on some smoked tomatoes, by all means use them.

1 small dried guajillo chile, soaked in very hot water
for about 15 minutes, drained, and finely chopped

1 cup [220 g] unsalted butter, cut into ½-in [12-mm] pieces

1 tsp smoked paprika

1 tsp kosher salt

1 clove Garlic Confit (page 64)

2 Tbsp sliced Shallot Confit (page 64)

¼ cup [65 g] Tomato Confit (page 60)

1 Tbsp red wine vinegar

In a food processor, combine the chile, butter, paprika, salt, garlic confit, shallot confit, tomato confit, and vinegar. Process until well blended, 3 to 5 minutes, scraping down the sides of the bowl at the end of each minute. The mixture should have an even red color and a smooth texture, with no lumps of cream-colored butter.

Store, tightly wrapped, in the refrigerator for up to 1 week.

TOMATO CONFIT

MAKES 2 CUPS [520 G] / These preserved tomatoes are amazingly versatile. We cook with them all year-round. When fresh tomatoes are out of season, canned San Marzano tomatoes can be prepared in the same way, adding depth of flavor and complexity to an ingredient that can otherwise taste ordinary. Be sure to use the tomato oil on anything that tastes better with a little olive oil and tomato, which is just about everything.

3 lb [1.4 kg] tomatoes, such as
Roma or Early Girl
Kosher salt
10 garlic cloves, smashed

10 fresh thyme sprigs
1 Tbsp dried oregano
Pinch of crushed red pepper flakes
2 cups [480 ml] extra-virgin olive oil, plus more as needed

Preheat the oven to 250°F [120°C]. Bring a large pot of water to boil over high heat. Prepare an ice-water bath by filling a large bowl with ice water.

Use a paring knife to score a small X in the bottom of each tomato. Plunge the tomatoes into the boiling water for 20 seconds, and immediately transfer them to the ice-water bath. Work in batches, if necessary, until all the tomatoes have been blanched.

When the tomatoes are cool, remove them from the water. With a sharp paring knife, peel the skin from the tomatoes; it should slip off easily. Cut the tomatoes into halves or quarters, depending on size, and gently pull the seeds out with your fingers. The tomatoes do not need to be perfectly seedless, but do your best to clean them so just the tomato flesh remains.

Place the tomatoes in a shallow baking dish or roasting pan and season with salt. Scatter the garlic, thyme, oregano, and red pepper flakes over the tomatoes. Pour the olive oil over all. Bake until the tomatoes are shriveled and browned around the edges, 3 to 4 hours. Turn them and move them around occasionally while baking so that the tomatoes closest to the edge of the pan don't burn. Remove from the oven and let cool to room temperature.

Store in an airtight container in the refrigerator for up to 1 month, completely covered with olive oil to prevent air from reaching them.

CHERRY TOMATO CONFIT

MAKES 4 CUPS [800 G] / This confit is somewhat luxurious and takes a bit of extra effort to produce, but the little pearls of tomato flesh are sweeter and more delicate than our regular Tomato Confit (page 60). We spoon these over grilled vegetables or fish. Try them in Grilled Summer Squash, Za'atar & Cherry Tomato Confit (page 181).

2 pt [760 g] Sun Gold cherry tomatoes, stemmed

2 cups [480 ml] extra-virgin olive oil, plus more as needed

4 garlic cloves, smashed

½ cup [15 g] basil leaves

1 tsp kosher salt

3 fresh thyme sprigs

Preheat the oven to 350°F [180°C]. Bring a large pot of water to boil over high heat. Prepare an ice-water bath by filling a large bowl with ice water.

Use a paring knife to score a small X in the bottom of each tomato. Plunge the tomatoes into the boiling water for 20 seconds, and immediately transfer them to the ice-water bath. Work in batches, if necessary, until all the tomatoes have been blanched.

When the cherry tomatoes are cool, remove them from the water. With your fingers, gently slip the tomatoes out of their skins and place them in a single layer in a baking dish. Pour the olive oil over the tomatoes and add the garlic, basil, salt, and thyme. Cover tightly with aluminum foil and bake for 30 minutes, or until the oil is hot but the tomatoes remain vibrant and whole. Let cool completely.

Store in an airtight container in the refrigerator for up to 2 weeks, completely covered with olive oil to prevent air from reaching them.

SHALLOT CONFIT

MAKES 8 CUPS [1.8 KG] / Sliced shallots cooked slowly and preserved in olive oil (pictured opposite) are handy for adding to vinaigrettes as well as to sautéed vegetables such as green beans, kale, sweet corn, Romano beans, and English peas. The shallot-flavored olive oil is arguably the most useful element of this recipe. Think of it as a shallot perfume that can enhance almost any dish.

2½ lb [1.2 kg] shallots, peeled and halved
3 cups [720 ml] extra-virgin olive oil, plus more as needed

6 fresh thyme sprigs
2 bay leaves, crushed

Preheat the oven to 350°F [180°C].

Place the shallots in an ovenproof casserole dish. Cover completely with the olive oil and sprinkle with the thyme and bay leaves. Cover tightly with aluminum foil. Bake until the shallots are fork-tender and taste sweet and mellow, 45 minutes to 1 hour. Remove from the oven and let cool completely.

Store in an airtight container in the refrigerator for up to 1 month, completely covered with olive oil to prevent air from reaching them.

GARLIC CONFIT

MAKES 4 CUPS [1 KG] / These slow-cooked cloves of garlic lend a more muted flavor to a dish than raw or even quickly sautéed garlic. And the garlic-scented oil is equally valuable.

2 cups [480 ml] extra-virgin olive oil, plus more as needed
8 heads garlic, cloves separated and peeled

12 fresh thyme sprigs
3 bay leaves, bruised

Preheat the oven to 350°F [180°C].

In a medium baking dish, combine the olive oil, garlic, thyme, and bay leaves. The garlic should be completely covered by about 1 in [2.5 cm] of oil. Bake until the garlic cloves are soft, fragrant, and lightly browned but still hold their shape, 45 minutes to 1 hour. Remove from the oven and let cool to room temperature.

Store in an airtight container in the refrigerator for up to 2 months, completely covered with olive oil to prevent air from reaching them.

GARLIC CHIPS & GARLIC OIL

MAKES 1 CUP [40 G] GARLIC CHIPS AND 1½ CUPS [360 ML] GARLIC OIL / Try to get your hands on some Spanish red garlic. This variety has larger cloves and tends to be easier to peel.

2 heads garlic, cloves separated and peeled   **2 cups [480 ml] extra-virgin olive oil or grapeseed oil**

Carefully cut the garlic cloves into slices 1 mm thick. The most important thing here is to get slices that are the same thickness so they fry up evenly.

Rinse the sliced garlic in a sieve under cold running water for about 2 minutes. This will help take out some of the natural bitterness in the garlic. Dry on a kitchen towel, patting the cloves to draw out as much water as you can.

In a small saucepan, heat the olive oil over medium heat until it is shimmering, about 200°F [90°C]. Carefully add the garlic slices and cook, stirring constantly and allowing the oil's temperature to rise to 250°F [120°C], until the garlic turns a light golden brown, 5 to 6 minutes. (You may need to lower the heat halfway through cooking to maintain that temperature.) With a slotted spoon, transfer the garlic to a paper towel–lined dish to drain. Let the oil cool to room temperature.

Store the garlic in an airtight container at room temperature for up to 3 days. Pour the oil into a jar and store in the refrigerator for up to 7 days.

CRISPY SHALLOTS & SHALLOT OIL

MAKES ABOUT ¾ CUP [35 G] CRISPY SHALLOTS AND 1½ CUPS [360 ML] SHALLOT OIL / Crisp fried shallots and the oil used to cook them are culinary gold. The shallots make a great garnish for almost any dish, and the oil can be used in salad dressings, on pastas, and as an embellishment for grilled fish. Use them anywhere you want to add texture and a sweet and savory onion flavor.

The key to frying shallots is to add them to warm oil and raise the temperature gradually while moving the shallots briskly around the pan. The bubbling action of the shallots in the oil will tell you when the temperature is right. The oil should hiss steadily, but not so much that the shallots spit out of the pan.

2 cups [480 ml] extra-virgin olive oil   **5 shallots, thinly sliced**

In a small saucepan, heat the olive oil over medium-high heat. As soon as the oil is warm, add the shallots and cook, stirring, until deep golden brown and the temperature of the oil is about 230°F [110°C], 10 to 15 minutes. Using a slotted spoon or a strainer, transfer the shallots to a paper towel–lined dish to drain. Let the oil cool to room temperature.

Store the shallots in an airtight container at room temperature for up to 3 days. Pour the oil into a jar and store in the refrigerator for up to 7 days.

ROASTED APPLE, ROSEMARY & BLACK PEPPER MOSTARDA

MAKES ABOUT 2½ CUPS [1.2 KG] / We make our mostardas to use with pâtés, rillettes, and other charcuterie items, but we also love them in sandwiches. You could just as easily slather this one on a crisp duck leg confit or a slow-roasted pork shoulder. The key is to get a nice balance between the sweet caramelized fruit and the sharp mustard and vinegar.

⅓ cup [75 ml] extra-virgin olive oil

2 lb [910 g] sweet-tart apples, such as Pink Lady, peeled, cored, and cut into small cubes

1 tsp kosher salt

1 tsp freshly ground black pepper

1 tsp chopped fresh rosemary leaves

2 Tbsp brown sugar

½ cup [125 g] Dijon mustard

½ cup [125 g] whole-grain mustard

1 tsp red wine vinegar

In a medium frying pan over medium-high heat, warm the olive oil until hot but not smoking. Add the apples, salt, pepper, and ½ tsp of the rosemary. Cook until the apples are caramelized and soft, 20 to 25 minutes. If they color too quickly, lower the heat a bit. Remove from the heat and let cool slightly.

In a food processor, combine the cooled apples with the remaining ½ tsp rosemary, the brown sugar, both mustards, and the vinegar. Pulse until not quite smooth, with some apple chunks remaining, 6 to 8 minutes.

Store in an airtight container in the refrigerator for up to 3 weeks.

PICKLED FRESNO CHILES

MAKES 1¾ CUPS [425 G] / I like the relatively subtle heat of a Fresno chile, as opposed to the more assertive nature of jalapeño and habanero chiles. Pickling further tempers the heat and brings out their sweetness. We often incorporate these (pictured top right) into herb salads to introduce a sour-spicy note to a dish that is otherwise mostly herbaceous and bitter.

BRINE
1 cup [240 ml] water
⅓ cup [80 ml] white wine vinegar
1 Tbsp sugar
1 Tbsp kosher salt

1 fresh bay leaf
2 whole cloves

12 Fresno chiles, or other medium-hot green or red chiles, seeds removed and sliced into 1/16-in- [2-mm-]thick rings

To make the brine: In a small saucepan, combine the water, vinegar, sugar, salt, bay leaf, and cloves. Bring to a boil, lower the heat, and simmer for 2 minutes. Remove from the heat and allow to steep for 20 to 30 minutes, then let cool to room temperature.

Pack the chiles into a 1-qt [1-L] glass jar with a lid. Pour the brine over the chiles. Let sit at room temperature for 4 hours before using.

Store, tightly sealed, in the refrigerator for up to 2 weeks.

PICKLED RED ONIONS

MAKES ABOUT 2 QT [900 G] / We make pickled onions (pictured center) almost exclusively to serve with Chicken & Duck Liver Pâté with Pickled Beets & Mustard Greens on Brioche Toasts (page 130). I have a hard time imagining one without the other. These also go great with pork or duck rillettes or smoked fish, or piled in a skirt steak sandwich with a dollop of aioli, a sprinkle of freshly grated horseradish, and some arugula.

BRINE
3 cups [720 ml] water
1¼ cups [300 ml] red wine vinegar
1 Tbsp cumin seeds
1 Tbsp yellow mustard seeds
1 tsp black peppercorns

5 fresh thyme sprigs
1 bay leaf
3 Tbsp plus 2 tsp sugar
2 Tbsp plus 1 tsp kosher salt

2 lb [910 g] red onions, thinly sliced

To make the brine: In a medium saucepan, combine the water, vinegar, cumin seeds, mustard seeds, peppercorns, thyme, bay leaf, sugar, and salt. Bring to a boil, lower the heat, and simmer for 3 or 4 minutes. Remove from the heat and allow to steep for 20 to 30 minutes, then let cool to room temperature.

Pack the sliced onions into a 2-qt [2-L] glass jar with a lid. Pour the brine over the onions. Let sit at room temperature for 1 hour before using. These are best after 2 to 3 days.

Store, tightly sealed, in the refrigerator for up to 1 month.

PICKLED EGGPLANT WITH ANCHOVIES & FRESNO CHILE

MAKES ABOUT 2 QT [900 G] / Of all the pickles we make, this might be my favorite. Grilling softens the eggplant, allowing it to absorb the brine more quickly, and it adds a smoky element. The buttery flesh turns almost custardlike after brining for a couple of days. The anchovies create an appealing and addictive umami effect.

BRINE
3 cups [720 ml] water
1¼ cups [300 ml] red wine vinegar
3 Tbsp plus 2 tsp sugar
2 Tbsp plus 1 tsp kosher salt
1 tsp allspice
½ tsp brown mustard seeds
½ tsp yellow mustard seeds
2 bay leaves
1 tsp black peppercorns

2 whole cloves
10 whole salt-packed anchovy fillets, halved lengthwise, boned, rinsed, and roughly chopped
1 Fresno chile, or another medium-hot green or red chile, cut thinly into rounds

1½ lb [680 g] Japanese eggplant, halved lengthwise
¼ cup [60 ml] extra-virgin olive oil
Kosher salt
Freshly ground black pepper

To make the brine: In a medium saucepan, combine the water, vinegar, sugar, salt, allspice, brown mustard seeds, yellow mustard seeds, bay leaves, peppercorns, and cloves. Bring to a boil, lower the heat, and simmer for 2 minutes. Remove from the heat and allow to steep for 20 to 30 minutes, then let cool to room temperature.

Once the liquid has cooled, strain through a fine-mesh strainer into a medium bowl and add the chopped anchovies and sliced chile.

Prepare a hot fire in a charcoal grill (or preheat a gas grill to high, or heat a grill pan over high heat).

In a medium bowl, toss the halved eggplant with the olive oil and season with salt and pepper. Grill, cut-side down, until charred, 1 or 2 minutes. Flip the eggplant over and allow grill marks to develop on the skin. The goal is to cook the eggplant until almost, but not quite, tender. Let cool completely.

Pack the eggplant into a 2-qt [2-L] glass jar with a lid so they are standing lengthwise. Pour the brine over the eggplant, the eggplant should be submerged. Let sit at room temperature for 1 hour before using.

Store, tightly sealed, in the refrigerator for up to 1 month.

PICKLED TURNIPS WITH MEYER LEMON

MAKES 2 QT [900 G] / Turnips have a crisp texture that lends itself well to pickling. Made with baby Japanese pink turnips, these pickles turn a beautiful pale pink. I like to leave the base of the stem intact so you can see it in cross-sectional slices. I like these with hummus and baba ghanoush as part of a Middle Eastern lunch spread. Their shape makes them ideal for sandwich building as well.

BRINE
3 cups [720 ml] water
¾ cup [180 ml] white wine vinegar
1 tsp allspice
1 tsp black peppercorns
2 whole cloves

2 bay leaves
3 Tbsp plus 2 tsp sugar
2 Tbsp plus 1 tsp kosher salt
¾ cup [180 ml] fresh lemon juice

1 lb 10 oz [735 g] baby Japanese pink turnips, cut into ⅛-in- [4-mm-] thick rounds

To make the brine: In a medium saucepan, combine the water, vinegar, allspice, peppercorns, cloves, bay leaves, sugar, and salt. Bring to a boil, lower the heat, and simmer for 2 minutes. Remove from the heat and allow to steep for 20 to 30 minutes, then let cool to room temperature. Add the lemon juice.

Pack the sliced turnips in a 2-qt [2-L] glass jar with a lid. Pour the brine over the turnips. Let sit at room temperature for at least 1 hour, or up to 3 hours, before using. These are best after 2 days.

Store, tightly sealed, in the refrigerator for up to 1 month.

To make pickled beets, make the brine as directed. Wash, peel, and stem 1 lb 10 oz [735 g] small red or gold beets. Cut the beets crosswise into ⅛-in- [4-mm-] thick rounds. Complete and store as directed.

SPICY SWEET CUCUMBERS

MAKES 4 QUARTS [3.6 KG] / This is one of my favorite "vinegared" pickles—most decidedly in the bread-and-butter category, with a sweet and slightly spicy profile. They can be eaten an hour or so after placing in the brine; quick pickling helps them keep a nice, crunchy texture.

BRINE
1 Tbsp mustard seeds
1 Tbsp coriander seeds
1½ tsp dill seeds
2 cups [480 ml] water
1 cup [240 ml] white wine vinegar
¼ cup plus 1 Tbsp [65 g] sugar
2 Tbsp kosher salt
¼ tsp ground turmeric
¼ tsp crushed red pepper flakes

2 lb [910 g] Persian or other pickling cucumbers, cut into ¾-in- [2-cm-] thick rounds
5 fresh dill sprigs
5 garlic cloves, thinly sliced

To make the brine: In a small, dry saucepan over medium heat, toast the mustard seeds, coriander seeds, and dill seeds until fragrant, about 3 minutes. Add the water, vinegar, sugar, salt, turmeric, and red pepper flakes. Bring to a boil, lower the heat, and simmer for 5 minutes. Remove from the heat and let cool.

In a 2-qt [2-L] canning jar, layer the cucumber rounds, dill sprigs, and garlic slices. Add the cooled brine to the jar. Let sit at room temperature for at least 1 hour (the flavor will be more intense if you let stand for up to 3 hours).

Store, tightly sealed, in the refrigerator for up to 1 month.

PRESERVED LEMONS

MAKES 12 LEMONS / When we're working with an ingredient pool that includes lots of lemon, these preserved lemons add a bright, briny flavor. They are very easy to make, look beautiful in a glass jar in your kitchen, and come in handy more often than you might imagine.

12 large lemons, washed well
3 Tbsp coriander seeds
3 Tbsp fennel seeds
2 cups [500 g] kosher salt

1 dried guajillo chile
6 fresh thyme sprigs
½ cinnamon stick, crushed
2 bay leaves, crumbled

Starting at the top of each lemon, cut a deep X into it, stopping about ¼ in [6 mm] from the base, so you are left with a quartered lemon held together at one end. Set aside.

In a small, dry pan, toast the coriander seeds and fennel seeds until fragrant and beginning to brown, about 3 minutes. In a medium bowl mix together the salt, toasted spices, chile, thyme, cinnamon stick, and bay leaves.

Working over a large bowl, stuff a lemon with a handful of the salt mixture, using your thumb to gently break into the flesh, allowing the juices to run out. Drop this lemon into the bottom of the bowl. Repeat until all the lemons have been stuffed. Pour any remaining salt over the lemons and gently toss.

Carefully pack the stuffed lemons and salt into a 2-qt [2-L] glass jar with a lid, pressing down so they are completely covered in their own juices. Pour in any juice and seasoning from the bowl. Seal the jar and let sit at room temperature until the rinds have softened, 3 to 4 weeks.

Store, tightly sealed, at room temperature for up to 6 months.

FERMENTED LEEKS

MAKES 2½ CUPS [500 G] / We cook leeks in various ways at Gjelina, playing up their natural sweetness through braising, charring, or, here, lacto-fermenting as one would sauerkraut. This is a pickle that elevates pâté or smoked fish, and takes an egg or tuna salad sandwich to new heights.

8 leeks, white and light-green parts only,
cut into ¼-in [6-mm] rings
1 Tbsp kosher salt

One 1-in [2.5-cm] piece fresh horseradish,
peeled and finely grated

Rinse the leeks in several changes of cold water to remove any dirt. Gently squeeze the excess water out of the leeks. Place the leeks in a mixing bowl and massage the salt into them, separating the rings and causing them to release some liquid. Stir in the horseradish.

Pack the leeks into a 1-qt [1-L] glass jar with a lid. Cover loosely with a clean kitchen towel and let sit at room temperature until the leeks have fermented and smell sour but are still crunchy, 3 to 4 weeks.

Store, tightly sealed, in the refrigerator for up to 3 months.

GIARDINIERA

MAKES 2 QT [900 G] / This classic Italian pickle blend is super to have on hand. Throw it in a sub-style deli sandwich or use it to offset a rich pâté or rillettes. Since we are in Southern California, we often use jalapeño or Fresno chiles instead of the more classic Italian hot pepper varieties. When I use dried oregano, I always choose Sicilian for its intense flavor.

BRINE
3 cups [720 ml] water
1¼ cups [300 ml] red wine vinegar
1 Tbsp coriander seeds
1 tsp cumin seeds
1 tsp yellow mustard seeds
5 fresh thyme sprigs
2 garlic cloves, smashed
3 Tbsp plus 2 tsp sugar
2 Tbsp plus 1 tsp kosher salt

1 head cauliflower
½ red onion, thinly sliced
¼ cup [35 g] pitted black olives,
such as Gaeta or kalamata
¼ cup [35 g] pitted green olives,
such as Castelvetrano or Lucques
1 medium-hot green or red chile,
preferably Fresno, thinly sliced
2 Tbsp dried oregano, preferably Sicilian

To make the brine: In a medium saucepan, combine the water, vinegar, coriander seeds, cumin seeds, mustard seeds, thyme, garlic, sugar, and salt. Bring to a boil, lower the heat, and simmer for 3 minutes. Remove from the heat and allow to steep for 20 to 30 minutes.

While the brine is steeping, cut the cauliflower into large florets. Slice the florets ¼ in [6 mm] thick and put in a medium bowl.

If the brine has cooled to room temperature, heat it up a bit. You want it to be hot but not boiling. Strain the brine through a fine-mesh sieve into the bowl with the cauliflower. Let sit at room temperature for about 1 hour, until the brine has cooled to room temperature. Add the onion, black and green olives, chile, and oregano. Mix with a large spoon and transfer to a 2-qt [2-L] glass jar with a lid.

Store, tightly sealed, in the refrigerator for up to 1 month.

KIMCHEE WITH GUAJILLO CHILE PASTE

MAKES 2 QT [900 G] / Guajillo is not the variety of chile that would normally be included in an authentic Korean kimchee, but I urge you to try it for yourself. The results are outstanding. I like my kimchee slightly sweet but more on the sour-salty end of the scale. This recipe hits that note.

2 heads napa cabbage

Kosher salt

GUAJILLO CHILE PASTE

3 dried guajillo chiles

2 Tbsp water

½ yellow onion, diced

6 garlic cloves, chopped

One 1-in [2.5-cm] piece fresh ginger, peeled and roughly chopped

1 Tbsp fish sauce

¼ cup [60 ml] white wine vinegar

Cut each head of cabbage into quarters, discarding the stem. Cut each quarter crosswise into 2-in- [5-cm-] thick pieces. In a large bowl, sprinkle the cabbage with 2 Tbsp salt. Massage the salt into the cabbage until it releases some water and feels wet. You want the cabbage to taste and feel salty, so add more, 1 tsp at a time, if needed.

To make the chile paste: In a small, dry frying pan, toast the guajillos until they darken slightly and become very aromatic, about 3 minutes. Let cool. Roughly chop the chiles and grind them into a powder in a spice grinder.

In a food processor, combine the ground guajillos with the water, onion, garlic, ginger, fish sauce, and vinegar. Pulse to make a loose paste.

Add the chile paste to the salted cabbage and mix until the cabbage is well coated. Pack the cabbage into a 2-qt [2-L] canning jar, pushing it down so that it is completely submerged in its own juices. Leave some headroom in the container so that the juices do not bubble over onto your counter. Cover and let stand at room temperature for 2 to 4 weeks. You will see small bubbles form in the mixture. Stir occasionally so that the flavors are distributed evenly, and to check for the rate of fermentation. As long as you keep the cabbage covered in liquid, you should not have any spoilage problems. Taste occasionally. It will get more and more sour and fizzy as time goes on. When you're happy with the flavor, place it in the refrigerator to slow down the fermentation process.

Store, tightly sealed, in the refrigerator for up to 3 months.

ROASTED OR GRILLED RED PEPPERS

MAKES 2 CUPS [410 G] / I wondered whether I should include a recipe for this kitchen staple. But I am convinced that peppers roasted at home, especially over fire, are so simple, satisfying, and superior to those you can buy in jars, it's worth inclusion for those who haven't made their own.

4 whole red bell peppers   **Olive oil**

Prepare a hot fire in a charcoal grill (or preheat a gas grill to high, or heat a large cast-iron grill pan over high heat).

Put the bell peppers on the grill (or in the grill pan) and cook, turning them until charred on all sides and starting to soften, about 10 minutes. Transfer the bell peppers to a bowl, cover with a kitchen towel, and set aside to steam. When cool enough to handle, gently slip off the skins with the kitchen towel and remove the seeds from the peppers. Slice the peppers into ¼-in [6-mm] strips. Transfer the strips to a glass jar with a tight-fitting lid. Pour olive oil over the peppers until completely covered.

Store in the refrigerator for up to 1 week.

GRILLED OR TOASTED BREAD

MAKES 12 TOASTS / I would not expect anyone to start a wood or charcoal fire just to make toasts, but if you happen to have one going, by all means use it to grill tasty bread. Ideally, grilled bread is made over an open charcoal or hardwood flame, so the bread is crispy on the outside, soft in the center, and slightly charred around the edges. My favorite non-grill option is to get a cast-iron skillet or grill pan very hot on the stove top, brush the bread on both sides with olive oil, and brown the bread in the pan. Otherwise it's perfectly fine to use a toaster or broiler setting on your oven or toaster oven.

Twelve ½-in- [12-mm-] thick slices rustic bread   **Olive oil for brushing**

Heat a large cast-iron skillet or grill pan over medium-high heat.

Brush the bread on both sides with olive oil. Cook the bread in batches until browned and toasted, about 3 minutes on each side. Set the slices in one layer on a cooling rack, lightly brushing the tops with olive oil. Repeat until all the bread has been grilled.

Serve within a few hours, or let cool completely and store in an airtight container for up to 2 days.

CHAPTER TWO
SALADS

A food critic once suggested that there are too many salads on the menu at Gjelina. That's a criticism that I can live with. It's true that I crave something leafy, either cooked or raw, just about every time I sit down to eat; but I don't think I'm the only one. Every day, the cooks working our salad station throw down crate after crate of black kale, Bloomsdale spinach, arugula, and dozens of other fresh greens as we work to satisfy our customers' appetites for salads. We regularly serve about three hundred of them daily. It seems to me that most of our guests like a menu that's heavy on the greens.

This hunger for salads has brought about a big shift in the number of diners who are open to and enthusiastic about eating greens that not so long ago were a hard sell. Salads based on dandelion, curly endive, mizuna, and tatsoi no longer require a lengthy explanation from our servers. Everyone from the most committed carnivore to the pickiest vegan now seems to understand that fresh greens are both a critical part of a healthful diet and often the best part of a meal.

Small farmers are reacting to this increased demand by seeking out new varieties of fresh lettuces to bring to the market. Greens that were once difficult to source, such as puntarelle and Little Gem, have become easier to find; every year it seems we discover a new and even more delicious one.

MIXED LETTUCES WITH YOGURT DRESSING & WARM CROUTONS

SERVES 4 TO 6 / Yogurt dressings are among my very favorites. I love how their rich creaminess is balanced by the acidity of good-quality Greek yogurt. These dressings are a great canvas for herbs, spices, and aromatics. And because the yogurt is so thick, it can be mixed with vinegar and oil without becoming too thin.

The warm, hand-torn croutons are a great addition here, helping to carry the creamy, decadent dressing while also creating some temperature contrast. These are great added to all kinds of salads, when you want to make something a little more substantial or you have an abundance of day-old bread.

GARLIC CROUTONS
3 to 4 Tbsp [45 to 60 ml] oil from Garlic Confit (page 64), or plain extra-virgin olive oil

Four 1-in- [6-mm-] thick slices day-old sourdough bread, country white, or baguette, torn into quarter-size pieces

Kosher salt

Freshly ground black pepper

YOGURT DRESSING
1 cup [240 ml] Greek-style yogurt

¼ cup [60 ml] cold water

2 garlic cloves, minced

1 large shallot, minced

2 Tbsp white wine vinegar

2 Tbsp fresh lemon juice

2 Tbsp chopped fresh flat-leaf parsley

2 Tbsp chopped fresh chives

1 Tbsp chopped fresh mint

¼ cup [60 ml] extra-virgin olive oil

Kosher salt

5 generous handfuls mixed greens, such as Little Gem, Deer Tongue, romaine, and butter lettuces; arugula; tatsoi; mizuna; mustard frills; and chicories, such as frisée, curly endive, escarole, and radicchio Treviso

5 radishes, black or standard red, thinly sliced

1 fennel bulb, thinly sliced

Kosher salt

Freshly ground black pepper

To make the croutons: In a medium frying pan, heat 3 Tbsp of the olive oil over medium heat. Add the pieces of bread, making sure not to crowd the pan. Cook, turning occasionally and adding another 1 Tbsp oil, if necessary, until the croutons are crisp on the surface but still slightly soft in the center, about 7 minutes. No need to be too fussy; an uneven color gives the croutons more character. Season with salt and pepper. Transfer to a plate lined with paper towels, and set aside until ready to toss the salad.

To make the dressing: In a small bowl, combine the yogurt, water, garlic, shallot, vinegar, lemon juice, parsley, chives, and mint. Whisk in the olive oil and season with salt. (Store in an airtight container in the refrigerator for up to 1 week. Bring to room temperature before using.)

In a large salad bowl, combine the mixed greens, radishes, and fennel and spoon the dressing down the sides of the bowl. Using your hands, toss the salad, pulling the dressing off the sides of the bowl as you do. Don't overdress; the greens should be lightly coated, not wet. Season with salt and pepper. Add the still-warm croutons to the salad. Add more dressing, if necessary, and serve immediately.

TUSCAN KALE SALAD WITH FENNEL, RADISH & RICOTTA SALATA

SERVES 4 TO 6 / Kale salads have become ubiquitous, especially in the green-minded state of California. But I believe Italians have been dressing *cavolo nero* with lemon juice and olive oil and serving it raw long before this recent infatuation. Also known as Tuscan and dinosaur kale, this particular variety has a strong fiber and dark-green-bordering-on-purple hue to its leaves. It's not hard to see why people equate it with healthful eating, as it evokes minerality and soil-rich nutrients, and it is remarkably resilient after harvest.

Oily, rich, and garlicky homemade bread crumbs elevate this salad far past a simple statement of mindful eating. I don't recommend leaving them out or substituting store-bought junk. And do seek out ricotta salata, a salted and pressed version of fresh ricotta with a creamy, salty flavor and a dry, almost crumbly texture.

1 Tbsp plus 2 tsp extra-virgin olive oil, plus more as needed

2 large bunches Tuscan kale, stemmed and cut into ¼-in- [6-mm-] wide strips

Kosher salt

2 Tbsp red wine vinegar, plus more as needed

1½ Tbsp fresh lemon juice, plus more as needed

6 radishes, thinly sliced

1 fennel bulb, trimmed and shaved with a vegetable peeler

1 large handful Garlic Croutons (see page 80), fully cooled

2 oz [55 g] ricotta salata cheese

Freshly ground black pepper

In a large bowl, drizzle the olive oil over the kale and sprinkle with salt. Massage the leaves until softened and tender, squeezing them firmly with your hands. This breaks down the cell walls, making the greens softer and more receptive to the dressing. Add the vinegar and lemon juice and continue to massage the kale. Add more vinegar, lemon juice, or salt if necessary, and make sure there is enough rich, velvety olive oil coating the leaves. Add the sliced radishes and shaved fennel.

Place the croutons on a work surface and, using a rolling pin or a chef's knife, crush into coarse crumbs.

With a vegetable peeler, shave the ricotta salata into the bowl. Toss gently to combine. Add the crouton crumbs and mix thoroughly. Season with salt and pepper. Transfer to a serving platter or individual plates and serve. This salad holds up well for several hours, but should be eaten the day it is made.

BLOOMSDALE SPINACH SALAD WITH HONEY-GARLIC DRESSING, FETA & PINE NUTS

SERVES 4 TO 6 / The silky, wrinkled leaves of Bloomsdale spinach, an heirloom variety, carry the more substantial garnishes of this salad really well. I love the way salty feta and olives work with the honey-sweetened, garlic-laced dressing of red wine vinegar and lemon juice. We use day-old ciabatta to make crostini-like croutons, which we rub with garlic as they come out of the oven and drench with lots of good olive oil.

CIABATTA CROUTONS
Twelve ⅛-in [4-mm] slices day-old ciabatta
¼ cup [60 ml] oil from Garlic Confit (page 64)
or plain extra-virgin olive oil

¼ cup [25 g] pine nuts

HONEY-GARLIC DRESSING
¼ cup [60 ml] red wine vinegar
3 Tbsp fresh lemon juice
3 garlic cloves, minced
1 shallot, minced
1 Tbsp buckwheat or wildflower honey

¾ cup [180 ml] extra-virgin olive oil
Kosher salt
Freshly ground black pepper

1 bunch Bloomsdale spinach
¼ cup [35 g] pitted buttery green olives,
such as Castelvetrano
¼ cup [35 g] pitted black olives, such as Gaeta or Niçoise
2 oz [55 g] French or Greek feta, crumbled
3 oz [85 g] sweet cherry tomatoes, halved
Kosher salt
Freshly ground black pepper

To make the croutons: Preheat the oven to 350°F [180°C]. Arrange the ciabatta slices on a baking sheet and brush both sides with oil. Bake until crisp all the way through, 8 to 10 minutes. Set aside, and leave the oven on.

On a small baking sheet, spread out the pine nuts in one layer. Toast the pine nuts in the oven until golden and fragrant, about 6 minutes, stirring the nuts after 3 minutes. Set aside.

To make the dressing: In a small bowl, combine the vinegar and lemon juice. Stir in the garlic and shallot, and let stand for several minutes. Whisk in the honey and then the olive oil. Season with salt and pepper. There should be a noticeable sweetness that balances the acidity of the vinegar and lemon. Keep in a warm spot until ready to use.

In a large bowl, combine the spinach, green and black olives, feta cheese, pine nuts, and croutons. Spoon the dressing around the sides of the bowl. Mix with the intention of breaking down the feta and the croutons without completely smashing them. Add the tomatoes and season with salt and pepper. Transfer to a serving platter or individual plates and serve immediately.

ESCAROLE & SUNCHOKE SALAD WITH SMOKED ALMONDS & PRESERVED LEMON

SERVES 4 TO 6 / Escarole hearts have a beautifully crunchy texture that holds up well to more substantial dressings and a delicately bitter flavor that makes them more interesting than typical romaine hearts. Try them in a chopped salad or your next Caesar.

Don't discard the outer leaves. They're a darker shade of green and have a bitter flavor and a denser texture that makes them more suitable for cooking. Use them in the Chicken & Escarole Soup with Charmoula & Lemon (page 231) or in the Grilled Chicories with Crispy Fried Eggs & Bacon Vinaigrette (page 98).

Sunchokes, also known as Jerusalem artichokes, have a reputation for being difficult to digest, but I've found that shaving raw sunchokes minimizes the negative effects, while bringing out their sweet taste and jicama-like crunchiness. Varieties range in color from off-white to pinkish. They're all delicious.

PRESERVED LEMON DRESSING
2 Preserved Lemons (page 73), rinsed, flesh scraped out, and peels roughly chopped
3 Tbsp white wine vinegar
1 Tbsp buckwheat or wildflower honey
Kosher salt
Freshly ground black pepper
1 cup [240 ml] extra-virgin olive oil

3 heads escarole
¼ cup [30 g] smoked almonds, roughly chopped
3½ oz [100 g] sunchokes, cut into thin slices with a mandoline or vegetable peeler
Kosher salt
Freshly ground black pepper
Chunk of Parmesan cheese for grating

To make the dressing: In a small bowl, combine the preserved lemons, vinegar, and honey. Season with salt and pepper. Whisk in the olive oil. (Store in an airtight container in the refrigerator for up to 1 week.)

For this recipe you want the pale interior leaves of the escarole. If you have large heads, peel off about one-third of the outer leaves (and refrigerate for another use). In a large bowl, combine the escarole hearts, smoked almonds, and sunchokes. Add the dressing and toss well. Season with salt and pepper. Transfer to a serving platter or individual plates, top with a generous grating of Parmesan cheese, and serve.

ARUGULA & RADICCHIO SALAD WITH CRISPY SHALLOTS & SHALLOT OIL—SHERRY VINAIGRETTE

SERVES 4 TO 6 / We especially like the way crisp fried shallots pair with the nuttiness of Parmesan cheese in this salad, while the shallot oil complements the musky flavor of good-quality sherry vinegar.

1 recipe Crispy Shallots & Shallot Oil (page 66)

¼ cup [60 ml] fresh lemon juice

¼ cup [60 ml] sherry vinegar

1½ tsp balsamic vinegar

1 Tbsp honey

Kosher salt

Freshly ground black pepper

1 bunch arugula

1 head radicchio, torn or cut into strips

Chunk of Parmesan cheese for shaving

Pour 1½ cups [360 ml] of the shallot oil into a small bowl (reserve the remaining oil for another use). Whisk in the lemon juice, sherry vinegar, balsamic vinegar, and honey and season with salt and pepper.

In a large salad bowl, combine the arugula and radicchio. Spoon the dressing over the top. Add a handful of the crispy shallots, and a light shaving of Parmesan. Toss well and transfer to individual plates. Top with more crispy shallots and Parmesan, if you like, and serve.

SPICY HERB SALAD WITH GINGER-LIME DRESSING

SERVES 4 TO 6 / We tend to have some version of this dish on our menu all year long; it's delicious on its own or as a contrasting side to roasted meats or braises. Bury a whole grilled fish in it or use it to set off a slab of pâté. Anytime you want sharp, bitter flavors, either as a contrast for a more fatty dish or simply to refresh your palate, this is the salad you should turn to.

The list of herbs suggested here is by no means intended as a strict template never to be varied. Let the market be your guide and grab whatever you stumble on that looks fresh and intriguing. Use a dozen herbs or just one or two. A version that includes only parsley or cilantro can be perfect. The Ginger-Lime Dressing is so piercing that when combined with the complex bittersweet notes of the herbs, the effect is reminiscent of a bracing tonic. The dressing recipe makes twice the amount you need to dress this salad, giving you enough on hand to quickly make the salad again later in the week.

GINGER-LIME DRESSING
1 Tbsp fresh lime juice
1 medium-hot green or red chile,
preferably Fresno, minced
1 shallot, minced
One ½-in [12-mm] piece peeled fresh ginger
1 garlic clove
½ tsp honey
½ cup [120 ml] extra-virgin olive oil
Kosher salt
Freshly ground black pepper

4 generous handfuls mixed fresh herbs, such as
parsley, cilantro, opal basil, Thai basil, lemon basil,
chives, tarragon, mint, shiso, dill, and fennel fronds
¾ cup [85 g] cherry tomatoes, halved
1 Japanese cucumber, cut into rounds
Kosher salt
Freshly ground black pepper

To make the dressing: In a small bowl, combine the lime juice, chile, and shallot. Using a Microplane grater, grate the ginger and garlic into the bowl. Add the honey and gradually whisk in the olive oil until well combined. Season with salt and pepper. (Store in an airtight container in the refrigerator for up to 3 days.)

In a salad bowl, combine the mixed herbs, cherry tomatoes, and cucumber. Season with salt and pepper. Drizzle in up to ¼ cup [60 ml] of the dressing and gently toss. The dressing should coat the herbs but not weigh them down. This salad is best eaten the day it is made.

SMOKED TROUT SALAD WITH GRAPEFRUIT & AVOCADO

SERVES 4 TO 6 / A stripped-down dressing of lemon juice and olive oil is all that's needed for this salad, where smoked fish is the featured player. This most basic combination of fat and acid carries the trout's gentle smokiness to every corner of the dish. And when the acidic sting of grapefruit (at Gjelina, we're fools for the ones from Shaner Farms), lush slices of avocado, and the peppery bite of arugula come into play, this simple salad rises to the level of a classic.

If you're curious about the process of smoking your own trout, I urge you to try the recipe on page 129. It's not hard to do, and the results are delicious.

Other citrus, such as orange or tangerine, works well here, too, but I think the intense acidity and floral qualities of grapefruit, and its cousins pomelo and oro blanco, are ideal.

8 oz [230 g] arugula
5 oz [140 g] high-quality store-bought smoked trout
2 tsp fresh lemon juice
1¼ tsp extra-virgin olive oil
Kosher salt

Freshly ground black pepper
1 grapefruit, pomelo, or oro blanco, or
a combination, peeled and sectioned
1 avocado, cut lengthwise in ¼-in [6-mm] slices
¼ red onion, cut in thin slices

Put the arugula in a large mixing bowl. Break up the trout into small chunks over the arugula. Drizzle with the lemon juice and olive oil and season with salt and pepper.

Add the grapefruit sections, avocado, and onion and toss gently, taking care not to break up the avocado slices while distributing them evenly throughout the salad. Transfer to a serving platter or individual plates and serve immediately.

GEMS WITH FUYU PERSIMMON, POMEGRANATE, CRISP GARLIC & BLUE CHEESE DRESSING

SERVES 4 TO 6 / A study in contrasts, this salad combines sweet, firm Fuyu persimmons; crunchy pomegranate seeds; crisp garlic; and a punchy blue-cheese dressing. Many blue cheeses work well here; we particularly like domestic ones such as Maytag from Iowa and Point Reyes from Northern California. I would suggest steering clear of the drier, more aged blue cheeses for this particular recipe.

Little Gem, a cross between romaine and butter lettuce, is found at some local farmers' markets. Its tender texture and small size—the leaves are perfect for eating whole—have made it a hit with consumers, and it's becoming more widely available. There are a few varieties; I like them all. Buy the freshest if you have a choice. If the greens wilt a bit on the ride home or have been sitting in your refrigerator too long, soak them in cold water mixed with a couple of drops of vinegar. This trick is a miraculous way of bringing greens back to life.

BLUE CHEESE DRESSING
1 cup [240 ml] buttermilk
6 oz [170 g] blue cheese, at room temperature
1 garlic clove, minced
1 shallot, minced
¼ cup [60 ml] extra-virgin olive oil
2½ Tbsp red wine vinegar
1 Tbsp Worcestershire sauce
Kosher salt
Freshly ground black pepper

3 Little Gem lettuce heads, leaves separated at the base
Kosher salt
Freshly ground black pepper
1 Fuyu persimmon
¼ cup [40 g] pomegranate seeds
1 Tbsp Garlic Chips (page 66)

To make the dressing: In a food processor, combine the buttermilk, blue cheese, garlic, shallot, olive oil, vinegar, and Worcestershire sauce. Season with salt and pepper, and pulse until almost smooth. The dressing should have the consistency of pancake batter—too thick and it will bury the other ingredients; too thin and it won't adhere to the lettuce properly. (Add more buttermilk if the dressing is too thick, and more cheese if it's too thin. And remember to adjust the seasoning.)

Put the lettuce in a large salad bowl, and spoon the dressing down the sides of the bowl. Using your hands, toss the salad by pulling the dressing off the bowl and massaging it evenly into the leaves. Season with salt and pepper. Add the persimmon and pomegranate seeds and mix thoroughly to coat with dressing. Transfer to salad plates, top with the garlic chips, and serve immediately.

DANDELION GREENS WITH LEMON-ANCHOVY DRESSING

SERVES 4 TO 6 / Bitter greens dressed with lemon and seasoned with anchovies are a combination of acid, bitter, and umami perfected in Italy over several centuries. At Gjelina, we've reworked this classic Roman salad to our liking by upping the anchovy. Dandelion greens can be an acquired taste, but I insist that you get acquainted with them. Once your taste adjusts to the bitter notes, you'll discover their subtle sweetness. If you find yourself with a more mature specimen, simply wilt it with garlic and olive oil and pair it with your favorite roast or braise. Or slap it down with a soulful plate of beans and rice.

LEMON-ANCHOVY DRESSING
6 to 8 anchovy fillets, finely chopped
2 garlic cloves, minced
¼ cup [60 ml] fresh lemon juice
½ cup [120 ml] extra-virgin olive oil
Kosher salt
Freshly ground black pepper

1 large handful Garlic Croutons (see page 80), fully cooled
2 large bunches dandelion greens
Kosher salt
Freshly ground black pepper
Chunk of Parmesan cheese for grating

To make the dressing: In a small bowl, combine the anchovy fillets and garlic with the lemon juice. Whisk in the olive oil and season with salt and pepper. (If you prefer a stronger dressing, by all means add more anchovies.)

Place the croutons on a work surface and, using a rolling pin or a chef's knife, crush into coarse crumbs.

Put the greens in a salad bowl and spoon the dressing over them. Sprinkle the crouton crumbs on top. Mix thoroughly, and season with salt and pepper. Transfer to salad plates, top each with a generous grating of Parmesan, and serve immediately.

GRILLED KALE WITH SHALLOT-YOGURT DRESSING & TOASTED HAZELNUTS

SERVES 4 TO 6 / I know for certain that I'm cooking in Southern California when I glance at my grill and see it covered with charred leafy greens. At Gjelina, we love the depth of flavor and savory deliciousness of a charred wedge of escarole or a bundle of curly endive. Grilling bitter or tough greens briefly on the hottest part of the grill, followed by several moments off to the side, is a great way to turn tough, bitter greens into a tender, smoky dish.

Tossing a bit of cold water over the greens before grilling ensures that they get some critical steam while still charring nicely around the edges. If the kale is on the young side, it may need only a tiny amount of water or none at all. If it's more mature, drizzle the kale with a bit more water to make sure the leaves become tender and the stems soften without burning.

SHALLOT-YOGURT DRESSING
1 cup [240 ml] Greek-style yogurt
¼ cup [55 g] Shallot Confit (page 64), roughly chopped
2 Tbsp extra-virgin olive oil or shallot oil from Shallot Confit
¼ cup [7 g] packed fresh mint leaves, chopped
2½ Tbsp fresh lemon juice
Kosher salt
Freshly ground black pepper

½ cup [80 g] hazelnuts
3 bunches Russian kale
⅓ cup [75 ml] extra-virgin olive oil
Flaky sea salt
Freshly ground black pepper
2 to 3 Tbsp water

Prepare a medium-hot fire in a charcoal grill (or preheat a gas grill to medium-high).

To make the dressing: In a small bowl, combine the yogurt, shallot confit, olive oil, mint, and lemon juice. Season with kosher salt and pepper. Let stand while you make the salad.

In a small, dry frying pan, toast the hazelnuts until fragrant, about 5 minutes. Let cool and coarsely chop.

In a large bowl, toss the kale with the olive oil and season with sea salt and pepper. Drizzle in the water and mix well. Put the kale on the hottest part of the grill. Once the leaves begin to char, about 30 seconds, flip them over to char the other side. Move the kale to a cooler spot on the grill, stacking the leaves on top of each other, and continue cooking until the leaves are slightly wilted, about 2 minutes. Transfer to a serving platter, drizzle with the dressing, and scatter the toasted hazelnuts on top. Season with sea salt and pepper and serve warm.

GRILLED CHICORIES WITH CRISPY FRIED EGGS & BACON VINAIGRETTE

SERVES 4 / This substantial salad, which includes eggs fried in olive oil and a dressing based on rendered bacon fat, is our riff on the easy-to-like theme of bacon and eggs.

We like to cook bacon slowly in olive oil to make lardons for dishes like Charred Brussels Spouts with Bacon & Dates (page 190). When we're done, we're left with a bacon fat–scented olive oil that's far too delicious to toss out, so we use it to enhance this basic vinaigrette.

Frying eggs in a generous quantity of olive oil yields crisp, browned-around-the-edges eggs with yolks that are delightfully runny. The key is to be generous with the oil, and as the eggs start to set, baste their tops and yolks slightly to set them while the edges crisp. Pull them from the pan when the yolks are warm but still very loose.

A standard Lodge cast-iron frying pan is the best egg-frying pan money can buy. It's very reasonably priced, and once adequately seasoned, has a nonstick surface.

BACON VINAIGRETTE
2 Tbsp rendered bacon fat
⅓ cup [75 ml] extra-virgin olive oil
¼ cup [60 ml] red wine vinegar
1 Tbsp honey

1 lb [455 g] chicories, such as endive, radicchio, curly endive, escarole, and frisée
5 Tbsp [80 ml] extra-virgin olive oil
Kosher salt
Freshly ground black pepper
2 Tbsp cold water
4 eggs

To make the dressing: In a small saucepan, melt the bacon fat over low heat. Remove from the heat and stir in the olive oil, vinegar, and honey. (Add more bacon fat if you want a porkier flavor, but keep a general 2:1 ratio of fat to acid.) The honey will balance the acidity of the vinegar but should not make the dressing overly sweet. Keep warm until ready to use.

Prepare a medium-hot fire in a charcoal grill (or preheat a gas grill to medium-high, or heat a grill pan over high heat).

In a large bowl, toss the chicories with 3 Tbsp of the olive oil and season with salt and pepper. Drizzle in the water, and mix well. Put the chicories on the hottest part of the grill (or in the grill pan). Once the leaves begin to char, about 30 seconds, move them to a cooler spot on the grill, stacking the leaves on top of each other, and continue cooking until the leaves are slightly wilted. Transfer to a salad bowl.

Add the remaining 2 Tbsp olive oil to a large cast-iron pan and warm over high heat until just beginning to smoke. Carefully crack the eggs and slide them into the pan. With a spatula, push the whites back as they spread to keep them from running into each other. As the whites begin to set, tilt the pan slightly so that the oil runs to one side and baste the eggs with the hot oil, paying special attention to the yolks. Once the eggs release from the pan and the edges begin to brown, season with salt and pepper, and remove from the heat.

Spoon the warm bacon vinaigrette over the chicories and toss. Adjust the seasoning, if necessary. Transfer to plates and set the eggs on top. Spoon a bit more of the vinaigrette over the eggs and serve immediately.

GRILLED ESCAROLE WEDGES WITH LEMON-ANCHOVY DRESSING & ROASTED PEPPERS

SERVES 4 / This riff on Caesar salad runs laps around the classic in terms of texture, contrast, and general tastiness. We leave the escarole wedges attached at the base for ease of grilling, and we like how it makes for a hearty steak of greens, to be eaten with a fork and knife. I like my Caesar dressing very anchovy-forward, but you can easily back down that element to suit your palate. Bread crumbs are a nice textural garnish here, but you can just as easily fry a few capers to give the dish an extra-briny crunch.

LEMON-ANCHOVY DRESSING
1 egg yolk
8 anchovy fillets
1 garlic clove
1 tsp whole-grain mustard
1 tsp capers, roughly chopped
3 Tbsp fresh lemon juice
¾ cup [180 ml] grapeseed oil
¼ cup [60 ml] extra-virgin olive oil
Kosher salt
Freshly ground black pepper
Dash of Tabasco sauce
Dash of Worcestershire sauce

1 large head escarole, cut into quarters through to the base, keeping the leaves intact
2 Tbsp extra-virgin olive oil
Kosher salt
Freshly ground black pepper
1 handful Garlic Croutons (see page 80), fully cooled
Fresh lemon juice for serving
1 Roasted or Grilled Red Pepper (page 77), cut into ¼-in [6-mm] strips
1 or 2 anchovy fillets
Chunk of Parmesan cheese for shaving

To make the dressing: In a food processor, combine the egg yolk, anchovy fillets, garlic, mustard, capers, and lemon juice. Process until well combined. Combine the grapeseed oil and olive oil in a measuring cup. With the food processor running, add to the egg yolk mixture, a few drops at a time at first and steadily increasing the flow as the mixture begins to emulsify. Season with salt and pepper. Add the Tabasco and Worcestershire sauce. The dressing should be thick and lemony, with a bold punch of anchovy. If the dressing seems too thick, thin with a couple of drops of cold water.

Prepare a hot fire in a charcoal grill (or preheat a gas grill to high, or heat a grill pan over high heat).

In a large bowl, gently toss the escarole with the olive oil and season with salt and pepper. Put the escarole wedges, cut-side down, on the hottest part of the grill (or in the grill pan) and cook, turning once, until well seared on both sides. Transfer to a serving platter.

Place the croutons on a work surface and, using a rolling pin or a knife, crush into coarse crumbs.

Top the greens with the dressing and a bit of fresh lemon juice. Garnish with the roasted peppers, anchovy fillets, and a shower of crouton crumbs. Shave some Parmesan over the salad and serve immediately.

GRILLED RED ROMAINE WITH BAGNA CAUDA

SERVES 4 TO 6 / Small heads of red romaine, like the ones we get from James Birch at Flora Bella Farm in Three Rivers, California, are the perfect vehicles for the warm garlic-and-anchovy bath known as bagna cauda. It's traditionally used as a dip, but when spiked with a bit of red wine vinegar and used as a dressing for the grilled red romaine, the result is a beautifully succulent, smoky dish. Be liberal with the anchovies and garlic—the heat tends to mellow them just enough so that your breath won't stink for the rest of the night. Use the other half of the recipe to dress raw cauliflower or use as a dip for cherry tomatoes.

**4 heads red romaine, cut in half through to the base
so that the leaves remain intact
3 Tbsp extra-virgin olive oil**

**Kosher salt
Freshly ground black pepper
½ recipe Bagna Cauda (page 54)**

Prepare a hot fire in a charcoal grill (or preheat a gas grill to high, or heat a grill pan over high heat).

In a large bowl, drizzle the romaine with the olive oil and season with salt and pepper. Put the romaine wedges, cut-side down, on the hottest part of the grill (or in the grill pan) and cook, turning once, until well charred on both sides. Transfer to a serving platter, drizzle with the bagna cauda, and serve warm.

CHAPTER THREE
PIZZAS & TOASTS

I see pizza as an obsession, subject to rules and personal hang-ups. But the toast portion of our menu is where anything goes. Having the two on our menu allows us to operate within limits some of the time, and with complete freedom at other times. And, let's admit it, a lot of things taste good on bread.

Every day, we are faced with the enviable problem of having a large quantity of leftover bread. This bounty has led us to many of my favorite dishes. With toast, there are few constraints. A topping of nut butter, banana, and honey is as respectable as roast beef with horseradish, mustard, and pickled red onions. At Gjelina, we feature all the staples we make in-house, from mostardas, jams, and pickles to smoked and pickled fish, pâtés, terrines, and rillettes on toast.

I love pizza from the bottom of my heart. When I was growing up in New Jersey, pizza was part of the fabric of my everyday life. It was my first food love and it still fills me with simple joy. The guys who threw pies at my neighborhood pizza shop were badasses, and their pizza was the best on the face of the earth as far as I could tell. I ate a ton of it and loved every bite. I still crave it almost daily and imagine that, by now, at least 50 percent of my body comprises dough, tomato, and mozzarella.

I will never forget the moment, after months of planning and construction, that we fired up the Gjelina pizza oven for the first time. It marked the beginning of a long, difficult process of learning how to produce a large volume of wood-fired pizzas in a busy restaurant day after day. I knew so little then; if I could have imagined the months of trial and error and painstaking, hairsplitting experimentation, I might not have done it. But I am grateful that I did. Pizza is at the very heart of this restaurant and I'm proud of our reputation for making great pies. I generally don't subscribe to any pizza voodoo. Special water? Strains of yeast from Italy? As far as I'm concerned, it's all misdirection to make people believe they cannot make great pizza. Utter nonsense. But pizza-making can be humbling. You need to be tuned in to the subtleties of the science of dough production. I've found that good technique always makes for a better pizza. With regard to dough, we have found that using small amounts of yeast or starter, making a very wet dough, and allowing for a long, slow rise result in the kind of charred, tender, crisp yet chewy crust we like. We opt for a relatively small 6½-oz [185-g] ball of dough and stretch it so thin that we can read the newspaper through it. The temperature in our wood-fired oven reaches about 800°F [425°C], which means that our pizzas are ready in roughly 2 minutes. Great pizzas can be made in a home oven fitted with a pizza stone and heated to 500°F [260°C].

I don't consider myself a pizza purist by any means, but the truth is that a couple of ripe tomatoes and some fresh burrata are simply better than more complex toppings. As far as I'm concerned, there are certain things that just don't belong on pizza. If I go to pizza shop and find BBQ sauce or Caesar salad on pizza, then I know I am not in my kind of joint. I have had passionate disagreements with people about a range of pizza-related topics, such as whether corn or avocado belong on a pizza (the answer to both is no for me), and have gotten nowhere. On the other hand, I have heard chefs discuss the merits of cooked tomato sauce versus uncooked tomato sauce and found that both sides have valid points.

A very hot oven, a very wet dough with a long fermentation, and a light hand with the toppings are the keys to making a great pizza. Keep these fundamentals in mind and your pizza can't help but be great.

GJELINA PIZZA DOUGH

MAKES THREE 6½-0Z [185-G] PORTIONS / We like a puffed-up, pillowy pizza crust with a charred surface and a tender, chewy crumb. A combination of fine-milled, low-gluten 00 Italian flour mixed with a higher-protein bread flour helps achieve this result. The dough is mixed and allowed to rise in bulk, and is coated with olive oil while being turned at 30-minute intervals, to help achieve the elasticity and strength needed to be pulled superthin. After 2 to 3 hours (depending on the ambient room temperature), we punch the dough down a final time and retard it in the walk-in fridge for a minimum of 24 hours. Then we divide it into 6½-oz [185-g] portions and allow a final rise before shaping the pies. We have found that a dough with some age has a more complex flavor, caramelizes to a more beautiful golden hue, and develops a crisper outer crust than a younger dough made under the same conditions.

I'm sure there are people shaking their fists in passionate disagreement while reading this. But, hey, there are many approaches equally logical, if conflicting, opinions on this topic. Run some experiments of your own and adjust this recipe to your liking. This recipe is among the simplest I've worked with, and the most reliable in quality and consistency. The dough should maintain a temperature of about 80°F [27°C] throughout the mixing process, so make sure your kitchen isn't too cool. And your results will be more reliable if you weigh the ingredients, even the water.

At Gjelina, we employ a wild yeast starter culture for our bread, but we rely on commercial yeast for pizza. The result is a crust with a lighter texture and a less assertive flavor.

1 cup plus 2 Tbsp [270 g] warm (87°F [30°C]) water

1 tsp [3 g] fresh yeast (baker's compressed fresh yeast)

1½ cups [170 g] 00 flour, preferably Antimo Caputo

1½ cups [180 g] bread flour, such as King Arthur's Sir Galahad, plus more for dusting

3 tsp [15 g] fine sea salt

2 Tbsp extra-virgin olive oil, plus more for brushing

Semolina flour for dusting

All-purpose flour for dusting

In a small bowl, combine the water and yeast, stirring until the yeast dissolves.

In the bowl of a stand mixer fitted with the dough hook attachment, combine the 00 flour and bread flour. Add the dissolved yeast to the flours and mix at medium speed just until the dough comes together, about 3 minutes. Drape a clean kitchen towel over the dough and let rest for 15 minutes. Add the salt and mix at medium-high speed for 5 to 7 minutes, until smooth and very elastic.

Coat a large glass or metal bowl with the olive oil. Fold the dough into thirds like a giant letter and put it in the bowl, turning it over several times to coat it with oil. Cover the bowl with plastic wrap and let the dough rise at warm room temperature until it has increased its volume by 50 to 75 percent, about 3 hours. Punch the dough down, fold in thirds, and rotate it 90 degrees, then fold in thirds again. Cover the bowl with plastic wrap and refrigerate for 1 to 2½ days. If the dough grows larger than the bowl, punch it down, and return to the refrigerator.

Divide the dough into three 6½-oz [185-g] pieces. Dust a little bread flour on your work surface, put the dough on the work surface, and, pressing down on it lightly with the palm of your hand, roll it in a circular motion, forming a boule (dough ball). If the dough is sliding around, there is too much flour on the work surface. Wipe some away if necessary. You need some friction between the work surface and the dough, but not so much that the dough sticks and makes a mess. Once the dough gathers into a tight ball and the outer layer of dough is pulled taut over the surface, check the bottom of the dough to see that the seam has sealed. If there is an opening on the bottom, you need to roll the dough more tightly or it will tear easily when stretched. Repeat with the remaining pieces of dough.

Transfer the dough balls to a baking sheet brushed with a bit of olive oil, leaving plenty of space between the balls so they have room to rise and expand. (The boule shape encourages an even, round, and more vertical rise, as opposed to a flatter, more irregular shape.) Brush the tops with a bit of olive oil, loosely cover with plastic wrap, and let rise at room temperature until doubled in size, 1½ to 3 hours.

In a small bowl, combine 2 to 3 Tbsp semolina flour and an equal amount of all-purpose flour and then mound the blended flours on your work surface. Put another 2 to 3 Tbsp all-purpose flour in a medium bowl. Put one of the dough balls in the bowl of all-purpose flour and turn to coat with the flour on all sides, handling the dough gently so as not to force out the air or misshape it.

Put the floured dough ball on top of the mound of flour on your work surface. With your fingertips, punch the air out of the dough and press your fingers into the center and extend outward to shape the mass into a small disk. Continue to press your fingers and palm down on the center of the dough while turning the dough with your other hand, pushing out the dough from the center but maintaining an airy rim around the perimeter. Continue stretching out the dough on the work surface with your hand by spreading your fingers as far as you can as you turn the dough.

Some of my guys with smaller hands use two hands to stretch the dough as it grows larger, using this technique: With the palms of your hands facing down, slip your hands under the dough, lift it up, and use the backs of both hands to gently pull on the dough while continuing to turn it. The dough should stretch easily, resting on the backs of your wrists and forearms, so do not pull on it too much. If it is superelastic, then the dough probably has not proofed enough. If the dough is supersoft and tears easily, it has proofed too much. You are done stretching out the dough when it is 10 to 12 in [25 to 30.5 cm] in diameter and thin enough so that you can read a newspaper through it. This takes a bit of practice so be patient, but under no circumstances should you resort to a rolling pin.

Follow the topping and baking instructions, as directed in the pizza recipes, repeating the stretching process for the remaining dough balls while the pizza you stretched and just topped cooks.

PIZZA POMODORO

MAKES ONE 10- TO 12-IN [25- TO 30.5-CM] PIZZA / This pizza is spectacular. We build it from our simple tomato sauce, tomato confit, oregano, and crushed red pepper, balanced with the right amount of olive oil and sea salt. This makes for a perfect base for mozzarella, burrata, anchovies, prosciutto, arugula, or some combination of these. If I could eat only one pizza for the rest of my life, it would be a pomodoro burrata, our version of a classic Margherita. The only trick to using burrata is to add it toward the end of the cooking process, baking only until it just melts. Plenty of good-quality, ripe extra-virgin olive oil drizzled over the top of this pizza is key to its tastiness.

Semolina flour for dusting

One 6½-oz [185-g] ball Gjelina Pizza Dough (page 104), proofed and stretched until 10 to 12 in [25 to 30.5 cm] in diameter

⅓ cup [75 ml] Pomodoro Sauce (page 59)

⅓ cup [80 g] Tomato Confit (page 60)

2 tsp best-quality olive oil

¼ tsp dried oregano, preferably Sicilian

¼ tsp flaky sea salt

¼ cup [7 g] fresh basil leaves

Crushed red pepper flakes for serving

Place a pizza stone on the middle rack of your oven and preheat the oven to the highest possible setting, at least 500°F [260°C], for 1 hour. Lightly dust a pizza peel or a rimless baking sheet with semolina flour.

Using your forearms or the backs of your hands, transfer the stretched round of dough to the prepared peel.

With a large spoon, gently spread the pomodoro sauce evenly across the dough, leaving a 1-in [2.5-cm] border without any sauce. Sprinkle the tomato confit in areas where there is less sauce. Drizzle with half of the olive oil and sprinkle with half the oregano and all the sea salt.

Slide the dough onto the pizza stone in the oven and bake, allowing it to bubble up and rise, 4 to 5 minutes. Once the rim starts to look pillowy and airy, using a pizza peel, turn the pizza 180 degrees to ensure that it browns evenly all over. It's ready when the rim is a deep golden brown and beginning to char and the bottom of the pizza is crisp, 4 to 5 minutes total.

Using the peel or rimless baking sheet, transfer the pizza to a cutting board or a baking sheet with a rim. Sprinkle with the remaining oregano and the basil and drizzle the rest of the olive oil over the top. Slice and serve hot, with crushed red pepper flakes on the side.

PIZZA POMODORO CRUDO

MAKES ONE 10- TO 12-IN [25- TO 30.5-CM] PIZZA / This is the ideal pizza to make in the summer when cherry tomatoes are abundant and as sweet as can be. Use any variety of cherry tomato you like, as long as it is on the smaller side. I especially like the bright yellow Sun Golds. The tomatoes give up some of their juice in the oven and combine with the olive oil in a way that is simply magical. This is Italian cooking as I know it, at its best. As basic as this sounds, if any part of the delicate balance of ingredients is compromised—the tomatoes are less than stellar or the olive oil has been open too long—the simple perfection of this pie is lost.

Semolina flour for dusting

One 6½-oz [185-g] ball Gjelina Pizza Dough (page 104), proofed and stretched until 10 to 12 in [25 to 30.5 cm] in diameter

2 cloves Garlic Confit (page 64), roughly chopped

6 oz [170 g] cherry tomatoes, halved

¼ tsp dried oregano, preferably Sicilian

Flaky sea salt

3 oz [85 g] stracciatella or burrata, torn into walnut-size pieces

1 tsp best-quality olive oil

¼ cup [7 g] fresh basil leaves

Place a pizza stone on the middle rack of your oven and preheat the oven to the highest possible setting, at least 500°F [260°C], for 1 hour. Lightly dust a pizza peel or a rimless baking sheet with semolina flour.

Using your forearms or the backs of your hands, transfer the stretched round of dough to the prepared peel.

Distribute the garlic confit over the dough, flicking the garlic oil that clings to your fingers onto the dough. Spread the cherry tomatoes around. They will not cover the entire area; there will be many gaps. Crumble half the oregano over the top, and season with a generous amount of salt.

Slide the dough onto the pizza stone in the oven and bake, allowing it to bubble up and rise, 4 to 5 minutes. Once the rim starts to look pillowy and airy, using the pizza peel, turn the pizza 180 degrees to ensure that it browns evenly all over. Open your oven and sprinkle on the stracciatella about 1 minute before the pizza is finished baking. It's ready when the rim is a deep golden brown and beginning to char and the bottom of the pizza is crisp, 4 to 5 minutes total.

Using the peel or rimless baking sheet, transfer the pizza to a cutting board or a baking sheet with a rim. Drizzle with the olive oil and sprinkle the remaining oregano on top. Season with more salt. If the basil leaves are small, leave them whole and scatter them over the top of the pizza; tear larger ones in half. Slice and serve hot.

PIZZA WITH SPINACH, FETA & GARLIC CONFIT

MAKES ONE 10- TO 12-IN [25- TO 30.5-CM] PIZZA / Watching through the oven door as the pile of spinach on top of the pizza cooks down and the dough slowly becomes covered with salty feta and creamy mozzarella is, simply, rad. We use an heirloom variety of spinach called Bloomsdale, which has very curly leaves that char on the edges in a beautiful way as they cook.

Semolina flour for dusting

One 6½-oz [185-g] ball Gjelina Pizza Dough (page 104), proofed and stretched until 10 to 12 in [25 to 30.5 cm] in diameter

2 cloves Garlic Confit (page 64), roughly chopped

4 cups [85 g] loosely packed spinach leaves, preferably Bloomsdale

1½ oz [40 g] feta cheese

1½ oz [40 g] mozzarella cheese, cut into ½-in [12-mm] cubes

Pinch of dried oregano, preferably Sicilian

2 tsp olive oil

Place a pizza stone on the middle rack of your oven and preheat the oven to the highest possible setting, at least 500°F [260°C], for 1 hour. Lightly dust a pizza peel or a rimless baking sheet with semolina flour.

Using your forearms or the backs of your hands, transfer the stretched round of dough to the prepared peel.

Distribute the garlic confit over the dough, flicking the garlic oil that clings to your fingers onto the dough. Pile the spinach on top, leaving a 1-in [2.5-cm] border, and scatter the feta and mozzarella over the spinach, allowing the cheese to nestle into the folds of the greens.

Slide the dough onto the pizza stone in the oven and bake, allowing it to bubble up and rise, 4 to 5 minutes. Once the rim starts to look pillowy and airy, using the pizza peel, turn the pizza 180 degrees to ensure that it browns evenly all over. It's ready when the rim is a deep golden brown and beginning to char, and the bottom of the pizza is crisp, 6 to 8 minutes total.

Using the peel or rimless baking sheet, transfer the pizza to a cutting board or a baking sheet with a rim. Crumble the oregano and sprinkle over the top. Drizzle with the olive oil. Slice and serve hot.

PIZZA WITH NETTLES, RACLETTE & FRESNO CHILE

MAKES ONE 10- TO 12-IN [25- TO 30.5-CM] PIZZA / The Alpine cheese raclette melts beautifully on a pizza, and its nutty flavor pairs deliciously with the salty green flavor of the nettles. We like to buy young nettles that we can throw directly on a pie without blanching first. As they mature, nettles' stingers become more of an obstacle, and they require gloved hands and a quick dip in boiling water before using as a topping.

Semolina flour for dusting

One 6½-oz [185-g] ball Gjelina Pizza Dough (page 104), proofed and stretched until 10 to 12 in [25 to 30.5 cm] in diameter

1½ oz [40 g] fresh young nettles

2 Tbsp best-quality olive oil

1 or 2 Fresno chiles, or another medium-hot green or red chile, cut into 12 thin slices, seeds removed

2 cloves Garlic Confit (page 64), roughly chopped

¼ tsp flaky sea salt

½ oz [15 g] raclette cheese

½ oz [15 g] mozzarella cheese, torn into small pieces

½ oz [15 g] Parmesan cheese, grated

Place a pizza stone on the middle rack of your oven and preheat the oven to the highest possible setting, at least 500°F [260°C], for 1 hour. Lightly dust a pizza peel or a rimless baking sheet with semolina flour.

Using your forearms or the backs of your hands, transfer the stretched round of dough to the prepared peel.

In a medium bowl, toss the nettles with the olive oil, chiles, garlic confit, and salt. Scatter the nettle mixture over the dough. With a vegetable peeler, shave the raclette over the top. Sprinkle with the mozzarella and Parmesan.

Slide the dough onto the pizza stone in the oven and bake, allowing it to bubble up and rise, 4 to 5 minutes. Once the rim starts to look pillowy and airy, using the pizza peel, turn the pizza 180 degrees to ensure that it browns evenly all over. It's ready when the rim is a deep golden brown and beginning to char and the bottom of the pizza is crisp, 6 to 8 minutes total.

Using the peel or rimless baking sheet, transfer the pizza to a cutting board or a baking sheet with a rim. Slice and serve hot.

PIZZA WITH MUSHROOMS & TRUFFLE-STUDDED GOAT CHEESE

MAKES ONE 10- TO 12-IN [25- TO 30.5-CM] PIZZA / The key to this pizza is to use whatever mushrooms look good and fresh at the market. We always have a pie made with just cremini mushrooms that has a bit more of a working-class personality but tastes amazing. This pizza, in contrast, is more upscale. Look for a truffle-studded ash-y goat cheese such as Truffle Tremor by Cypress Grove.

Semolina flour for dusting

One 6½-oz [185-g] ball Gjelina Pizza Dough (page 104), proofed and stretched until 10 to 12 in [25 to 30.5 cm] in diameter

4 oz [115 g] mushrooms, such as cremini or chanterelle, sliced ¼ in [6 mm] thick if large; small ones halved or left whole

2 Tbsp best-quality olive oil

¼ tsp Maldon sea salt

2 oz [55 g] truffled goat cheese, such as Truffle Tremor

1½ oz [40 g] fontina cheese

¼ tsp fresh thyme leaves

Place a pizza stone on the middle rack of your oven and preheat the oven to the highest possible setting, at least 500°F [260°C], for 1 hour. Lightly dust a pizza peel or a rimless baking sheet with semolina flour.

Using your forearms or the backs of your hands, transfer the stretched round of dough to the prepared peel.

In a small bowl, toss together the mushrooms, olive oil, and sea salt. Scatter the mushrooms generously over the dough, almost covering the whole base. Crumble the goat cheese over the mushrooms. With a vegetable peeler, shave the fontina over the top. Be somewhat sparing with the cheese, as it will spread in the oven.

Slide the dough onto the pizza stone in the oven and bake, allowing it to bubble up and rise, 4 to 5 minutes. Once the rim starts to look pillowy and airy, using the pizza peel, turn the pizza 180 degrees to ensure that it browns evenly all over. It's ready when the rim is a deep golden brown and beginning to char, and the bottom of the pizza is crisp, 6 to 8 minutes total.

Using the peel or rimless baking sheet, transfer the pizza to a cutting board or a baking sheet with a rim. Scatter the thyme leaves on top. Slice and serve hot.

PIZZA WITH ASPARAGUS, SOTTOCENERE & SUNNY EGG

MAKES ONE 10- TO 12-IN [25- TO 30.5-CM] PIZZA / After you've tried making a couple of pizzas in your home oven and mastered the timing, try this one. Of course, a runny egg on top of just about anything has a way of making people happy. We put one egg in the center of the pizza, which breaks when you slice the pie and oozes all over the top. It also gives you something to swipe your crust through. Sottocenere is an ash-rubbed, truffle-studded cow's milk cheese with a subtle creamy texture and a flavor of sweet spices like cinnamon and nutmeg, which permeates the cheese as it ages.

In an 800°F [425°C] oven, the egg and pizza cook at a very similar rate. This may not be the case in your home oven, so you might want to start the pizza without the egg, and crack one over the pizza about halfway through the baking process. You want the egg whites to be set, but the yolk still very runny. It may take a couple of shots to get it right, but your flawed experiments will still be tasty.

Semolina flour for dusting
One 6½-oz [185-g] ball Gjelina Pizza Dough (page 104), proofed and stretched until 10 to 12 in [25 to 30.5 cm] in diameter
2 cloves Garlic Confit (page 64), roughly chopped
⅓ cup [75 g] sliced Shallot Confit (page 64)

4 large asparagus, shaved with a vegetable peeler into thin slices
3 oz [85 g] sottocenere cheese, or another nutty, creamy cheese, such as fontina
1 egg
Flaky sea salt
Freshly ground black pepper

Place a pizza stone on the middle rack of your oven and preheat the oven to the highest possible setting, at least 500°F [260°C], for 1 hour. Lightly dust a pizza peel or a rimless baking sheet with semolina flour.

Using your forearms or the backs of your hands, transfer the stretched round of dough to the prepared peel.

Distribute the garlic confit and shallot confit over the dough, flicking the garlic oil that clings to your fingers onto the dough. Top with the shaved asparagus and the sottocenere, leaving a small space in the center of the pie for the egg.

Slide the dough onto the pizza stone in the oven and bake for 2 to 3 minutes. Using the pizza peel, turn the pizza 180 degrees to ensure that it browns evenly all over. Crack the egg into a small ramekin or bowl and carefully transfer the egg to the center of the pizza. Continue cooking until the rim is a deep golden brown and beginning to char, 3 to 5 minutes longer.

Using the peel or rimless baking sheet, transfer the pizza to a cutting board or a baking sheet with a rim. Sprinkle with salt and pepper. Slice and serve hot.

PIZZA WITH ANCHOVIES & ROASTED PEPPER

MAKES ONE 10- TO 12-IN [25- TO 30.5-CM] PIZZA / I have a serious love for anchovies, so of course we feature them on pizza. They're a natural addition to a standard pomodoro or margherita pizza, but this combination is just a bit better with the addition of sweet roasted peppers and smoked mozzarella.

Semolina flour for dusting

One 6½-oz [185-g] ball Gjelina Pizza Dough (page 104), proofed and stretched until 10 to 12 in [25 to 30.5 cm] in diameter

⅓ cup [80 g] Tomato Confit (page 60)

¼ cup [50 g] Roasted or Grilled Red Peppers (page 77)

8 to 10 whole salt-packed anchovies, halved lengthwise, boned, and rinsed

3 oz [80 g] smoked mozzarella cheese, torn into rough ½-in [12-mm] pieces

Dried oregano, preferably Sicilian, for sprinkling

2 Tbsp best-quality olive oil

Place a pizza stone on the middle rack of your oven and preheat the oven to the highest possible setting, at least 500°F [260°C], for 1 hour. Lightly dust a pizza peel or a rimless baking sheet with semolina flour.

Using your forearms or the backs of your hands, transfer the stretched round of dough to the prepared peel.

Distribute the tomato confit and roasted peppers over the dough, followed by the anchovies and mozzarella.

Slide the dough onto the pizza stone in the oven and bake, allowing it to bubble up and rise, 4 to 5 minutes. Once the rim starts to look pillowy and airy, using the pizza peel, turn the pizza 180 degrees to ensure that it browns evenly all over. It's ready when the rim is a deep golden brown and beginning to char, and the bottom of the pizza is crisp, 6 to 8 minutes total.

Using the peel or rimless baking sheet, transfer the pizza to a cutting board or a baking sheet with a rim. Crumble the oregano and sprinkle over the top. Drizzle with the olive oil. Slice and serve hot.

PIZZA WITH GUANCIALE, CASTELVETRANO OLIVES & FRESNO CHILE

MAKES ONE 10- TO 12-IN [25- TO 30.5-CM] PIZZA / For anyone not yet acquainted with guanciale, it is the delicately spiced, unsmoked cousin to bacon. It has much more fat than bacon, and a sweet, subtle flavor. And it crisps perfectly when it cooks. Here, we pair it with buttery green Castelvetrano olives, the mild heat of Fresno chile, and a scattering of roughly chopped rosemary.

Semolina flour for dusting

One 6½-oz [185-g] ball Gjelina Pizza Dough (page 104), proofed and stretched until 10 to 12 in [25 to 30.5 cm] in diameter

⅓ cup [75 ml] Pomodoro Sauce (page 59)

4 Castelvetrano olives, pitted and broken into quarters

1 Fresno chile, or another medium-hot green or red chile, sliced and seeds removed

1½ oz [40 g] mozzarella cheese, torn into small pieces

1½ oz [40 g] Asiago cheese

1½ oz [40 g] thinly sliced guanciale

2 pinches of roughly chopped fresh rosemary

Place a pizza stone on the middle rack of your oven and preheat the oven to the highest possible setting, at least 500°F [260°C], for 1 hour. Lightly dust a pizza peel or a rimless baking sheet with semolina flour.

Using your forearms or the backs of your hands, transfer the stretched round of dough to the prepared peel.

With a large spoon, gently spread the pomodoro sauce evenly across the dough, leaving a 1-in [2.5-cm] border without any sauce. Scatter the olives, chile, and mozzarella on top. With a vegetable peeler, shave the Asiago over the top. Add the guanciale last so that it will get crisp as it cooks.

Slide the dough onto the pizza stone in the oven and bake, allowing it to bubble up and rise, 4 to 5 minutes. Once the rim starts to look pillowy and airy, using the pizza peel, turn the pizza 180 degrees to ensure that it browns evenly all over. It's ready when the rim is a deep golden brown and beginning to char, and the bottom of the pizza is crisp, 6 to 8 minutes total.

Using the peel or rimless baking sheet, transfer the pizza to a cutting board or a baking sheet with a rim. Sprinkle the rosemary on top. Slice and serve hot.

PIZZA WITH BACON & RADICCHIO

MAKES ONE 10- TO 12-IN [25- TO 30.5-CM] PIZZA / Look for thinly sliced bacon, which can go right on the pizza and will crisp as it cooks. We're big fans of the applewood-smoked Nueske's bacon from Wisconsin. Grilling the radicchio before it goes on the pizza gives it an added smokiness and helps ensure that it will cook through. You could just sauté it quickly in olive oil instead, or even put it on the pizza raw.

Semolina flour for dusting
One 1-in [2.5-cm] wedge radicchio
1 tsp best-quality olive oil
Flaky sea salt
Freshly ground black pepper

One 6½-oz [185-g] ball Gjelina Pizza Dough (page 104), proofed and stretched until 10 to 12 in [25 to 30.5 cm] in diameter
⅓ cup [80 g] Tomato Confit (page 60)
1½ oz [40 g] fontina cheese
6 slices thinly sliced bacon
Fresh thyme leaves for sprinkling

Place a pizza stone on the middle rack of your oven and preheat the oven to the highest possible setting, at least 500°F [260°C], for 1 hour. Lightly dust a pizza peel or a rimless baking sheet with semolina flour.

Prepare a hot fire in a charcoal grill (or preheat a gas grill to high).

In a small bowl, toss the radicchio with the olive oil and season with salt and pepper. Cook on the hottest part of the grill until grill marks develop, about 2 minutes. Flip and cook on the other side until charred, about 1 minute longer. Remove from the grill and let cool. When cool enough to handle, chop the grilled radicchio into 1-in [2.5-cm] pieces.

Using your forearms or the backs of your hands, transfer the stretched round of dough to the prepared peel.

Distribute the tomato confit over the dough, followed by the chopped radicchio. With a vegetable peeler, shave the fontina over the top. Drape the bacon slices over the radicchio, making sure that it is on top of the other ingredients so that it can crisp as it cooks in the oven.

Slide the dough onto the pizza stone in the oven and bake, allowing it to bubble up and rise, 4 to 5 minutes. Once the rim starts to look pillowy and airy, using the pizza peel, turn the pizza 180 degrees to ensure that it browns evenly all over. It's ready when the rim is a deep golden brown and beginning to char, and the bottom of the pizza is crisp, 6 to 8 minutes total.

Using the peel or rimless baking sheet, transfer the pizza to a cutting board or a baking sheet with a rim. Sprinkle with the thyme. Slice and serve hot.

PIZZA WITH LAMB SAUSAGE & BROCCOLI RABE

MAKES ONE 10- TO 12-IN [25- TO 30.5-CM] PIZZA / Sausage and broccoli rabe is one of this world's great marriages and a perfect topping for pizza. For quick-cooking pizzas, look for a young Asiago; it melts better than the harder, aged Asiago. I find the lamb sausage and mint an interesting combination, but you can use pork sausage and oregano for a more traditional pairing, if you prefer.

Semolina flour for dusting
2 Tbsp best-quality olive oil
3 broccoli rabe stalks, roughly chopped
1 clove Garlic Confit (page 64), roughly chopped
2 pinches of crushed red pepper flakes
Kosher salt

One 6½-oz [185-g] ball Gjelina Pizza Dough (page 104), proofed and stretched until 10 to 12 in [25 to 30.5 cm] in diameter
⅓ cup [80 g] Tomato Confit (page 60)
1½ oz [40 g] Asiago cheese
3 oz [85 g] Lamb Sausage (page 297)
2 Tbsp freshly grated Pecorino Romano cheese
1 Tbsp chopped fresh mint

Place a pizza stone on the middle rack of your oven and preheat the oven to the highest possible setting, at least 500°F [260°C], for 1 hour. Lightly dust a pizza peel or a rimless baking sheet with semolina flour.

In a medium frying pan over medium-high heat, warm the olive oil until hot but not smoking. Add the broccoli rabe, garlic confit, and a pinch of red pepper flakes and season with salt. Cook until bright green and al dente, about 3 minutes. Set aside to cool.

Using your forearms or the backs of your hands, transfer the stretched round of dough to the prepared peel.

Distribute the tomato confit over the dough, followed by the sautéed broccoli rabe. With a vegetable peeler, shave the Asiago over the top. Pinch off small pieces of the sausage and distribute it evenly over the pie.

Slide the dough onto the pizza stone in the oven and bake, allowing it to bubble up and rise, 4 to 5 minutes. Once the rim starts to look pillowy and airy, using the pizza peel, turn the pizza 180 degrees to ensure that it browns evenly all over. It's ready when the rim is a deep golden brown and beginning to char, and the bottom of the pizza is crisp, 6 to 8 minutes total.

Using the peel or rimless baking sheet, transfer the pizza to a cutting board or a baking sheet with a rim. Sprinkle the Pecorino, mint, and remaining pinch of red pepper flakes on top. Slice and serve hot.

EGGPLANT CAPONATA & BURRATA ON TOASTED BAGUETTE

SERVES 4 / Our caponata is a riff on the classic Sicilian dish by way of North Africa. It's a great addition to grilled tuna or chicken, and makes a cool starter on grilled bread with burrata.

2 Tbsp pine nuts

¼ cup [60 ml] extra-virgin olive oil, plus 2 Tbsp

1 lb [455 g] globe eggplant, cut into cubes

Kosher salt

Freshly ground black pepper

½ red onion, diced

1 Roasted or Grilled Red Pepper (page 77), sliced

2 Tbsp dried currants or golden raisins

2 tsp pomegranate molasses or sweet balsamic vinegar

¼ cup [60 ml] Pomodoro Sauce (page 59)

2 whole salt-packed anchovies, halved lengthwise, boned, rinsed, and chopped

1 Tbsp plus 1 tsp red wine vinegar

Pinch of crushed red pepper flakes

1 clove Garlic Confit (page 64)

2 Tbsp roughly chopped arugula

2 Tbsp roughly chopped fresh flat-leaf parsley

2 Tbsp roughly chopped fresh basil

1 Tbsp roughly chopped fresh mint

4 slices baguette, cut on a long diagonal so they are 6 in [15 cm] long and 1 in [2.5 cm] thick

8¼ oz [230 g] burrata cheese

In a small, dry frying pan over medium heat, toast the pine nuts just until fragrant and beginning to brown, 3 to 5 minutes. Let cool.

In a large frying pan over medium-high heat, warm the ¼ cup [60 ml] olive oil until hot but not smoking. Add the eggplant, season with salt and pepper, and cook until starting to soften, about 5 minutes. Work in batches to avoid crowding the pan. Remove the eggplant to a medium bowl and set aside.

Add the 2 Tbsp olive oil to the pan and, when it's hot, add the red onion. Sauté until just starting to soften, about 5 minutes. Stir in the bell pepper. Add the toasted pine nuts and currants to the pan and cook for 1 minute. Stir in the pomegranate molasses and pomodoro sauce. Season with salt and transfer to the bowl with the eggplant. Stir to combine and set aside to cool for 10 minutes. Stir in the anchovies, red wine vinegar, red pepper flakes, garlic confit, arugula, parsley, basil, and mint. Season with salt and pepper. The eggplant should be slightly saucy and have a nice sweet-and-sour balance from the tomato sauce, vinegar, and pomegranate molasses. (This holds very well at room temperature for up to 4 hours, or refrigerated in an airtight container for up to 4 days.)

Grill or toast the bread according to the method on page 77.

Place the toasted bread on a serving plate. Generously smear each slice of toast with burrata and top with a generous coating of the caponata. Serve at room temperature or slightly warm.

MUSHROOM TOAST

SERVES 4 / Our customers freak out over this dish, and there is a good reason why—seared mushrooms, lashed with house-made crème fraîche, a splash of wine, and a few herbs, mounded on top of grilled bread is always a crowd-pleaser. We make no claims for inventing this combination, but we proudly carry the torch. There's a classic version that calls for brioche and wild spring morels, with an optional shower of black truffles. A similar, far less opulent version, can be made with everyday cremini mushrooms and simple ciabatta or a baguette. We opt for a variety of mushrooms supplied by our friend Matt Parker at Shiitake Happens, including nameko, clamshell, pioppini, chanterelle, and hen of the woods, in addition to porcini, matsutake, and the seasonal morels we occasionally score.

Buttermilk stirred into good-quality heavy cream left out to culture for a few days yields a decadent crème fraîche with limitless possibilities. Real farmstead raw-milk crème fraîche is very difficult to come by, but if you are lucky enough to have access to it, by all means use it here. Do not substitute store-bought sour cream. It doesn't hold up to the heat and may break and curdle the sauce.

Unlike the other toasts in this chapter, this is best served piping hot, before the crème fraîche starts to set. Small portions can be served as an appetizer, but a large slab of this toast alongside a glass of earthy red is the way I prefer to take it down.

One 6-in [15-cm] hunk ciabatta, halved horizontally and then crosswise to yield 4 pieces

3 Tbsp extra-virgin olive oil, plus more for toasting the bread

1 lb [455 g] mushrooms, such as nameko, hen of the woods, chanterelle, porcini, matsutake

6 cloves Garlic Confit (page 64), sliced

Kosher salt

Freshly ground black pepper

½ cup [120 ml] dry white wine

1¼ cups [300 ml] Buttermilk Crème Fraîche (page 55)

1 Tbsp chopped fresh flat-leaf parsley

½ tsp fresh thyme leaves

Grill or toast the bread according to the method on page 77. Set aside.

Heat a large frying pan over high heat. Add the olive oil and, when hot, add the mushrooms, in batches if necessary so as not to crowd the pan. It's important that the mushrooms sear and not steam. Cook, without stirring, until the mushrooms are well browned, about 3 minutes. Give the mushrooms a good toss to turn them and then briefly sear on the other side.

Add the garlic confit to the pan, and season with salt and pepper. Add the wine and cook until reduced by half, about 2 minutes. With a wooden spoon, stir in the crème fraîche until well incorporated. Cook until slightly thickened, season with more salt and pepper if necessary, and stir in the parsley and thyme.

Place the toasted bread on individual plates. Spoon the mushrooms and pan sauce on top, dividing it evenly. Serve hot.

SMOKED OCEAN TROUT RILLETTES & FERMENTED LEEKS ON RYE TOAST

SERVES 4 / We cure a lot of ocean trout, which leaves us with a large amount of belly and collar scraps. Although the kitchen staff consumes most of the precious collars, we often smoke the belly pieces—you will need wood chips for this recipe—and fashion them into rillettes, which are especially decadent (if you can find belly, use it instead of the fillet here). Arctic char or sockeye or king salmon fillets make good substitutes for the ocean trout. If not using immediately, pack the rillettes into a jar with a lid, top with clarified butter, and refrigerate for up to 5 days. This toast is equally delicious in the morning with coffee and in the evening with a glass of wine.

SMOKED OCEAN TROUT RILLETTES
1 lb [455 g] ocean trout fillet
Kosher salt
Freshly ground black pepper
¾ cup [170 g] Buttermilk Crème Fraîche (page 55)
¼ cup [7 g] chopped fresh dill
Zest of 1 lemon
3 Tbsp extra-virgin olive oil

½ cup [125 g] Fermented Leeks (page 73)
¼ cup [40 g] Pickled Red Onions (page 69)
¼ cup [30 g] Pickled Fresno Chiles (page 69)
¼ cup [7 g] fresh dill leaves
Best-quality olive oil for drizzling
Squeeze of fresh lemon juice
Flaky sea salt
Four 5-in [12-cm] slices sprouted-rye bread

To make the trout rillettes: Season the ocean trout with kosher salt and pepper and allow to sit while you prepare your smoker.

In a medium bowl, cover a handful of wood chips with water and let soak for about 10 minutes. Prepare a medium-hot fire on one side of a charcoal grill (or preheat one side of a gas grill to medium-high). The ideal temperature for smoking the fish is 180° to 220°F [80° to 105°C]. Wrap the soaked chips loosely in aluminum foil and, with a sharp knife, punch a few holes in the foil. Put the foil packet of wood chips over the hot coals (or gas flame) on one side of the grill. It will start to smoke in about 10 minutes.

Once fully smoking, place the fish on the cool side of the grill. Cover the grill and smoke the fish until it registers 165°F [74°C] on an instant-read thermometer, about 20 minutes, depending on the thickness of the fish (smoking could take up to 40 minutes if it's large).

Transfer the smoked fish to a bowl to cool. When cool enough to handle, use your hands to flake the fish, removing any pin bones or skin as you work. With a wooden spoon, stir in the crème fraîche, dill, and lemon zest, using a whipping motion to thoroughly incorporate all the ingredients. Season with salt and pepper and drizzle in the olive oil.

In a small bowl, mix the fermented leeks, pickled onions, pickled chiles, and dill leaves. Drizzle in a touch of best-quality olive oil and a squeeze of lemon juice and season with sea salt.

Grill or toast the bread according to the method on page 77.

Place the toasted bread on a serving plate. Spread each piece of toast with a generous layer of the rillettes, at least ¼ in [6 mm] thick. Top each toast with some of the dressed leek mixture and cut in half. Serve at room temperature.

CHICKEN & DUCK LIVER PÂTÉ WITH PICKLED BEETS & MUSTARD GREENS ON BRIOCHE TOASTS

SERVES 4 / I can think of few better ways to serve chicken liver pâté, and this is my fallback, especially for parties. Pickled beets and red onions lend a spicy edge to the rich pâté. Small, curly mustard greens are an ideal garnish, but arugula, watercress, or another peppery green will work, too.

1 bunch curly mustard green frills, arugula, or watercress

1 tsp extra-virgin olive oil

½ tsp fresh lemon juice

Dash of aged balsamic vinegar

Flaky sea salt

Freshly ground black pepper

Four 1-in- [2.5-cm-] thick slices brioche

1 lb [455 g] Rustic Chicken & Duck Liver Pâté (page 290), at room temperature

¼ cup [40 g] Pickled Red Onions (page 69)

1 pickled beet, homemade (see variation, page 71) or store-bought, cut into thin strips

Tear the mustard green frills into 2-in [5-cm] lengths. In a mixing bowl, toss the frills with the olive oil, lemon juice, and balsamic vinegar and season with salt and pepper.

Grill or toast the bread according to the method on page 77.

Place the toasted bread on a serving plate. Slather a generous layer of pâté on each toast, taking care not to crush the delicate bread. The layer of pâté should be as thick as the toast itself. Sprinkle a bit of salt over the pâté and grind some pepper on top. Scatter the pickled red onions and beet over the pâté and cut each toast in half. Garnish with the dressed mustard frills. Serve at room temperature.

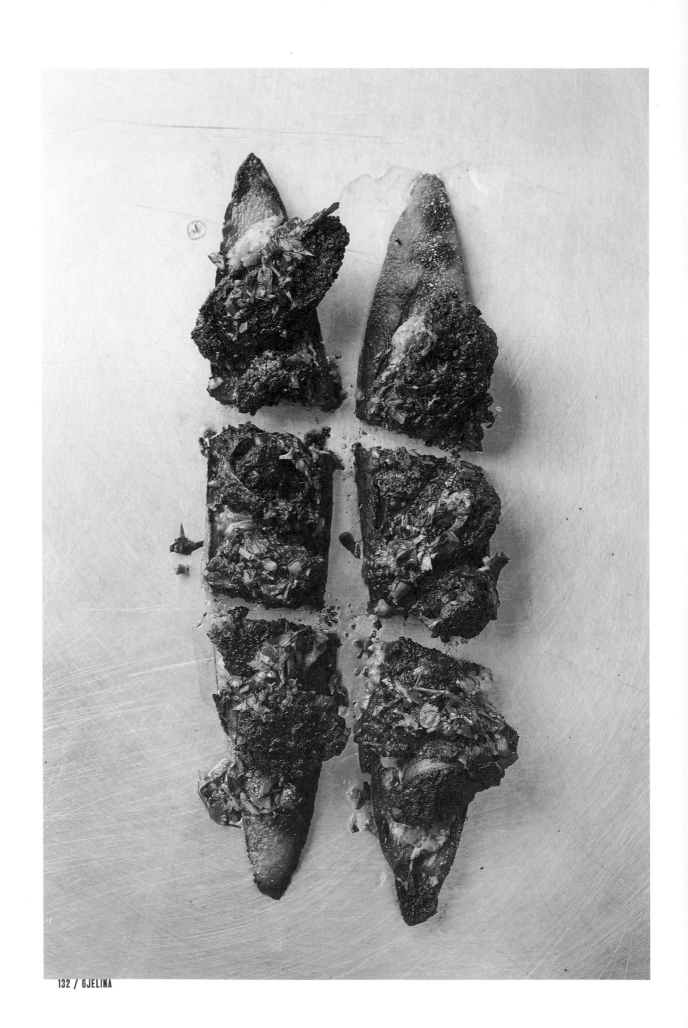

SEARED MORCILLA WITH ROASTED APPLE, ROSEMARY & BLACK PEPPER MOSTARDA & CHIMICHURRI ON TOASTED BAGUETTE

SERVES 4 / When it's seared, blood sausage (*morcilla* in Spanish) turns a deep purplish black, a hue that contrasts beautifully with bright green chimichurri. Mostarda adds sweetness, but use it sparingly; you really want the flavor of the blood sausage to shine.

2 Tbsp extra-virgin olive oil

1 lb [455 g] Blood Sausage (page 298), cut on the bias into ¾-in [2-cm] slices

4 slices baguette, cut on the bias into 1-in- [2.5-cm-] thick slices

¼ cup [60 g] Roasted Apple, Rosemary & Black Pepper Mostarda (page 67)

¼ cup [50 g] Chimichurri (page 51)

Heat a large frying pan over high heat. Add the olive oil and blood sausage slices, cut-side down. Cook, without moving, until the sausage is well seared and the slices release easily from the pan, 4 to 5 minutes. Flip the slices and sear for about 2 minutes longer. Transfer to a plate and let cool.

Grill or toast the bread according to the method on page 77.

Place the toasted bread on a serving plate. Spread each toast with 1 Tbsp of the mostarda. Shingle the slices of blood sausage on top. Cut each toast into three manageable pieces and drizzle with the chimichurri. Serve immediately.

CHAPTER FOUR
VEGETABLES

When Gjelina was in its construction phase, people would often ask me what the "concept" was for the new restaurant, which is a question I generally try to avoid. I would reply somewhat sheepishly that I wanted to focus primarily on small seasonal vegetable dishes, and more often than not people would look at me with a good-luck-with-that kind of expression and walk off.

Admittedly, paying top-dollar Los Angeles rents and selling eight-dollar vegetable sides did seem a little off. Our menu offerings are actually much wider ranging, but the reality is that our vegetable dishes attract people and serve as the centerpiece of the Gjelina dining experience. Our focus on vegetables made us a twice-a-week (or more) kind of establishment for many folks in our neighborhood, rather than a place you only go to occasionally for a celebratory steak or fish.

Listing the daily selection of vegetables in the dead center of the menu is our way of directing the diner's attention toward these dishes. Our wood-fired oven has been great for cooking vegetables and has a way of bringing a rustic soulfulness to pretty much anything that goes in there.

At home you most likely do not have a wood-burning oven, but you can come close to getting the same textures and flavors from your vegetables that we do with a cast-iron frying pan and a very hot oven. Even a basic charcoal grill is a respectable way to up the ante and take a break from your standard stir-fried or steamed vegetables. At Gjelina, we rarely steam or boil vegetables. More often we sear vegetables and then add small amounts of liquid to briefly simmer and meld the flavors, or blanch something quickly before slapping it on the grill or in a searing hot pan.

To add flavor to our vegetable dishes, we draw from an arsenal of pestos, pistous, gremolatas, aiolis, harissas, and other little sauces and emulsions featured in chapter one. These are generally easy to make and hold up well at room temperature, so they can be made in advance and applied effortlessly.

Most of the vegetable dishes in this chapter are delicious served at a range of temperatures, so if prepping ahead of time suits you, feel free. Definitely bring these dishes to the table on a platter whenever possible, as the casual, generous spirit of that presentation suits them.

I am very interested in participating in a shift in how food is produced, taking inspiration from the past to help address some very current and pressing concerns about safe and healthful food production. There are interesting environmental, health, and socioeconomic issues that come up in this conversation, none of which I am an expert in. Regardless, putting out food that tastes better is my primary job as a chef, and I have found that buying farm-fresh ingredients really is the easiest way to make a quantum leap into better cooking and eating. Less common varieties of everyday items like carrots, onions, and potatoes—generally found only in local markets—are much more inspiring to cook with than commodity-grade industrial foods. They simply have more presence and personality and encourage more sensitivity from the cook. Small farm stands and farmers' markets are becoming more widespread and are a practical way for people in many types of communities to access good raw foods.

Allow the availability of the fresh foods that are in season to dictate what you are cooking (within reason). Look for the farmers whose stands best reflect what's currently growing in your area, and learn to groove with the ebb and flow of foods throughout the growing season. I still have to remind myself to simply react to what looks best at the market when making my decisions for our menus. I do my best cooking when riffing on what's available.

BABY RADISHES WITH BLACK OLIVE & ANCHOVY AIOLI

SERVES 4 AS A SIDE DISH / While it is difficult to improve on the classic presentation of raw radishes with butter and sea salt, here a little bit of anchovy introduces an umami note that makes a remarkable contrast with the peppery young radish.

Make this when you stumble upon baby radishes so perfect that even separating the delicate tops from the bulbs seems like a crime. It's gratifying to chomp down on the bulb and its greens in the same bite. Look for small radishes, 4 to 6 in [10 to 15 cm] long, with vibrant leafy greens.

1 bunch baby radishes, with tops intact **Flaky sea salt**
¼ cup [40 g] Black Olive & Anchovy Aioli (page 57)

Wash the radishes thoroughly, rinsing off the grit that hangs out between the leaves. Dry thoroughly.

Spread out the radishes on a platter. Drizzle with the aioli, hitting some of the radishes and leaves, and pour the rest in a puddle on the side, to use for dipping. Sprinkle with salt and serve immediately.

SAUTÉED GREEN BEANS, SMOKED ALMONDS, SHALLOT CONFIT & PRESERVED LEMON

SERVES 4 TO 6 AS A SIDE DISH / If your green beans are large and sturdy, blanch them before sautéing, but if you happen upon some young and tender haricots verts, simply toss them into the hot pan without bothering to cook them first.

3 Tbsp Shallot Oil (page 66) or olive oil

10 oz [280 g] green beans, stem ends trimmed

Kosher salt

Freshly ground black pepper

¼ cup [55 g] Shallot Confit (page 64)

¼ cup [30 g] smoked almonds, coarsely chopped

1 Tbsp minced Preserved Lemons (page 73), rind only

½ cup [120 ml] Vegetable Stock (page 222)

¼ tsp aged balsamic vinegar

Juice of ½ lemon

In a large frying pan over medium-high heat, warm the shallot oil until hot but not smoking. Add the green beans to the hot pan, season with salt and pepper, and cook until the beans begin to blister, about 2 minutes. Add the shallot confit, smoked almonds, and preserved lemon rind and continue cooking until all the ingredients are heated through, about 1 minute longer. Add the stock, bring to a boil, and cook until the sauce begins to thicken, about 5 minutes longer. Stir in the balsamic vinegar and the lemon juice.

Transfer to a serving platter, season again with salt and pepper, and serve warm.

SNAP PEAS & TENDRILS WITH PROSCIUTTO, SOFFRITO & MINT

SERVES 4 TO 6 AS A SIDE DISH / One of our favorite ways to prepare fresh snap peas is to sear them in a hot pan and then add a bit of liquid to finish the cooking with a quick hit of steam. When you select the pea tendrils, make sure they are not too tough. Use only the most delicate leaves and stems. We like to slice an end piece of prosciutto to make smaller, irregularly shaped shavings of ham, but center-cut slices work fine.

¼ cup [60 ml] extra-virgin olive oil

1 lb [455 g] sugar snap peas, stemmed, tough strings removed, and halved on a sharp bias, plus 1 bunch pea tendrils

¼ cup [60 g] Soffrito (page 46)

Kosher salt

Freshly ground black pepper

½ cup [120 ml] Chicken Stock (page 223)

1 Tbsp chopped fresh mint

Pinch of crushed red pepper flakes

Juice of ½ lemon

4 thin slices prosciutto, torn into 3-in- [7.5-cm-] long strips

In a medium sauté pan over high heat, warm the olive oil until hot but not smoking. Add the sugar snap peas to the pan and cook, without stirring, until they begin to brown, about 2 minutes. Stir in the soffrito and season with salt and pepper. Add the stock and cook until it reduces slightly, about 1 minute. Add the pea tendrils, mint, red pepper flakes, and lemon juice and quickly toss in the pan. Season with more salt and pepper if necessary.

Transfer to a serving platter, garnish with the prosciutto, and serve warm.

PAN-ROASTED ROMANESCO WITH GOLDEN RAISINS, TAHINI & SUMAC

SERVES 4 TO 6 AS A SIDE DISH / There is something so mesmerizing about the spiraling sacred geometry found in the florets of romanesco. A cousin to cauliflower, romanesco's sweet nuttiness is also brought out by charring over high heat. Be sure to break the heads into same-size florets so that they can stand up to the high heat. Golden raisins and tahini give this dish a juxtaposition of sweet and savory; lemon and sumac contribute bright flavors. Don't be shy with the sumac; a liberal use defines the dish.

¼ cup [85 g] tahini

Juice of 2 lemons

1 garlic clove, minced

2 Tbsp cold water

2 Tbsp extra-virgin olive oil, plus more for cooking

Kosher salt

Freshly ground black pepper

2 medium heads romanesco, trimmed and chopped into 1-in [2.5 cm] florets

¼ cup [45 g] golden raisins

2 Tbsp Vegetable Stock (page 222) or water

1 Tbsp ground sumac

Flaky sea salt

Best-quality olive oil for drizzling

In a small bowl, combine the tahini with the lemon juice, garlic, and cold water. Whisk in the extra-virgin olive oil. The sauce should be thin enough to drizzle with a spoon. (If it is too thick, add in more cold water, 1 Tbsp at a time.) Season with kosher salt and pepper.

Heat a large frying pan over high heat. Add enough extra-virgin olive oil to coat the bottom of the pan, and warm until hot but not smoking. Add the romanesco, cut-side down, and cook until deep golden brown in color, 3 to 4 minutes. Stir with tongs or a wooden spoon and cook for 2 to 3 minutes longer. Turn the heat to medium and add the raisins. Season with kosher salt and cook, stirring, until the raisins soften, 1 to 2 minutes. Add the stock and allow the ingredients to steam briefly. Taste a piece of romanesco for seasoning and doneness; it should be tender.

Transfer to a serving platter, drizzle the tahini sauce on top, sprinkle with sumac, and garnish with sea salt and a drizzle of best-quality olive oil. Serve warm or at room temperature.

SEARED OKRA, BLACK OLIVES, TOMATO CONFIT, PINE NUTS & CHILE

SERVES 4 TO 6 AS A SIDE DISH / This quick stew is substantial enough to be the main event with a little rice and salad, but it has enough finesse to sit alongside proteins such as whole grilled fish or grilled lamb.

Get a hard sear on the okra without moving it too much. Add salt late in the game to keep the vegetable's gelatinous goodness from oozing out and making a mess of things.

2 Tbsp pine nuts

¼ cup [60 ml] extra-virgin olive oil

1 lb [455 g] okra, cut into 1-in [2.5-cm] pieces

½ cup [130 g] Tomato Confit (page 60)

¼ cup [35 g] pitted black olives, such as Gaeta or kalamata

1 clove Garlic Confit (page 64), chopped

1 cup [240 ml] dry white wine

½ cup [120 ml] Vegetable Stock (page 222)

Kosher salt

¼ cup [7 g] chopped fresh mint

2 tsp red wine vinegar

Pinch of crushed red pepper flakes

In a small, dry frying pan over medium heat, toast the pine nuts just until fragrant and beginning to brown, 3 to 5 minutes. Set aside.

In a medium sauté pan over high heat, warm the olive oil until almost smoking. Add the okra to the pan and cook, without moving, until well seared, about 2 minutes. Add the tomato confit, black olives, and toasted pine nuts to the pan and cook for 1 minute longer. With a wooden spoon, stir in the garlic confit, and immediately add the wine to the pan to avoid burning the garlic. Continue stirring to incorporate the wine into the tomato mixture, about 1 minute. Stir in the stock and cook until the sauce thickens and begins to coat the okra, 3 to 5 minutes. Season with salt and stir in the mint, vinegar, and red pepper flakes.

Transfer to a serving platter and serve warm.

BRAISED SWEET CORN, CHILE, CILANTRO, FETA & LIME

SERVES 4 TO 6 AS A SIDE DISH / This dish is a riff on Mexican-style corn on the cob with chile, lime, and queso fresco. Here, I use briny feta and little bits of Fresno chile and cilantro leaves. Be sure to use the corn milk that tends to get left behind when you shave the kernels off the cob. It is an amazing way to add some creamy richness to the dish without butter or cream. Also, try to shave the corn kernels from the cob at the last possible moment; the sugar starts to convert to starch as the kernels sit. For this dish we make a corn cob–enriched stock. Vegetable stock or water can easily be substituted, but corn stock is a delicious thing to have around and well worth the effort, if you're feeling ambitious. Use any remaining stock to make a rad corn chowder.

Organic sweet corn, which is not genetically modified, is difficult to find these days. If you do happen to find some, buy it and give that farmer some support. The texture of organic corn can be a bit starchy and it's nowhere near as sweet as GMO corn, with its off-the-chart sugar levels. But you'll be rewarded with a deep, old-fashioned corn flavor that's all but lost in modern corn.

6 ears corn, shucked	1 shallot, minced
Kosher salt	2½ oz [70 g] feta cheese, crumbled
3 Tbsp extra-virgin olive oil	Juice of 1 lime
2 medium-hot green or red chiles, preferably Fresno, minced	¼ cup [7 g] fresh cilantro leaves

Using a knife, shave the corn kernels off the cobs into a medium bowl and set aside. Working over a small bowl, scrape the cobs with the back of the knife to extract the milk. Set aside the milk. Cut the scraped cobs into 2-in [5-cm] pieces.

In a 1-gl [3.8-L] saucepan over high heat, combine the cob pieces with cold filtered water to cover and season with salt. Bring to a boil, cover the pan, turn the heat to medium-low, and simmer until the stock becomes cloudy and is deliciously corn scented, 20 to 30 minutes. Strain and discard the cobs. Set aside ½ cup [120 ml] of this corn stock and reserve the rest for another use.

In a medium sauté pan over medium heat, warm the olive oil until hot but not smoking. Add the chiles and shallot and cook until tender, but not browned, about 3 minutes. Add the corn kernels and season with salt. Add the corn stock, the milk from the corn cobs, and half the feta cheese and cook until the liquid has reduced slightly, 2 to 3 minutes. Season with additional salt and stir in the lime juice. Remove from the heat and stir in half the cilantro leaves.

Transfer to a serving platter, sprinkle with the remaining feta cheese and cilantro leaves, and serve warm.

BRAISED SPICED ROMANO BEANS WITH YOGURT & MINT

SERVES 4 TO 6 AS A SIDE DISH / These are not the quickly cooked, bright-green take on fresh beans that you might expect from a California-based cookbook. This recipe takes its inspiration from the Middle East: these beans are long-cooked and the exotic personality of the spices is muted rather than bright. Black lime is a dehydrated citrus that is used throughout the Middle East. Track down some if you can, as their flavor is distinctive. Substitute the juice of a fresh lime or two or omit lime entirely and this will still be very tasty.

¼ cup [60 ml] Greek-style yogurt

Juice of 1 lime

3 Tbsp extra-virgin olive oil

Kosher salt

Freshly ground black pepper

½ yellow onion, minced

3 cloves garlic, minced

2 tsp ground black lime, plus more for sprinkling

1 tsp coriander seeds toasted and ground

1 tsp fennel seeds, toasted and ground

2 cups Pomodoro Sauce (page 59)

1 cup Vegetable Stock (page 222) or Chicken Stock (page 223), plus more as needed

1 lb [455 g] romano beans, stem end trimmed

2 Tbsp red wine vinegar

¼ cup [7 g] mint leaves

In a small bowl, combine the yogurt, lime juice, and 2 Tbsp of the olive oil. Add water, 1 tsp at a time, so the mixture is thick but pourable. Season with salt and pepper. Set aside.

In a deep, heavy-bottomed pot over medium-high heat, warm the remaining 1 Tbsp olive oil until hot but not smoking. Add the onion and garlic and cook until just starting to brown, 2 to 3 minutes. Add the black lime, coriander seeds, and fennel seeds and cook until fragrant, 1 minute. Add the pomodoro sauce and stock and bring to a simmer. Stir in the romano beans, coating with the sauce, and bring back to a simmer. Season with salt, turn the heat to medium-low, and cook at a slow, steady simmer until the beans soften and darken in color, 15 to 20 minutes. If needed, add more stock, 1 Tbsp at a time, to keep the pan from drying out. Remove from the heat and add the vinegar. Taste for seasoning, adding more salt if desired.

Transfer to a serving platter and drizzle with the lime yogurt. Scatter the mint leaves over all, sprinkle with a bit more ground black lime, and serve warm or at room temperature.

BRAISED FAVA BEANS, LEMON, BLACK PEPPER & PECORINO

SERVES 4 TO 6 AS A SIDE DISH / I find the fresh, grassy, green flavor of fava beans irresistible. In Southern California, favas generally have a short season, and tend to disappear just as quickly as they arrive. We work hard to capture their spring flavor while we can. If we find very young beans no bigger than the nail on my pinky finger, we pop them from their pods and don't bother to peel the beans. If the beans are any bigger, blanch them and peel the inner skin. Just be sure not to overcook them, as they cook twice, briefly, in this recipe.

The puckering brininess of a good raw-milk pecorino provides the perfect counterpoint for the fava's sweetness. Look for the black-peppercorn studded variety called "pepato." This is also a good time to reach for a high-quality, green olive oil. The simplicity of this dish allows it to shine.

1½ lb [680 g] fresh young fava beans, shelled

3 Tbsp extra-virgin olive oil

Kosher salt

Freshly ground black pepper

½ cup [120 ml] Vegetable Stock (page 222)

Juice of ½ lemon

2 Tbsp torn fresh mint leaves

1 oz [30 g] pecorino pepato

Best-quality olive oil for drizzling

If working with medium to large fava beans, prepare an ice-water bath by filling a large bowl with ice water. Blanch the beans in lightly salted boiling water for about 15 seconds and plunge them into the ice-water bath. Remove them from the bath and peel them once they are cool.

In a medium sauté pan over medium-high heat, warm the extra-virgin olive oil until hot but not smoking. Add the fava beans to the pan, and season with salt and pepper. Add half of the stock and bring to a quick simmer. The idea is to add just enough liquid to heat the beans without overcooking them, which will destroy their natural sweetness. Continue adding stock, about 1 Tbsp at a time, tasting the beans for doneness as you go. Larger beans will take a little longer, 2 to 3 minutes. Once the beans are tender and the liquid has almost evaporated, add the lemon juice and mint.

Transfer to a serving platter. With a vegetable peeler, shave the pecorino over the top, then drizzle with best-quality olive oil. Serve warm.

BRAISED GREEN CHICKPEAS WITH POMEGRANATE & FETA

SERVES 4 TO 6 AS A SIDE DISH / Fresh chickpeas are sold in a dense bunch of branches, with generally just one or two beans per pod. They're a major pain to clean. One of my kitchen guys from Oaxaca, Mexico, told me that in his pueblo they often throw the whole branch on the grill so they char and steam in the pods, and then pick the beans out to eat at once. Here, we shell them raw and cook them gently to retain some of their delicate sweetness. You can make this with any shelling bean, such as favas or cranberry beans.

3 Tbsp extra-virgin olive oil
2 shallots, finely chopped
1 carrot, peeled and finely chopped
1 celery rib, finely chopped
1 Tbsp pomegranate molasses
Kosher salt
1 lb [455 g] shelled green chickpeas
4 cups [960 ml] Vegetable Stock (page 222)

3 fresh thyme sprigs
1 bay leaf
¼ cup [7 g] chopped fresh mint
½ lemon
3 oz [85 g] feta cheese
¼ cup [40 g] pomegranate seeds
Best-quality olive oil for drizzling

In a medium, heavy-bottomed pot over medium heat, warm the extra-virgin olive oil until hot but not smoking. Add the shallots, carrot, and celery and cook until softened but not brown, about 5 minutes. Add the pomegranate molasses and season with salt. Stir in the chickpeas, and add the stock, thyme, and bay leaf. Bring to a gentle simmer, cover partially with a lid, and continue to cook at a slow, steady simmer, stirring occasionally, until the chickpeas start to soften but still have some bite, about 10 minutes. Remove from the heat and allow the chickpeas to cool slightly in the cooking liquid. Remove the bay leaf.

Warm the chickpeas gently in some of their cooking liquid, reducing it slightly. Once it's starting to coat the chickpeas, stir in half of the chopped mint and squeeze in the lemon juice.

Transfer to a serving bowl and crumble the feta cheese on top. Scatter the pomegranate seeds over all, add the remaining mint leaves, and drizzle with best-quality olive oil. Serve warm.

ROASTED ARTICHOKES WITH CALABRIAN CHILE, ANCHOVY & CRISPY SHALLOTS

SERVES 4 TO 6 AS A SIDE DISH / This recipe makes good use of the small- to medium-size artichokes that are available in early spring through late summer. Roast them, which intensifies their flavor and yields a crispy, tender texture. Small artichokes tend to not have the fuzzy choke that has to be trimmed, so you can use them whole. The vegetal artichoke flavor marries beautifully with anchovy, but leave out the fish if you prefer a vegetarian dish. Fresno chiles or crushed red pepper flakes can be substituted for heat if you can't find Calabrian chiles, which are usually sold in a jar. You can also sub in a tablespoon of Calabrian chile paste.

½ lemon

5 lb [2.3 kg] small or medium artichokes

Extra-virgin olive oil for cooking

6 salt-packed anchovies, rinsed and deboned

6 Calabrian chiles, roughly chopped

½ cup [120 ml] white wine

Kosher salt

½ bunch parsley

½ bunch mint

2 Tbsp chopped marjoram or oregano

¼ cup [60 ml] Vegetable Stock (page 222) or water (optional)

2 Tbsp Crispy Shallots (page 66)

Preheat the oven to 450°F [230°C]. Fill a bowl with cold water and squeeze the lemon into it.

Remove the outer leaves from the artichokes until you reach the paler, more tender inner leaves (about two-thirds of the artichoke comes off). Slice off the rough tips of the artichoke leaves. If using larger artichokes, use a small paring knife to remove the tough fibers where the leaves connect to the base and continue trimming down the stem so that the more tender part of the artichoke heart is revealed. Halve and scoop out any hairy choke that may be inside the heart (most of the smaller artichokes have not developed this yet). As you work, drop the trimmed artichokes into the bowl of lemon water.

In a large frying pan over high heat, add enough olive oil to coat the bottom of the pan. Add the artichokes, using tongs to place the cut side against the pan bottom to get a good sear. Cook until beginning to brown, 3 to 4 minutes, then transfer the pan to the oven and roast until the artichokes are deeply roasted and crispy at the edges, 5 to 7 minutes.

Carefully return the pan back to the stove top over medium-high heat and add the anchovies and chile. Stir for 1 minute, then add in the wine. Season with salt, bring to a simmer, then stir in the parsley, mint, and marjoram. Smash the anchovies with a wooden spoon; they should be evenly distributed throughout the artichokes. Check the artichokes for doneness. If they are still firm to the tip of a knife, add the stock and continue cooking for 2 to 3 minutes longer.

Transfer to a platter and scatter the crispy shallots over all. Serve warm or at room temperature.

ROASTED FENNEL WITH ORANGE & CRUSHED RED PEPPER FLAKES

SERVES 4 TO 6 AS A SIDE DISH / This is a stunning side that goes particularly well with fish, or stands up on its own. I love when you can use multiple parts of the plant in a single dish; with fennel you can use the bulb, stem, fronds, and the pollen that's harvested from the flowers. Use the best citrus you can find and feel free to substitute tangelos or mandarins.

2 fennel bulbs
2 blood or cara cara oranges
¼ cup [60 ml] extra-virgin olive oil
Flaky sea salt
½ cup [120 ml] fresh orange juice

¼ [60 ml] cup white wine
¼ cup [60 ml] Vegetable Stock (page 222) or Chicken Stock (page 223)
Pinch of crushed red pepper flakes
Freshly ground black pepper
Pinch of fennel pollen (optional)

Cut the fennel bulb into wedges. Cut the stems into thin slices, reserving the fronds. Set aside.

Section one of the oranges by cutting off both ends. Set it on one end, and use a paring knife to cut away the peel and pith in strips, starting at the top and following the curves to the bottom. Then, holding the orange in one hand, carefully insert the blade of the knife between the flesh and the membrane to cut out the sections without any membrane attached. The sections should come out easily. Repeat with the remaining orange, and set aside.

In a large frying pan over high heat, warm the olive oil. Add the fennel wedges, using tongs to place the cut sides against the pan bottom to get a good sear. Cook until the fennel is caramelized, about 3 minutes. Flip, lower heat to medium-high, and cook on the other side until caramelized, another 3 minutes. Season with salt, toss in the fennel stems, and continue to cook until the stems are well-browned, another 2 minutes. Add the orange juice, wine, and stock, and let reduce until the sauce is thickened and the fennel is deeply seared and starting to soften, 2 to 3 minutes. Add the red pepper flakes and season with lots of salt and pepper.

Pour onto a serving platter. Garnish with the fennel fronds, orange segments, and fennel pollen. Serve warm or at room temperature.

ROASTED CAULIFLOWER WITH GARLIC, PARSLEY & VINEGAR

SERVES 4 TO 6 AS A SIDE DISH / Surprisingly, this is one of our most requested recipes. It's baffling to me because it's one of the easiest things we make. The key is to get a char on the cauliflower, caramelizing the sugars and bringing out the vegetable's natural sweetness. That's easy to do in our 900°F [480°C] wood-fired pizza oven, but I've had excellent results making this at home in my 500°F [260°C] gas oven. I like to serve this as a starter with pizza. The same roasting technique works equally well with Romanesco and broccoli.

1 head cauliflower, trimmed and chopped into large florets	3 cloves Garlic Confit (page 64)
⅓ cup [75 ml] extra-virgin olive oil	2 Tbsp chopped fresh flat-leaf parsley
Kosher salt	¼ tsp crushed red pepper flakes
Freshly ground black pepper	2 Tbsp red wine vinegar

Preheat the oven to 500°F [260°C].

In a medium bowl, toss the cauliflower with the olive oil and season with salt and pepper.

Heat a large cast-iron frying pan over high heat. Dump the cauliflower into the hot pan and cook until starting to brown, about 3 minutes. Transfer the pan to the oven and roast the cauliflower, undisturbed, until well seared, about 5 minutes longer. With a spatula, turn the cauliflower and cook on the other side until well seared, about 3 minutes longer.

Remove from the oven, add the garlic confit, parsley, red pepper flakes, and vinegar and stir to distribute the seasonings and toast the garlic slightly. Season with salt and pepper.

Transfer to a serving platter. Serve warm or at room temperature.

ROASTED ACORN SQUASH WITH HAZELNUTS, BROWN BUTTER & ROSEMARY

SERVES 4 TO 6 AS A SIDE DISH / Brown butter and acorn squash are classic fall flavors. In fact, this would be right at home as a side dish for Thanksgiving dinner. This dish makes no apologies for its richness, so don't skimp on the brown butter. Though you may not normally think of eating the peel of a hard squash, it gets deliciously crisp as it roasts. You won't want to leave it on the plate. The brown butter is delicious on vegetables and pasta, or as a sauce for fish.

¼ cup [30 g] roughly chopped hazelnuts

4 Tbsp [55 g] unsalted butter

1 acorn squash, halved and seeded

¼ cup [60 ml] water

1 Tbsp dark brown sugar

Kosher salt

1 tsp chopped fresh rosemary leaves

½ cup [120 ml] Vegetable Stock (page 222)

½ tsp fresh lemon juice

Freshly ground black pepper

In a small, dry frying pan over medium heat, toast the hazelnuts until fragrant, about 3 minutes. Set aside and let cool.

Preheat the oven to 425°F [220°C].

In a small saucepan over medium heat, melt and cook the butter, skimming the solids from the surface until the butter is clear. Turn the heat to low, and cook until the butter develops a nutty aroma and turns from yellow to a deep brown. Remove from the heat and let cool. (Store in an airtight container in the refrigerator for up to 3 weeks.)

Put the squash halves in a large roasting pan, cut-side down. Add the water to the pan, cover with aluminum foil, and roast for 25 minutes. Remove the foil, and continue roasting until the squash is lightly browned, about 10 minutes longer. Cut the squash halves into bite-size pieces and transfer to a serving platter.

In a small sauté pan over medium-high heat, warm the brown butter. Add the toasted hazelnuts and brown sugar and season with salt. Stir in the rosemary and cook until the rosemary becomes fragrant and the sugar has dissolved into the butter, about 3 minutes. Add the stock, a little bit at a time, and continue to cook until you have an emulsified, slightly thickened pan sauce. Remove from the heat and stir in the lemon juice.

Pour the brown butter sauce over the squash and season with pepper. Serve warm.

ROASTED BEETS WITH TOPS, HERBED YOGURT & HORSERADISH

SERVES 4 TO 6 AS A SIDE DISH / Look for small, golf-ball-size beets that you can roast with their leafy tops. We add a little water to the roasting pan to create steam, which keeps the greens from burning while they roast. A little beef stock lends a savory note, which I like, especially in winter. Skip that if you want to make this a vegetarian dish. These are nice paired with a slow-cooked beef rib, or as part of an offering of winter vegetables.

HERBED YOGURT

¼ cup [60 ml] Greek-style yogurt

1 tsp chopped fresh flat-leaf parsley

1 tsp chopped fresh mint

1 tsp chopped fresh dill

1 tsp chopped fresh tarragon

1 tsp snipped fresh chives

Zest and juice of 1 lime

1 Tbsp extra-virgin olive oil

Kosher salt

Freshly ground black pepper

1½ lb [680 g] baby beets with greens still attached, halved lengthwise

¼ cup [60 ml] extra-virgin olive oil

Kosher salt

Freshly ground black pepper

¼ cup [60 ml] water, plus more as needed

¼ cup [60 ml] Beef Stock (page 226; optional)

2 tsp sherry vinegar

One 1-in [2.5-cm] piece fresh horseradish

Flaky sea salt

Best-quality olive oil for drizzling

To make the herbed yogurt: In a medium bowl, combine the yogurt with the parsley, mint, dill, tarragon, chives, lime zest, lime juice, and extra-virgin olive oil. Season with kosher salt and pepper, and set aside.

Preheat the oven to 400°F [200°C].

In a large bowl, toss the beets with the extra-virgin olive oil and season with kosher salt and pepper. Transfer the beets to a baking sheet, add the water, and roast until the beets feel tender when pierced with the tip of a knife, about 25 minutes. Add more water if the greens dry out or begin to burn. Remove from the oven and let cool slightly. Leave the oven at the same temperature.

With a kitchen towel, gently pull the skins off the beets. Don't worry if some still clings to the beets, since a little skin left on is fine. There is often a bit of tough plant matter near the stem, which should slide off easily.

Return the beets to the oven and roast about 5 minutes longer. Remove from the oven and immediately add the stock (if using) and vinegar.

Transfer to a serving platter along with the pan juices. Drizzle the herbed yogurt on top. With a Microplane, grate the horseradish over all. Season with sea salt and drizzle with best-quality olive oil. Serve warm or at room temperature.

ROASTED BEETS WITH AVOCADO, ORANGE, TOASTED HAZELNUTS & SHERRY VINEGAR

SERVES 4 TO 6 AS A SIDE DISH / This is a nice recipe to turn to in early fall, when avocados hit the market in full force. After a long summer of sunny days, avocados are rich and oily and ideal to feature alongside roasted baby beets spiked with sherry vinegar. Hass, Reed, and Bacon are a few of the many varieties of avocados we have access to in California. They're all fantastic when at their peak. Marinating the beets to slightly pickle them results in a beautiful beet-juice-tinted sherry vinaigrette, which we pour over the finished dish.

1½ lb [680 g] red baby beets,
1 to 2 in [2.5 to 5 cm] in diameter
4 Tbsp [60 ml] extra-virgin olive oil
2 Tbsp water
Kosher salt
Freshly ground black pepper

1 Tbsp plus 1 tsp sherry vinegar
1 Tbsp fresh orange juice, plus 2 oranges
2 Tbsp hazelnuts
1 ripe avocado, cut in ¼-in- [6-mm-] thick slices
Flaky sea salt
Best-quality olive oil for drizzling

Preheat the oven to 400°F [200°C].

In a roasting pan, toss the beets with 2 Tbsp of the extra-virgin olive oil and the water and season with kosher salt and pepper. Roast until the beets look caramelized and feel tender when pierced with the tip of a knife, about 25 minutes. When cool enough to handle, slip the skins off the beets and cut into quarters.

In a medium bowl, toss the beets with the remaining 2 Tbsp olive oil, the sherry vinegar, and orange juice. Season with kosher salt and pepper and let stand until the beets have absorbed the flavors of the dressing, about 30 minutes.

In a small, dry frying pan over medium heat, toast the hazelnuts until fragrant, 3 to 5 minutes. Lay out on a work surface and let cool. With the bottom of a heavy pan, crush the nuts.

Section one of the oranges by cutting off both ends. Set it on one end, and use a paring knife to cut away the peel and pith in strips, starting at the top and following the curves to the bottom. Then, holding the orange in one hand, carefully insert the blade of the knife between the flesh and the membrane to cut out the sections without any membrane attached. The sections should come out easily. Repeat with the remaining orange, and set aside.

Arrange the beets on a serving platter with the avocado slices, and sprinkle them with sea salt and pepper. Distribute the orange sections throughout the salad and sprinkle with the crushed toasted hazelnuts. Finish with a drizzle of best-quality olive oil. Serve immediately.

ROASTED SUNCHOKES WITH PARSLEY SALSA VERDE

SERVES 4 TO 6 AS A SIDE DISH / The young sunchokes that pop up in the fall and early winter are amazingly sweet and delicious. I think they're at their best simply roasted in their skins. Their coarse peels char and caramelize in the oven and have lots of little pockets where the salsa verde collects. They're sturdy and can stand up to red meats, but they're also delicate enough to work with poultry or a whole grilled fish. We roast them in our wood oven to give them a beautiful crust, but you can do the same at home with a cast-iron pan in a screaming-hot oven—an excellent technique for cooking any root vegetable.

2 lb [910 g] sunchokes, cut into 1- to 2-in [2.5- to 5-cm] pieces
2 Tbsp extra-virgin olive oil
Kosher salt

Freshly ground black pepper
½ cup [120 ml] Parsley Salsa Verde (page 51)
Flaky sea salt
½ lemon

Preheat the oven to 500°F [260°C]. Put a large cast-iron frying pan on the center rack and heat until the pan is very hot, about 15 minutes.

In a medium bowl, toss the sunchokes with the olive oil and season with kosher salt and pepper. Pour them into the hot pan in the oven, spreading them out in a single layer. Roast, without stirring, until they begin to brown, 3 to 5 minutes. Give the pan a rough shake to toss the sunchokes, and continue cooking until well caramelized and soft but not mushy, about 5 minutes longer.

Transfer to a serving platter and spoon the salsa verde on top. Sprinkle with sea salt and squeeze a little fresh lemon juice on top. Serve warm or at room temperature.

ROASTED PURPLE POTATOES WITH AIOLI, HORSERADISH, PICKLED RED ONION & DILL

SERVES 4 TO 6 AS A SIDE DISH / Purple potatoes are amazingly sweet. For this recipe, we look for what are called a "creamer" size. About only 1 in [2.5 cm] in diameter, they have less starch than larger, more mature potatoes. We like to gently steam or boil them, and then partially smash them on the countertop, exposing their neon-bright flesh. Finally, we sear them in a hot cast-iron pan to be sure we end up with lots of tasty, crisp-fried potato bits.

1½ lb [680 g] purple potatoes, about 1 in [2.5 cm] in diameter
Kosher salt
¼ cup [60 ml] extra-virgin olive oil
Flaky sea salt
Freshly ground black pepper

½ cup [80 g] Basic Aioli (page 56)
One 2-in [5-cm] piece fresh horseradish
¼ cup [7 g] fresh dill leaves
¼ cup [40 g] Pickled Red Onions (page 69)
Juice of ½ lemon

In a large pot over medium-high heat, combine the potatoes with water to cover and season with kosher salt. Bring to a boil, lower the heat to a simmer, and cook until the potatoes feel tender when pierced with a knife but are not falling apart, about 15 minutes depending on their size. Drain and transfer the potatoes to a work surface to cool.

When cool enough to handle, cover one potato at a time with a kitchen towel and gently smash with the palm of your hand to break the skin and expose some of the flesh. You want to end up with relatively flat, irregular pieces. Don't worry if they break into smaller pieces.

Heat a large cast-iron frying pan over high heat. Add the olive oil, and then add only as many potatoes as will fit in a single layer. Don't crowd the pan. Cook until the potatoes are well seared, with a nicely browned, crisp exterior, 4 to 5 minutes. Turn and cook on the other side until well browned and crisp, another 3 minutes. Transfer the potatoes to a serving platter and repeat until all the potatoes are cooked.

Season the potatoes with lots of sea salt and pepper. Drizzle the aioli on top. With a Microplane, grate the horseradish over all. Garnish with the dill leaves and pickled red onions and squeeze the lemon juice over all. Serve warm or at room temperature.

ROASTED YAMS WITH HONEY, ESPELETTE & LIME YOGURT

SERVES 4 TO 6 AS A SIDE DISH / This is my favorite of a slew of recipes we have tinkered with over the years using yams. Yams are abundant and cheap in the winter months and customers find them soul-satisfying and delicious. This recipe plays salty against sweet and spicy against creamy; the lime and green onions provide the high notes. Tossing yams in honey before roasting them helps to bring out their sweetness and encourages a crusty caramelized exterior.

½ cup [120 ml] Greek-style yogurt
Juice of 2 limes
3 Tbsp extra-virgin olive oil
Sea salt
Freshly ground black pepper

2 medium to large yams
2 Tbsp honey
1 Tbsp espelette pepper or crushed red pepper flakes
Flaky sea salt
2 green onions (white and green parts), sliced thinly on the bias

Preheat the oven to 425°F [220°C].

In a small bowl, combine the yogurt with the lime juice and 1 Tbsp of the olive oil. Season with sea salt and pepper. Set aside.

Cut the yams lengthwise into eight wedges (about 1 in [2.5 cm] in diameter). In a medium bowl, toss the yams with the honey, ½ Tbsp of the espelette pepper, and the remaining olive oil. Season with sea salt and pepper. Marinate for 10 minutes, tossing once or twice to coat.

Transfer the yams to a rimmed baking sheet and roast until they are nicely caramelized around the edges and soft when pierced with a knife at the thickest part, 25 to 35 minutes.

Transfer to a serving platter, drizzle yogurt over all, and garnish with the green onions and remaining espelette pepper. Season with flaky salt. Serve warm.

OVEN-ROASTED PARSNIPS WITH HAZELNUT PICADA

SERVES 4 TO 6 AS A SIDE DISH / Cutting the parsnips into irregular sticks, a bit like making hand-cut *frites*, provides lots of surface area for them to brown and make these more flavorful. The hazelnut picada adds a nutty, herbaceous note and a delicious bit of crunch. We start by browning the parsnips on the stove top and then move them to the oven to ensure a deeply caramelized exterior with crispy edges. Then we rock them on the stove top again at the end to ensure they are as crisp as possible. This is a good technique for small potatoes, as well.

HAZELNUT PICADA
½ cup [40 g] hazelnuts, roughly chopped
1 large handful Garlic Croutons (see page 80), fully cooled
2 Tbsp chopped fresh flat-leaf parsley
1 Tbsp oil from Garlic Confit (page 64)
½ tsp finely grated lemon zest

1 lb [455 g] parsnips, peeled and cut into ¼- to ½-in- [6- to 12-mm-] thick irregular sticks
2 Tbsp extra-virgin olive oil
Kosher salt
Freshly ground black pepper
Juice of ½ lemon
Flaky sea salt

Preheat the oven to 500°F [260°C].

To make the hazelnut picada: In a small, dry frying pan over medium heat, toast the hazelnuts until fragrant, about 3 minutes. Let cool.

Place the croutons on a work surface and, using a rolling pin or chef's knife, crush into coarse crumbs.

In a mortar with a pestle or in a food processor, combine the hazelnuts, crouton crumbs, parsley, garlic oil, and lemon zest. Smash or process the ingredients to a rough paste. I like the picada to be very coarse. If using a food processor, pulse briefly, checking often to avoid overprocessing. Set aside until ready to use.

In a medium bowl, toss the parsnips with the olive oil and season with kosher salt and pepper. Heat a large, dry frying pan over medium-high heat. When hot, transfer the parsnips to the pan, taking care not to splatter yourself in the process, and cook on the stove top until beginning to brown, about 5 minutes. Transfer the frying pan to the oven and roast until tender and well browned, moving the parsnips around a couple of times to brown all sides, about 15 minutes longer. Return the pan to the stove top over high heat and cook until well caramelized and the edges are crisp and browned, about 5 minutes longer.

Transfer to a serving platter and squeeze the lemon juice over all. Scatter the picada on top, and season with sea salt. Serve hot.

PAN-ROASTED BABY CARROTS, ORANGE, CILANTRO, SESAME & SPICED YOGURT

SERVE 4 TO 6 AS A SIDE DISH / The cool, stubby Thumbelinas are our favorite carrots for this dish, but any small carrot works well. Just don't confuse those mechanically formed carrot pieces sold in plastic bags for baby carrots. Look for small varieties at your farmers' market in the fall and winter. Generally, you can just scrub these before using and forget about peeling them. I like to serve these alongside a couple of other vegetable dishes, and with roasted or braised meats.

2 lb [910 g] Thumbelina or other small carrots, cut into 1½-in [4-cm] lengths

6 Tbsp [90 ml] extra-virgin olive oil

Kosher salt

Freshly ground black pepper

2 tsp fresh thyme leaves

½ cup [120 ml] fresh orange juice

1 Tbsp sesame seeds

¼ cup [60 ml] dry white wine

¼ cup [60 ml] Chicken Stock (page 223) or Vegetable Stock (page 222)

¼ cup [60 ml] Spiced Yogurt (page 55)

½ cup [15 g] fresh cilantro leaves

In a medium bowl, combine the carrots with 3 Tbsp of the olive oil and season with salt and pepper. Add the thyme leaves and 2 Tbsp of the orange juice. Let stand at room temperature.

In a small, dry frying pan over medium heat, toast the sesame seeds until fragrant, about 3 minutes. Set aside and let cool.

Preheat the oven to 450°F [230°C].

In a roasting pan or a sauté pan large enough to hold the carrots in a single layer, heat the remaining 3 Tbsp olive oil over high heat. Add the carrots and cook until they begin to brown, 2 to 3 minutes. Transfer the pan to the oven and cook until the carrots caramelize around the edges but are still a bit firm, 5 to 7 minutes.

Return the pan to the stove top over medium heat, and add the wine, remaining 6 Tbsp [90 ml] orange juice, and the stock. Cook, stirring with a wooden spoon to scrape up the browned bits stuck to the bottom of the pan, until the liquids thicken and begin to coat the carrots, 2 to 3 minutes longer. Season with salt and pepper.

Transfer to a serving platter. Drizzle the spiced yogurt on top, sprinkle with the toasted sesame seeds, and garnish with the cilantro. Serve warm.

PAN-ROASTED BABY TURNIPS WITH THEIR GREENS & CHIMICHURRI

SERVES 4 TO 6 AS A SIDE DISH / Little pink, red, or white turnips that are tender enough to eat raw often have tender greens that are perfect for this dish. Choose an ovenproof pan that can go from the oven to the stove top. Leave any really small turnips whole. Larger ones should be halved or quartered.

3 bunches baby turnips, with their greens
2 Tbsp extra-virgin olive oil
Kosher salt
Freshly ground black pepper

4 Tbsp [60 ml] Vegetable Stock (page 222)
or Chicken Stock (page 223)
¼ cup [50 g] Chimichurri (page 51)
Juice of ½ lemon

Preheat the oven to 450°F [230°C]. Put a large cast-iron frying pan on the center rack and heat until the pan is very hot, about 15 minutes.

Separate the turnips from their greens. In a medium bowl, toss the turnips with the olive oil and season with salt and pepper.

Add the turnips to the hot pan and roast until just softened, 4 to 6 minutes, depending on the size and variety of turnip.

Return the pan to the stove top over medium-high heat, stir in the turnip greens, and sauté briefly. Add 2 Tbsp of the stock, followed by the chimichurri, and stir to combine. Add up to the remaining 2 Tbsp stock if you need to loosen the sauce. Taste and adjust the seasoning.

Transfer to a serving platter, squeeze on the lemon juice. Serve warm.

GRILLED JUMBO ASPARAGUS WITH GRIBICHE & BOTTARGA

SERVES 4 TO 6 AS A SIDE DISH / This is a riff on the classic Asparagus with Sauce Gribiche, incorporating the lovely red mullet bottarga from my friends at Cortez Bottarga. Try to score the fattest jumbo asparagus possible in early spring; if you're not seeing it, ask a local farmer if they have some extra jumbo or if they are willing to cultivate it. Big, fat asparagus really is ideal for this preparation. If you are lucky enough to stumble onto jumbo white asparagus, it's truly amazing prepared this way. I've only encountered beautiful white asparagus in France, where it has a very short season, and is celebrated by the chefs there.

2 eggs

2 bunches jumbo asparagus

1 tsp extra-virgin olive oil

1 Tbsp capers, roughly chopped

1 shallot, minced

2 Tbsp minced parsley

2 Tbsp minced dill

Juice of 1 lemon

1 Tbsp white wine vinegar

1 tsp Dijon mustard

Kosher salt

Freshly round black pepper

2 Tbsp crushed Garlic Croutons (see page 80)

1 oz [30 g] bottarga

In a heavy-bottomed stockpot, cover the eggs with 1 in [2.5 cm] cold water. Place over medium-high heat and bring to a boil. Turn off the heat and let rest for 3 minutes, then remove the eggs from the water with a slotted spoon. Rinse the eggs under cool water, peel, and roughly chop. Set aside.

Prepare an ice-water bath by filling a large bowl with cold water and ice. Peel the bottom third of the asparagus stalks with a vegetable peeler so they are uniformly thick. Bring a large saucepan of salted water to a boil over high heat. Add the asparagus and cook until tender but firm, 1 minute. Using tongs, transfer to the ice-water bath. Cool completely. Drain and toss with the olive oil.

In a small bowl, combine the capers, shallot, parsley, dill, lemon juice, vinegar, and mustard. Stir to blend. Gently fold in the chopped egg. Season with salt and pepper. Set the gribiche aside.

Meanwhile, heat a large grill pan over medium-high heat (or heat a gas grill to medium-high).

Season the asparagus with salt and pepper, then transfer to the hot grill. Cook until seared, 2 to 3 minutes, then flip and cook the other side until seared, 1 to 2 minutes.

Transfer to a serving platter and scatter the gribiche over all. Sprinkle with the crouton crumbs and grate the bottarga generously over all. Serve warm or at room temperature.

GRILLED EGGPLANT, MOJO DE AJO & BASIL SALSA VERDE

SERVES 4 TO 6 AS A SIDE DISH / Meaty eggplant takes to the grill so well, and it pairs beautifully with acidic, herbaceous sauces. Don't bother pre-salting the eggplant slices; just slather them with mojo de ajo, plenty of salt and pepper, and grill the hell out of them. They are meaty enough to pass as a main course, accompanied by a few more vegetable dishes. In summer, there are a bunch of cool varieties at the market in a range of shapes and sizes. They are all good in their own ways, but I especially like the Chinese and Japanese varieties for grilling.

1 lb [455 g] eggplants, sliced ¾ in [2 cm] thick
¼ cup [60 ml] Mojo de Ajo (page 54)
Kosher salt

Freshly ground black pepper
¼ cup [50 g] basil salsa verde (see variation, page 51)

Prepare a hot fire in a charcoal grill (or preheat a gas grill to high).

Meanwhile, on a baking sheet, spread out the eggplant slices in a single layer and brush generously on both sides with mojo de ajo. Season with salt and pepper and let stand at room temperature until the grill is ready.

Put the eggplant slices on the hottest part of the grill and cook until seared on the bottom, about 3 minutes. Turn the slices 90 degrees and continue cooking until grill marks form. Turn the slices over and move to a cooler spot on the grill. Cook, basting occasionally with mojo de ajo until beautifully caramelized, 5 to 7 minutes.

Transfer to a serving platter and garnish with the salsa verde. Serve warm.

GRILLED SUMMER SQUASH, ZA'ATAR & CHERRY TOMATO CONFIT

SERVES 4 TO 6 AS A SIDE DISH / Drenching grilled squash in oily California za'atar and tomato confit makes plenty of delicious dipping sauce for bread. There are many varieties of summer squash, all of them tasty and suitable for this dish. They are among the most plentiful vegetables when the growing season peaks, and with the exception of the precious baby varieties, they tend to be quite inexpensive. Cut the squash on the thicker side so that the slices can cook long enough to establish deep grill marks before they turn mushy.

We make this dish with quickly blanched Romano beans, which are equally delicious.

1 lb [455 g] mixed summer squash,
cut into ¾-in- [2-cm-] thick slices
¼ cup [60 ml] extra-virgin olive oil
Kosher salt
Freshly ground black pepper

2 Tbsp California Za'atar (page 46)
½ cup [100 g] Cherry Tomato Confit (page 62)
2 Tbsp red wine vinegar
¼ cup [7 g] fresh mint leaves, cut into thin ribbons

Prepare a hot fire in a charcoal grill (or preheat a gas grill to high).

Meanwhile, on a baking sheet, spread out the squash slices in a single layer and drizzle with half the olive oil, turning to coat both sides. Season with salt and pepper and let stand at room temperature until the grill is ready.

Put the squash slices on the hottest part of the grill and cook until seared on the bottom, about 4 minutes. Turn and cook until well seared on the other side, 2 to 3 minutes longer. The squash should be cooked through, but not mushy.

In a large bowl, gently toss the grilled squash slices with the za'atar, tomato confit, vinegar, and mint. Season with salt and pepper.

Transfer to a serving platter. Serve warm.

GRILLED KABOCHA SQUASH WITH MINT-POMEGRANATE PESTO

SERVES 4 TO 6 AS A SIDE DISH / I love the dense-fleshed kabocha squash. It's beautiful when simply steamed and seasoned with a little flaky salt and olive oil, or in a salad with walnuts, pomegranate seeds, and radicchio Treviso. Red kuri squash has an identical flavor but a more delicate skin, and it makes an excellent substitute. Here, we roast the kabocha until it's softened, and then slap it in a grill pan to char the edges. If you make the pesto in advance, this is very easy to pull together. If you're looking for a protein to serve this with it, rich meats such as duck, rabbit, pigeon, and even goat come to mind. This would also be cool served with wild rice and wilted broccoli rabe leaves.

1 kabocha or red kuri squash,
halved across the equator and seeded
¼ cup [60 ml] water
2 Tbsp extra-virgin olive oil

Kosher salt
Freshly ground black pepper
½ cup [120 ml] Mint-Pomegranate Pesto (page 48)
Flaky sea salt

Preheat the oven to 425°F [220°C].

Put the squash halves, cut-side down, in a large roasting pan. Add the water, cover with aluminum foil, and roast until the squash has softened, about 35 minutes. Remove from the oven and transfer the squash to a platter or cutting board to cool. Cut the cooled halves into thirds. (Store in the refrigerator for up to 1 day.)

Heat a large grill pan over high heat.

Drizzle the squash pieces with the olive oil, turning to coat, and season with kosher salt and pepper. Cook the squash pieces until well charred, about 5 minutes. Resist the urge to meddle. The pieces will release easily from the pan once they begin to blacken. Turn the pieces over and cook the other side until charred, 3 to 4 minutes longer.

Transfer to a serving platter, spoon the pesto on top, and season with sea salt. Serve warm.

GRILLED KING OYSTER MUSHROOMS WITH TARRAGON BUTTER

SERVES 4 TO 6 AS A SIDE DISH / These substantial mushrooms lend themselves well to grilling and topping with a compound butter as you would a good steak. The tarragon in the butter pairs unexpectedly well with the aromatic quality of the mushrooms. Don't feel like you have to cook these to death. A medium-cooked mushroom has delicate flavors that dissipate when cooked for too long. It's a no-brainer to pair these with grilled meats, but they're also tasty alongside grilled wild king salmon.

TARRAGON BUTTER
4 Tbsp [55 g] unsalted butter, at room temperature
1 Tbsp chopped fresh tarragon
1 tsp chopped fresh flat-leaf parsley
1 tsp snipped fresh chives
1 garlic clove, minced
1 tsp finely grated lemon zest

10 oz [280 g] king oyster mushrooms, halved lengthwise
¼ cup [60 ml] extra-virgin olive oil
Kosher salt
Freshly ground black pepper
½ lemon
Flaky sea salt

To make the tarragon butter: In a small bowl, use a fork to combine the butter with the tarragon, parsley, chives, garlic, and lemon zest. Set aside at room temperature until ready to serve.

Prepare a hot fire in a charcoal grill (or preheat a gas grill to high).

In a medium bowl, toss the mushrooms with the olive oil and season with kosher salt and pepper. Cook the mushrooms on the hottest part of the grill until they begin to caramelize, about 4 minutes. Turn them 90 degrees and cook for another 2 minutes. Flip the mushrooms and continue cooking until caramelized on the other side, about 3 minutes. Brush some of the tarragon butter over the mushrooms. It will drip off as it melts. Move the mushrooms away from any resulting flare-ups to keep them from burning. Brush with additional butter.

Transfer to a serving platter, squeeze lemon juice over all, and season with sea salt. Serve warm.

GRILLED BROCCOLINI WITH GARLIC, CRUSHED RED PEPPER FLAKES & RED WINE VINEGAR

SERVES 4 TO 6 AS A SIDE DISH / This dish reminds me of the steamed broccoli buried in garlic that I used to eat at red-sauce Italian joints in New Jersey. At Gjelina, we use Broccolini, which has longer stems that lend themselves well to grilling. If the stems are tough, we blanch the Broccolini before we cook them, but when they're young and tender, they can go straight to the grill. We like these with a generous amount of red wine vinegar, garlic, and red pepper flakes, but dial those seasonings back to suit your palate. Bagna Cauda (page 54) is a nice alternative if you like anchovies. I have also tried substituting bitter leafy broccoli rabe, which has an amazing peppery personality. I love it, but I have been nearly pelted with rocks from regular customers who prefer Broccolini.

3 bunches Broccolini

2 Tbsp extra-virgin olive oil

Kosher salt

Freshly ground black pepper

3 cloves Garlic Confit (page 64)

½ tsp crushed red pepper flakes

2 Tbsp red wine vinegar

If the Broccolini stems are thicker than ¾ in [2 cm], prepare an ice-water bath by filling a large bowl with cold water and ice. Blanch the Broccolini in lightly salted boiling water for about 15 seconds and plunge them into the ice-water bath to stop the cooking. (If your Broccolini stems are not thick, skip this step.)

Prepare a hot fire in a charcoal grill (or preheat a gas grill to high).

In a medium bowl, toss the Broccolini with the olive oil and season with salt and pepper. Put the Broccolini on the hottest part of the grill and cook until they start to crisp and turn brown, 3 to 5 minutes. Flip the Broccolini and cook the other side, 3 minutes longer. Return to the bowl; add the garlic confit, red pepper flakes, and vinegar; and toss well. Season with additional salt and pepper.

Transfer to a serving platter. Serve hot or at room temperature.

POTATO, LEEK & CHARD GRATIN WITH TALEGGIO

SERVES 4 TO 6 AS A SIDE DISH / This dish is made to serve with braised meats. A fatty, meltingly tender short rib stacked alongside is especially appealing to me, but a stew of vegetables or beans and greens would also be a great accompaniment. The preparation is a bit lengthy, but you can assemble the gratin a day ahead of cooking. Any variety of chard will do, although the red-veined will tint the dish pink. Taleggio cheese has a beautiful, ripe, funguslike aroma that gives this dish great character.

1 Tbsp olive oil

1 bunch Swiss chard, stemmed and deveined

2 large leeks (white and light green parts only), sliced ¼ in [6 mm] thick

Kosher salt

Freshly ground black pepper

3 lb [1.4 kg] Yukon gold potatoes, unpeeled, sliced ⅛ in [3 mm] thick

1½ cups [360 ml] heavy cream

3 Tbsp fresh thyme leaves

1⅓ cups [120 g] freshly grated Parmesan cheese

10 oz [225 g] Taleggio cheese, cut into ½-in [12-mm] chunks

3 Tbsp unsalted butter, cut into small chunks

¼ cup [30 g] fresh bread crumbs

Preheat the oven to 375°F [190°C]. Butter a 5-qt [4.7-L] baking dish, 2 in [5 cm] deep.

In a large cast-iron frying pan over medium heat, warm the olive oil until hot but not smoking. Add the chard and cook until the leaves are pliable, about 5 minutes. Remove the chard from the pan and set aside to cool. Add the leeks to the hot pan and cook until softened, about 5 minutes. Let cool, and season with salt and pepper. Roughly chop the cooled chard.

Arrange a third of the potato slices on the bottom of the prepared baking dish, overlapping them slightly. Pour in a third of the cream to cover the potatoes, and sprinkle with a third of the leeks, a third of the thyme, and a fourth of the Parmesan. Season with salt and pepper. Dot with a fourth of the Taleggio and a fourth of the butter, followed by a third of the chard. You will be repeating the layers two more times. Don't forget to season each layer as you go; potatoes can handle a decent amount of salt, so don't be shy.

Press down with your hands on the surface of every layer to make the ingredients lay flat and to get a sense of how much cream you'll need. You want just enough so that the entire mass is well moistened and decadent, but not enough so the gratin is a soupy mess. Finish layering by topping the chard with the remaining fourth of Parmesan, Taleggio, and butter. (If baking the next day, cover and refrigerate.) Top with the bread crumbs.

Cover with aluminum foil and bake until the potatoes are tender when pierced with the tip of a knife, about 1 hour. Increase the oven temperature to 425°F [220°C]. Remove the foil, and bake until bubbling and browned, about 15 minutes longer. Remove from the oven and allow to rest for 15 minutes to set. Serve warm.

CHARRED BRUSSELS SPROUTS WITH BACON & DATES

SERVES 4 TO 6 AS A SIDE DISH / This dish is so popular (we sell about four hundred orders of it a week) that our cooks grumble when the first crates of Brussels sprouts roll in. They know that these tiny cabbages will soon dominate their days and nights. For this recipe, look for smaller-than-golf-ball-size sprouts that are firm and tight. Be patient and let them get a good char on the cut side, almost to the point of burning. It brings a toasty, nutty flavor that contrasts with the sweet dates and sharp vinegar. You may have to adjust the cooking time to accommodate smaller sprouts, in early winter, or the larger ones as they mature throughout the season. We generally leave very tiny ones whole and quarter the larger ones, which we do not like as much.

3 oz [85 g] bacon, cut into ¼-in- [6-mm-] wide matchsticks

2 Tbsp extra-virgin olive oil

1 lb [455 g] Brussels sprouts, halved through the stem end

Kosher salt

Freshly ground black pepper

¼ cup [85 g] pitted soft fresh dates

1 cup [240 ml] Chicken Stock (page 223)

1 Tbsp plus 1 tsp red wine vinegar

Heat a large cast-iron frying pan over medium-high heat, and cook the bacon with the olive oil until the bacon has rendered most of its fat but is still juicy, about 10 minutes. Transfer the bacon to a paper towel–lined plate, and increase the heat to high. If there is excessive fat in the pan, you can drain some, but reserve in case the pan dries out. The sprouts will suck up the fat.

Add the Brussels sprouts to the pan, turning them over with tongs, if necessary, to make sure that the cut sides are down. Sear hard, without shaking the pan, until well charred and beginning to blacken, 5 to 7 minutes. Resist the temptation to meddle with them. The idea is to get a very deep, penetrating sear that nearly blackens the sprouts but keeps them relatively green inside. Flip the Brussels sprouts, and season with salt and pepper.

Add the dates and the reserved bacon to the pan, toss well, and cook until the sprouts begin to color, 2 to 3 minutes. Add the stock to the pan, a little bit at a time. With a wooden spoon, smash the dates into the sauce, breaking them into smaller pieces as the pan sauce reduces. Once the dates are incorporated into the sauce, add the vinegar.

Continue cooking until the sauce is thick enough to coat the Brussels sprouts, 2 to 3 minutes. Be careful not to reduce the sauce too much, or it will become cloyingly sweet and sticky. The sprouts should still be bright green and somewhat firm inside, but tender to the bite.

Transfer to a serving platter. Serve warm.

SWEET POTATO HASH

SERVES 4 TO 6 AS A SIDE DISH / I turn to this hash often as it's perfect topped with an egg or served alongside grilled meat such as pork & fennel sausage (see page 300) or grilled lamb chops. I use virgin coconut oil here for flavor and its high smoke point, which allows you to really rock the potatoes to a deep golden, crispy brown without burning the oil.

There seems to be a bit of confusion about the difference between a yam and a sweet potato. For this recipe, I'm talking about the red-skinned, white-fleshed, sweet potatoes also known as boniato, or Cuban or Japanese sweet potatoes. Any of these varieties work well here as they cook up without turning mushy and get beautifully crispy in the coconut oil.

3 Tbsp virgin coconut oil

1 large sweet potato, skin on, cut into ¾-in [2-cm] cubes

½ red onion, chopped

2 poblano chiles, seeded, stemmed, and chopped

1 jalapeño chile, sliced into thin rings

Kosher salt

Freshly ground black pepper

4 green onions (white and green parts), thinly sliced on the bias

1 bunch cilantro, leaves chopped and stems thinly sliced

1 or 2 limes

Heat a deep, heavy-bottomed pot over high heat. Add the coconut oil and let it melt and coat the bottom of the pan. Add the sweet potato and stir to coat with oil, then sear, without stirring, until brown, 2 to 3 minutes. Flip the cubes and sear, without stirring, 2 to 3 minutes. Stir in the red onion, poblanos, and jalapeños; season with salt and pepper; and turn the heat to medium-high. Cook, stirring occasionally, until the onion and chiles begin to brown and the potatoes are a deep, golden brown, 3 to 4 minutes. Test a potato for doneness; it should be crispy without, with a soft, creamy interior. Stir in the green onions and cilantro. Taste for seasoning, and squeeze in lime juice to taste.

Transfer to a serving platter. Serve hot.

When pasta is concerned, I prefer to keep it simple. Garlic and olive oil or a pomodoro sauce is every bit as satisfying as more complicated or luxurious preparations, especially if perfectly prepared. Putting some extra effort into making your own pasta is a quick way to take your cooking to a higher level and get more interesting results. Making pasta, like anything handmade, requires learning the "feel" throughout the process, and it was a challenge to offer precise measurements via written recipes. However, unlike bread, which has an active yeast variable, pasta dough is a relatively predictable dough and is easily mastered by a home cook with a little practice.

You can substitute high-quality dried pasta in any recipe that includes homemade pasta. Although homemade pasta can be a luscious, layered taste experience, and a seemingly endless number of shapes can be fashioned, a well-made dish of dried semolina spaghetti is among my favorite things to eat. I was shocked, as many Americans have been, the first time I witnessed a well-crafted spaghetti pomodoro being made by an Italian chef. Like any native New Jerseyan, I ate my share of respectable Italian-American versions of this dish growing up. But I noticed that across the ocean, the pasta was cooked al dente, and there was much less sauce than I was used to. In fact, when I first laid eyes on it, the Jersey boy in me wanted to ladle a scoop of red sauce over the top. When I ate it, I understood something about this pasta was changing me, making me pause to truly register the distinct flavors of the noodles themselves.

I like the new wave of artisan dried pastas that have hit the market, but I still think some of the old-school Italian imports like Barilla are very good. I am partial to the number 7 thickness of spaghetti, especially for pasta pomodoro, although other sizes can be used just as well. I recommend giving a little thought to the size of the noodle and how it works with the sauce you plan to use with it. Like goes with like: Fine-gauge noodles work best with creamy and fine-textured sauces; pasta shapes and noodles with a coarse surface pair well with chunky, rustic sauces.

When you cook dried store-bought pasta, paying close attention to doneness and the method for bringing the pasta together with the sauce will transform your approach to cooking pasta and the plate of pasta you sit down to eat. Getting just enough sauce to barely coat the pasta, layering the right amount of best-quality olive oil on top, and tying the whole thing together with a couple of drops of the pasta cooking water, which is viscous with starch and flavor and helps to create an emulsified sauce, lends an almost creamy texture that replaces the need for copious amounts of sauce. It also allows you to experience the texture of the pasta the way it is intended. The al dente texture of the pasta brings spunk and finesse to the dish; a fully cooked spaghetti can get heavy and dull fast. Give a firmer texture a shot.

Even people who appreciate my cooking often challenge me on our lightly sauced pasta when they first see it, as it really does look a little plain. Just try it and resist the urge to dump more sauce over it or to grate copious amounts of Parmesan on top.

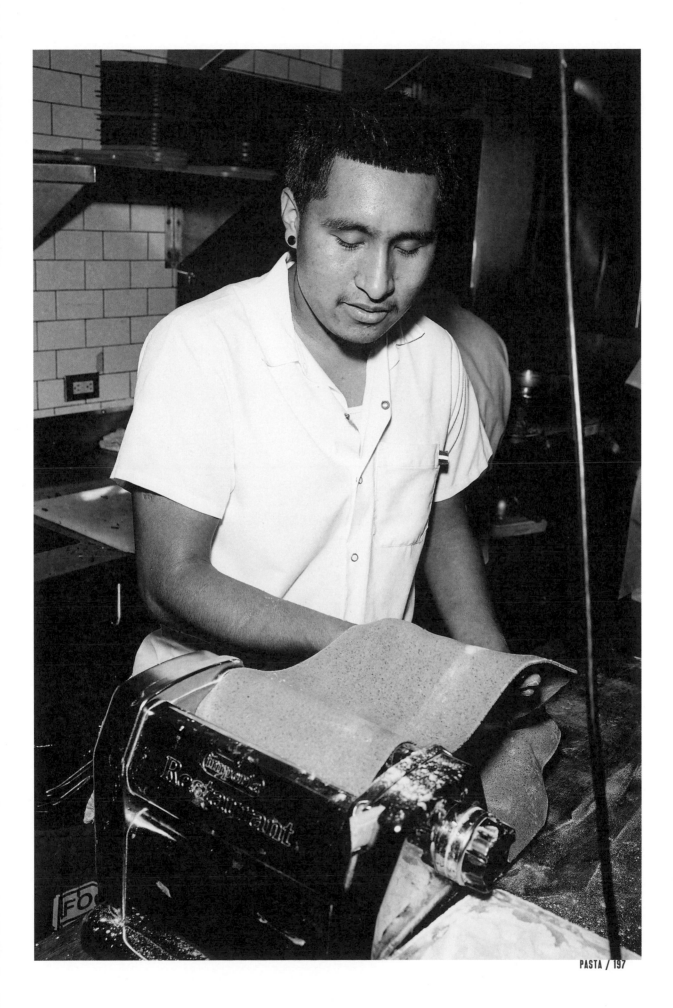

SPAGHETTI POMODORO

SERVES 2 / Many have argued with me on this one, but I stick to my guns: A tomato sauce of just good-quality ripe tomatoes, olive oil, sea salt, and basil is the still the best pasta recipe I've encountered, and also the simplest. Occasionally I add a bit of sugar to take the acid edge off the tomatoes, but only as necessary. This recipe makes just enough for two servings, as I think it is easier to nail it in a smaller quantity. Don't forget the finishing oil! Holding back on the oil added in the beginning of the dish so that you can drizzle in a little high-quality olive oil at the end allows the green olive flavor to permeate the dish.

¾ cup [180 ml] Pomodoro Sauce (page 59)

6 fresh basil leaves

Pinch of dried oregano, preferably Sicilian (optional)

Flaky sea salt

6 oz [170 g] dried spaghetti, preferably no. 7 thickness

2 Tbsp olive oil

Crushed red pepper flakes for serving (optional)

Freshly grated Parmesan cheese for serving

Bring a large pot of salted water to a boil over high heat.

Place the pomodoro sauce in a 10-in [25-cm] stainless-steel sauté pan over medium-high heat and slowly bring up to a simmer. Stir three of the basil leaves and the oregano (if using) into the sauce. Taste for salt and adjust as necessary. The sauce should just reduce slightly. Remove from the heat while the pasta cooks.

Drop the pasta into the boiling water and cook at a rolling boil for 4 minutes, stirring often. It is done when a noodle will drape over your tongs when raised out of the water. It will still be very firm. (I know it says 7 to 9 minutes on the box—ignore it.) Using the tongs, remove the spaghetti from the boiling water, transferring it directly to the sauce.

Place the pan over medium-high heat, and cook the spaghetti in the sauce. Splash in additional pasta water as necessary, 1 Tbsp at a time, to keep the sauce at the ideal thickness (not too thin to ladle over pasta and not so solid that it can't be ladled over) and continue to cook for 2 minutes. Turn off the heat. Tear the remaining three basil leaves into the sauce. Add the olive oil, toss, and taste for seasoning again. The spaghetti should be well seasoned, with a fruity olive oil overtone. You can add crushed red pepper flakes if you like it spicy.

Divide the pasta among two plates. Serve immediately, offering Parmesan at the table.

SPAGHETTI WITH ANCHOVIES, CRUSHED RED PEPPER FLAKES, GARLIC & OREGANO

SERVES 2 / Once you start eating anchovies, it doesn't take long before you can really handle a strong dose of their delightfully umami, briny flavor. I have found anchovy lovers really appreciate when the ingredient is rightly placed front and center. And this recipe is for them, as it packs an assertive anchovy punch. If you cannot find salt-packed anchovies, you can use good-quality oil-packed anchovies.

Like the previous recipe, as well as cacio e pepe, bottarga and bread crumbs, carbonara, aglio e olio, and puttanesca, the dish is enhanced by precise cooking of the spaghetti and the time spent cooking it together with the sauce and a small amount of pasta water.

2 Tbsp olive oil

4 oz [115 g] whole salt-packed anchovies, halved lengthwise, boned, and rinsed

2 garlic cloves, minced

1 tsp crushed red pepper flakes

Pinch of dried oregano, preferably Sicilian

6 oz [170 g] dried spaghetti, preferably no. 7 thickness

1 Tbsp crushed Garlic Croutons (see page 80)

Freshly grated Parmesan cheese for serving

Bring a large pot of salted water to a boil over high heat.

Place a 10-in [25-cm] stainless-steel sauté pan over medium-high heat and add the olive oil, anchovies, and garlic. Sauté for 1 or 2 minutes in the hot oil, breaking up the anchovies with tongs or a wooden spoon, and browning the garlic slightly. Add the crushed red pepper flakes and oregano and stir into the olive oil. Remove from the heat.

Drop the pasta into the boiling water and cook at a rolling boil for 4 minutes, stirring often. It is done when a noodle will drape over your tongs when raised out of the water. It will still be very firm. (I know it says 7 to 9 minutes on the box—ignore it.) Using the tongs, remove the spaghetti from the boiling water, transferring it directly to the pan with the anchovies and garlic. Add 2 Tbsp of the pasta cooking water.

Place the pan over medium-high heat and cook the spaghetti with the anchovies and garlic for 2 minutes, adding small amounts of additional pasta cooking water if necessary to coat the noodles. Taste the sauce for seasoning. (You should not have to add any additional salt to this dish.)

Divide the pasta among two plates and sprinkle with the crouton crumbs. Serve immediately, offering Parmesan at the table.

ORECCHIETTE WITH CHICKEN HEARTS, TURNIP GREENS, PECORINO & BLACK PEPPER

SERVES 4 / I love how the bouncy texture of chicken hearts plays off the knobby little orecchiette (the name means "little ears," which they faintly resemble). Chicken hearts are not always available at a standard supermarket meat counter, but if you ask your butcher, you might discover that he or she may have some stashed aside, or can easily get them if given a day or two's notice. Orecchiette are a relatively simple form to make, but require a bit of patience. So this is a good opportunity to put any extra hands around your home to work. We press the little dough nuggets over the slats of a bamboo sushi mat to give a ribbed texture on one side and a finger indentation on the other.

A bit of finesse is required to brown the hearts, while making sure the centers remain pink. Removing them from the pan before reducing the pan juices helps to keep them from overcooking. Time the cooking of the pasta with the preparation of the sauce, so that the dish can come together quickly.

ORECCHIETTE
1 cup [160 g] semolina flour, plus more for dusting
5 Tbsp [80 ml] water, at room temperature
Fine sea salt

3 Tbsp extra-virgin olive oil
3 garlic cloves, sliced
1 shallot, sliced
4 oz [115 g] turnip or radish greens,
cut into ½-in [12-mm] ribbons

Kosher salt
Freshly ground black pepper
8 oz [230 g] chicken hearts, halved
1 cup [240 ml] white wine
1 cup [240 ml] Chicken Stock (page 223)
1 tsp aged balsamic vinegar
Chunk of Pecorino Romano cheese for grating
Best-quality olive oil for drizzling

To make the orecchiette: Put the semolina flour in a medium bowl, and drizzle in 3 Tbsp of the water. With your hands, start to incorporate the water. The idea is to form small clumps of dough, making sure the flour doesn't stick to the bowl. Sprinkle in a large pinch of sea salt and continue mixing the ingredients together. Drizzle in another 1 to 2 Tbsp water and continue mixing. The dough should start to come together in a very dry mass. Do not add more water than necessary to get a cohesive dough, and be patient, adding 1 Tbsp at a time, as the flour will absorb the water slowly, so you will generally need less than you think. The amount of water needed will vary, depending on the freshness of your semolina and the humidity of your environment.

Once you have a cohesive dough, turn it out onto a work surface lightly dusted with semolina flour. Knead the dough by folding and pressing it with the palm of your hand, smashing the dough flat and then folding the outer edge toward the center and again pressing down. Continue to knead assertively until the dough is smooth and silky, 3 to 5 minutes. Wrap the dough in plastic wrap and let rest at room temperature at least 20 minutes, or for up to 2 hours.

Continued

Flatten the dough into a 1-in- [2.5-cm-] thick disk, and cut off a ¾-in- [2-cm-] wide strip. Using your hands, roll the strip of dough on the work surface to make a smooth snake of dough of uniform thickness. Continue rolling until you have a long noodle ¼ in [6 mm] thick. Repeat with the remaining dough.

Cut the dough into ½-in- [12-mm-] long pieces and dust with a bit of additional semolina. With your thumb, firmly press each dough piece against a bamboo sushi mat or into the palm of your hand. Pull downward with your thumb, so that the opposite edge of the dough curls over the depression that you made. (This is an easy motion once you get the hang of it and is something you could even teach a three-year-old to do.) Continue to smash all the dough pieces, forming little, irregular, ear-shaped pasta curls. Place them on a semolina-dusted baking sheet and cover with a kitchen towel while you prepare the sauce.

In a large frying pan over medium-high heat, warm 2 Tbsp of the extra-virgin olive oil until hot but not smoking. Add the garlic and shallot and cook until soft and translucent, about 2 minutes. Add the turnip greens and cook just until wilted, about 1 minute. Season with kosher salt and pepper and transfer to a plate to cool.

In the same pan, add the remaining 1 Tbsp olive oil and increase the heat to high. When the oil is very hot but not smoking, add the chicken hearts and cook until well seared, about 3 minutes. Flip the hearts, season with kosher salt and pepper, and sear for another 2 minutes. Transfer to the plate with the turnip greens.

Add the wine and stock to the pan and cook until reduced by half, 2 to 3 minutes. Return the hearts and turnip greens to the pan, toss, and taste for seasoning. The pan juices should still be slightly loose.

Meanwhile, bring a large pot of salted water to a boil over high heat. Add the orecchiette and cook just until tender, 1 to 1½ minutes.

With a slotted spoon, transfer the orecchiette to the pan with the chicken hearts and greens. Cook until the pan juices have reduced slightly and coat the pasta. Remove from the heat, add the balsamic vinegar, and season with pepper.

Transfer to a serving bowl, grate Pecorino over the orecchiette, and drizzle with best-quality olive oil. Toss once more and serve hot.

RICOTTA GNOCCHI WITH CHERRY TOMATO POMODORO

SERVES 6 / This tomato sauce made from extra-sweet cherry tomatoes is slightly indulgent but still doable in summer, when tomatoes are everywhere and growing out of control. The sauce takes on a silky texture that complements the pillowy texture of the ricotta gnocchi very well. This seems to be a dish that pleases young children as much as more astute diners.

RICOTTA GNOCCHI
1½ cups [180 g] all-purpose flour, plus more for dusting
1 lb [455 g] strained ricotta cheese
Pinch of kosher salt
Pinch of freshly grated nutmeg
1 egg, lightly beaten

CHERRY TOMATO POMODORO
2 pt [760 g] cherry tomatoes, stemmed
¼ cup [60 ml] extra-virgin olive oil
1 tsp kosher salt
1 tsp dried oregano, preferably Sicilian
Pinch of crushed red peppers flakes
½ bunch fresh basil, leaves only

Best-quality olive oil for drizzling
Freshly grated Parmesan cheese for serving

To make the gnocchi: On a work surface, spread out ½ cup [60 g] of the flour in a 9-in [23-cm] circle. Crumble the ricotta cheese over that and sprinkle another ½ cup [60 g] flour on top. Sprinkle the salt and nutmeg over. With your fingertips, gently gather the ricotta, incorporating the flour a little as you do, working the cheese and flour into a mound, with a volcano-shaped well in the center. Pour about three-fourths of the beaten egg into the well in the dough, and use a fork to combine the dough and egg until it has become a rough mass. Gently fold the mass with a bench scraper repeatedly until the dough has mostly come together into a ragged mass. Begin to gently knead, adding up to an additional ¼ cup [30 g] flour, until you have a smooth mass. Use small, quick motions and light touches—just enough to bring the dough together; assertive handling develops gluten, which will make your gnocchi tough.

Wrap the dough in plastic wrap and let rest for 20 minutes. Cover the work surface with the remaining ¼ cup [30 g] flour. Unwrap the dough and gently shape into a 1-in- [2.5-cm-] thick disk. Cut the disk into six strips and gently roll each strip into a log about ½ in [12 mm] in diameter. With a knife, cut each log into 1-in [2.5-cm] segments. Press each one into the tines of a fork, leaving a finger imprint on one side of the dumpling and a fork impression on the other. Transfer to a baking sheet and dust with additional flour.

To make the pomodoro: In a medium saucepan over medium heat, combine the cherry tomatoes, extra-virgin olive oil, and salt. Cook, stirring occasionally, until the tomatoes burst and release their liquid. Simmer until thickened, about 30 minutes. Pass the sauce through a food mill into a large frying pan. Season with the oregano, crushed red pepper flakes, and basil leaves. Continue to simmer to meld the flavors, 5 to 10 minutes longer.

Bring an extra-large pot of salted water to a boil over high heat. Add the gnocchi and boil just until they float to the surface, about 2 minutes. With a slotted spoon, transfer the gnocchi to the pan with the sauce and toss gently.

Transfer to a large serving platter. Drizzle with best-quality olive oil. Serve immediately, offering Parmesan at the table.

SQUID INK CHITARRA WITH ANCHOVIES

SERVES 2 / This pasta, which is named for the guitarlike tool on which it's traditionally cut, is all about the texture. We roll our chitarra on the thicker side and cut the noodles quite narrow. They end up about the same size as spaghetti, but squared off instead of round, with a bouncy texture that suits lighter sauces like this one. Squid ink is readily available online and in many fish stores and specialty markets, but you could just omit it from this recipe if you prefer dried chitarra or spaghetti. The benefit of the ink is more for color than flavor, but it really does yield a deep, stunning hue that seems both mysterious and oceanic.

SQUID INK CHITARRA
2 cups [240 g] all-purpose flour
1 tsp fine sea salt
2 eggs, plus 2 egg yolks
1 Tbsp squid ink
1 tsp extra-virgin olive oil
Semolina flour for sprinkling

2 Tbsp extra-virgin olive oil
1½ cups [285 g] cherry tomatoes

12 whole salt-packed anchovies, halved lengthwise, boned, and rinsed
4 garlic cloves, minced
½ cup [120 ml] dry white wine
¼ tsp crushed red pepper flakes
2 tsp dried oregano, preferably Sicilian
1 small handful Garlic Croutons (see page 80), fully cooled
Best-quality olive oil for drizzling
Freshly grated Parmesan cheese for serving

To make the chitarra: In a medium bowl, sift the flour and sprinkle in the sea salt. In a small bowl, whisk the eggs and egg yolks lightly and whisk in the squid ink and the olive oil. Drizzle about three-fourths of the egg–squid ink mixture over the flour mixture. With your fingertips, mix the liquid into the flour to form little pebbles. Massage the dough, pressing and squeezing the small pebbles into a shaggy mass. Add more of the remaining egg–squid ink mixture only as necessary, in order to bring the dough together into a cohesive mass. It will seem dry, but it will bind into a mass; the flour will absorb the liquid as it sits.

On a lightly floured work surface, knead the dough briskly until smooth and elastic, 3 to 5 minutes. Wrap the dough in plastic wrap and let rest at room temperature for 20 minutes.

Sprinkle a baking sheet with semolina flour. With a pasta machine, roll the dough into a sheet about ¹⁄₁₆ in [2 mm] thick. Sprinkle semolina on the surface of the dough, and cut into four 4-by-10-in [10-by-25-cm] sheets. Fold the sheets in thirds like a letter and, with a sharp knife, cut the sheets into strips about ¹⁄₁₆ in [2 mm] wide. This may seem difficult as first, but you will get the rhythm of it with some practice. Don't sweat it too much. The imperfect nature of the cuts adds to the pasta's character. Repeat with the remaining pasta sheets. Spread out the cut pasta on the prepared baking sheet, and cover with a kitchen towel.

Bring a large pot of salted water to a rolling boil over high heat.

In a medium frying pan over high heat, warm the extra-virgin olive oil until hot but not smoking. Add the cherry tomatoes and cook until charred and blistered, 2 to 3 minutes. Turn the heat to medium and stir in the anchovies and minced garlic. Cook, breaking up the anchovies with a wooden spoon, until the garlic is lightly browned, about 1 minute. Add the wine and reduce by half. Add the crushed red pepper flakes and oregano. Remove from the heat and set aside.

Place the croutons on a work surface and, using a rolling pin or a chef's knife, crush into coarse crumbs.

Drop the pasta into the boiling water and cook at a rolling boil for 2 minutes, until just cooked but still very firm. With a slotted spoon, tongs, or a wire-mesh strainer, transfer the pasta to the pan with anchovy sauce, along with about ¼ cup [60 ml] of the pasta cooking water. Cook, tossing gently, until the pasta is well coated with the sauce, adding 1 to 2 Tbsp of additional cooking water as needed if the sauce is too thick. Taste and adjust the seasoning. The pasta water and anchovies should provide plenty of salt, and you probably won't need more. The pasta water helps to emulsify the sauce and gives it a creamy texture, so don't underestimate its role.

Divide the pasta and sauce among two plates, top with the crouton crumbs, and drizzle with best-quality olive oil. Serve immediately, offering Parmesan at the table.

RYE RAGS WITH SAUSAGE, MUSHROOMS & FENNEL

SERVES 4 / We cut pasta sheets into elongated haphazard shapes that resemble a small pile of rags when cooked. The larger, rye-flavored sheets of dough hold up beautifully to the substantial ragout of mushrooms cooked with sausage and fennel.

RYE RAGS
1 cup [100 g] rye flour
1 cup [120 g] bread flour
2 eggs, at room temperature
Fine sea salt
2 Tbsp water, at room temperature
Semolina flour for dusting

1 large slice rye bread
1 tsp extra-virgin olive oil, plus 4 Tbsp [60 ml] or as needed
½ tsp caraway seeds
1 garlic clove

8 oz [230 g] Pork & Fennel Sausage (see page 300), or sweet Italian sausage, removed from their casings
½ fennel bulb, finely chopped, plus 2 Tbsp chopped fennel fronds
6 oz [170 g] shiitake mushrooms
¼ cup [65 g] Tomato Confit (page 60)
Kosher salt
½ cup [120 ml] white wine
1½ cups [360 ml] Chicken Stock (page 223)
Pinch of crushed red pepper flakes
Freshly grated Parmesan cheese for serving

To make the rye rags: In a medium bowl, sift the rye flour and bread flour together. In a small bowl, gently whisk the eggs and drizzle them into the flours. With your fingers, mix to form a rough dough. Sprinkle in some sea salt and continue to mix until you have a shaggy dough. Add the water 2 tsp at a time, just adding it until the dough comes together. The flour will absorb the water as you knead, so add as little water as you can and still gather it into a shaggy dough.

On a lightly floured work surface, knead the dough until silky and smooth, about 3 minutes. Wrap in plastic wrap and let rest at room temperature for 20 minutes.

Lightly flour the work surface again if it needs it. You need some friction with the work surface, so don't use too much flour, but sprinkle a light dusting if the dough starts to stick. Use a rolling pin to roll the dough about 1⁄16 in [2 mm] thick. I like to roll the dough around the rolling pin and flip it over from time to time so that I roll both sides of the dough from the center out to the edge.

With a knife, cut the dough into irregular-shaped rectangles 3 to 5 in [7.5 to 12 cm] long. The more random they are, the more beautiful they look in the bowl. Dust the pasta rags with semolina flour, place on a baking sheet, and cover with a kitchen towel while you make the sauce.

Preheat the oven to 350°F [180°C].

Brush the bread with the 1 tsp olive oil and toast in the oven until completely dried, 15 to 20 minutes.

In a small, dry frying pan over medium heat, toast the caraway seeds until fragrant, about 3 minutes.

Continued

Rub the toasted bread with the garlic clove, and then break the bread into pieces with your hands. Transfer to a food processor along with the toasted caraway seeds. Pulse to make small bread crumbs, stopping before they turn to dust. Or smash the bread and caraway seeds with a mortar and pestle. If the crumbs seem very dry, moisten with a bit more oil and set aside.

In a large frying pan over medium-high heat, warm 2 Tbsp olive oil until hot but not smoking. Add the sausage, breaking it apart with a wooden spoon, and cook until well browned, about 2 minutes. Transfer to a plate, leaving as much of the rendered fat as possible in the pan. Add the fennel and mushrooms to the pan and cook until beginning to brown, 2 to 3 minutes. Add up to another 2 Tbsp oil to the pan if it begins to look dry. Add the tomato confit and cook until lightly browned and fragrant, about 1 minute longer. Adjust the heat so you are searing and not steaming your ingredients. Season with kosher salt. Add the wine and stock to the pan and cook, stirring with a wooden spoon to scrape up any browned bits from the bottom of the pan, until the sauce begins to thicken, about 3 minutes.

Meanwhile, bring a large pot of salted water to a boil over high heat. Add the rye rags and cook just until tender, 1 to 1½ minutes, depending on the thickness of the pasta and how long they sat before cooking. With a slotted spoon, tongs, or a wire-mesh strainer, transfer the pasta to the pan with the sausage and mushrooms.

Cook over high heat just until the pasta is well coated with the sauce, 2 to 3 minutes. If the sauce is too thick, loosen it with a few spoonsful of the pasta cooking water. Toss in the fennel fronds and crushed red pepper flakes.

Transfer to a serving bowl and sprinkle with the seasoned bread crumbs. Serve immediately, offering Parmesan at the table.

TUNA & BUCKWHEAT-PASTA GRATIN

SERVES 6 / This is a riff on the classic tuna-noodle casserole (which I grew up on and adore), but it incorporates an earthy and substantial buckwheat pasta from northern Italy known as pizzoccheri. Because of buckwheat's relatively low gluten content, you have to be quite thorough and firm in kneading to get a cohesive dough that rolls out smoothly. A buckwheat noodle will always have a more substantial and hardy texture, which I love, but it's not for everybody. This is a beautiful wintery, Alpine pasta dish, with classic northern Italian and American roots. You can swap in a short pasta such as fusilli, penne, or even dried egg noodles if you want to go for store-bought and still get a killer result. Simply adjust your pasta cooking times accordingly, leaving some room for the pasta to cook and come together with the other ingredients in the oven.

Tuna conserva is great for sandwiches and for flaking into salads, so you may want to make extra. You can also substitute a good-quality canned albacore tuna packed in olive oil.

BUCKWHEAT PASTA

1½ cups [180 g] coarse buckwheat flour, preferably Anson Mills Rustic Aromatic Buckwheat Flour

½ cup [60 g] bread flour, plus more for sprinkling

1 tsp fine sea salt

2 eggs, at room temperature

¼ cup [60 ml] warm (130°F [54°C]) water, plus more if needed

Semolina flour for dusting

TUNA CONSERVA

3 cups [720 ml] extra-virgin olive oil, plus more if needed

2 shallots, halved

1 fennel bulb, quartered

1 garlic head, halved through the equator

1 dried guajillo chile

3 bay leaves

3 fresh thyme sprigs

Zest of 2 lemons, cut into large strips

2 lb [910 g] albacore tuna loin, cut into 4-oz [115-g] medallions

Kosher salt

1 Tbsp unsalted butter

1 Tbsp extra-virgin olive oil

1 red onion, thinly sliced

2 celery ribs, cut into ¼-in [4-mm] slices

4 garlic cloves, sliced

¼ head green cabbage, cored and cut into ½-in [12-mm] strips

Kosher salt

Freshly ground black pepper

1 cup [240 ml] white wine

1 cup [240 ml] Chicken Stock (page 223)

3 Tbsp roughly chopped fresh flat-leaf parsley

1½ cups [360 ml] Buttermilk Crème Fraîche (page 55)

6 oz [170 g] Gruyère cheese, grated

2 handfuls Garlic Croutons (see page 80), fully cooled

½ cup [60 g] freshly grated Parmesan cheese

To make the pasta: In a medium bowl, sift the buckwheat flour and bread flour together. Sprinkle in the sea salt. In a small bowl, whisk the eggs. Drizzle the eggs over the flours and, with your fingers, mix them together. Drizzle in the warm water, mixing constantly with your hands and pressing and squeezing the small pebbles of dough into a cohesive mass.

Continued

On a lightly floured work surface, knead the dough until it is very smooth and silky, 3 to 5 minutes. If the dough is sticking, sprinkle with bread flour and continue to knead. Add a small amount of water if the dough seems too dry. The important thing is to get a very smooth dough that can be handled without breaking. A stiffer dough is generally better than a softer one in terms of strength. Without letting the dough rest, press it into a 1-in- [2.5-cm-] thick disk. With a rolling pin, roll the dough from the center to the edge in all directions until the dough is 1/16 in [2 mm] thick. With a knife, cut the dough into 1/4-in- [6-mm-] wide strips. Then cut them crosswise to create 4- to 5-in- [10- to 12-cm-] long strands of pasta. Dust with semolina flour, transfer to a baking sheet, cover with a kitchen towel, and set aside.

To make the tuna conserva: In a medium enameled Dutch oven over medium-low heat, combine the olive oil, shallots, fennel, garlic, guajillo, bay leaves, thyme sprigs, and lemon zest. Heat the oil, stirring occasionally, until it reaches 180° to 200°F [80° to 95°C].

Season the tuna medallions with kosher salt and place in the warm oil. The tuna should be just barely submerged. Add more oil if necessary. Poach the tuna until it registers 150°F [65°C] at its center and is medium pink in its thickest part, 10 to 12 minutes. Remove from the heat and allow the tuna to cool in the oil. (If not using immediately, transfer the tuna and the seasoned oil to an airtight container and store in the refrigerator for up to 10 days.)

In a large pot over medium-high heat, melt the butter in the olive oil. Add the onion, celery, and garlic and cook until translucent, about 5 minutes. Stir in the sliced cabbage and season with kosher salt and pepper. Turn the heat to medium, and cook until the cabbage is tender and beginning to brown, 6 to 8 minutes. Add the wine and stock. Bring to a boil and continue boiling to reduce by about two-thirds, about 2 minutes. Remove from the heat, and stir in the parsley, crème fraîche, and Gruyère to make a rich sauce.

Weigh out 8 to 10 oz [225 to 280 g] of the tuna conserva, and drain. Add it to the sauce, flaking it over the pot with your hands and folding it in gently so as to not break it apart completely.

Preheat the broiler.

Bring a large pot of salted water to a boil over high heat. Add the pasta and boil until tender, 1½ to 2 minutes. With a slotted spoon, transfer the cooked pasta to the pot with the sauce and mix well. The sauce should coat the noodles but still be quite saucy. It is important to have some extra sauce so that it can continue reducing under the broiler while it browns without getting too thick. Add a bit of the pasta water if necessary to achieve this. If the sauce looks too loose, place over medium-high heat and reduce for 1 or 2 minutes before transferring to the oven.

Transfer the mixture to a 9-by-12-in [23-by-30.5-cm] baking dish.

Place the croutons on a work surface and, using a rolling pin or a chef's knife, crush into coarse crumbs.

Top the pasta with the crouton crumbs and Parmesan. Broil until the top is browned and the sauce is bubbling, 5 to 7 minutes, depending on your broiler, so watch it carefully. Remove from the oven and let sit for a few minutes, then serve.

KABOCHA SQUASH & GOAT CHEESE AGNOLOTTI WITH BROWN BUTTER & WALNUT PICADA

SERVES 4 TO 6 / Agnolotti can be an intimidating pasta shape to take on at home and for good reason. Attempting them for the first time is like giving yourself a master course in pasta making. But once you become familiar with the process, these are very achievable and satisfying to make, and the result is well worth the effort. The pillow of squash–goat cheese filling with a hood of pasta that captures the earthy, walnut-laced butter is super-tasty and fun to eat.

SQUASH AND GOAT CHEESE FILLING
One 1-lb [455-g] piece kabocha squash, seeded and halved
Extra-virgin olive oil for drizzling, plus 1 tsp
3 oz [85 g] ash-rind, semiripe goat cheese, such as Humboldt Fog, at room temperature
1 Tbsp freshly grated Parmesan cheese
Kosher salt
Freshly ground black pepper

AGNOLOTTI DOUGH
2 cups [240 g] all-purpose flour, plus more as needed
½ tsp fine sea salt
2 eggs, plus 2 egg yolks
1 Tbsp extra-virgin olive oil
Semolina flour for dusting

1 egg
2 Tbsp milk

WALNUT PICADA
¼ cup [30 g] chopped walnuts
Zest of 1 lemon
2 Tbsp chopped fresh flat-leaf parsley
1 Tbsp fresh thyme leaves
1 tsp chopped fresh rosemary leaves
2 tsp extra-virgin olive oil or oil from Garlic Confit (page 64)
Flaky sea salt

4 Tbsp [55 g] unsalted butter
¼ cup [55 g] sliced Shallot Confit (page 64)
½ tsp sherry vinegar
1 tsp freshly squeezed lemon juice
Freshly ground black pepper
Freshly grated Parmesan cheese for serving

To make the filling: Preheat the oven to 425°F [220°C]. On a baking sheet, drizzle the squash halves with olive oil, turn them cut-side down, and roast until very soft and beginning to caramelize around the edges, 30 to 45 minutes. Remove from the oven and let cool.

Scrape out the squash flesh and transfer to a food processor. Pulse until smooth.

In a large piece of cheesecloth, wrap the puréed squash in a tight bundle. Set in a colander set over a bowl, and let drain at least 4 hours, or up to overnight. Squeeze with your hands by twisting the cheesecloth to remove any extra water. Unwrap the drained squash and transfer to a medium bowl.

Add the goat cheese, Parmesan, and 1 tsp olive oil to the squash purée and stir to incorporate all the ingredients. (I like it when the goat cheese is ribboned throughout instead of perfectly blended.) Season with kosher salt and pepper to be sure the flavors are balanced. Transfer to a resealable plastic bag, and let stand at room temperature until ready to use.

To make the dough: In a medium bowl, sift the all-purpose flour and sprinkle in the fine sea salt. In a small bowl, whisk the eggs and the egg yolks together. Stir olive oil into the eggs. Drizzle about three-fourths of the egg mixture over the flour. With your fingertips, mix the egg mixture into the flour to form little pebbles. Massage the dough, pressing and squeezing the small pebbles into a shaggy mass. Add more of the remaining egg mixture only as necessary, in order to bring the dough together into a cohesive mass, and start to press the mixture together with your hands to form a shaggy dough. It will seem dry, but it will bind into a mass; the flour will absorb the liquid as it sits.

Turn out the dough onto a lightly floured work surface. Knead until it is very smooth and silky, 3 to 5 minutes, adding more flour only as needed 1 Tbsp at a time. (Add 1 tsp water if the dough seems too dry.) The important thing is to get a very smooth dough that can be handled without breaking. A stiffer dough is generally better than a softer one for filled pasta in terms of strength and resulting texture. Wrap the dough in plastic wrap and allow to rest at room temperature at least 20 minutes, or up to 6 hours.

Flatten the dough into a disk and feed it though a pasta machine set at its widest setting. Repeat two more times. Fold the dough into thirds like a letter, turn it 90 degrees, and feed it through the machine. Repeat this folding and feeding pattern two more times or until the dough is very smooth and elastic.

Now set the machine at its next to widest setting. Fold the dough and feed it through. Continue to set the machine at a progressively thinner setting before you fold and feed the dough through the machine, rolling the pasta out into a long, even sheet. As the sheet gets longer, start to fold the pasta over itself as it comes out, so you don't have too long of a piece, which can be cumbersome. As you work, add just enough all-purpose flour to the surface of the dough as needed as you go. If you started with relatively stiff dough, you should not need very much additional flour. When the machine is at its thinnest setting, fold and feed it though two times. The dough should be about 1 mm thick and about 5 ft [1.5 m] long. Cut the dough in half lengthwise so you have two long strips about 2½ in [6 cm] wide. Fold one of the strips over on itself several times and cover with a kitchen towel. The dough should be dry enough so that it doesn't stick to itself, but if it does, sprinkle with semolina flour before folding. Dust a baking sheet with semolina flour and set aside.

In a small bowl, beat the egg with the milk to make an egg wash.

Cut off the tip of one corner of the plastic bag holding the filling. Working quickly, pipe a ½-in- [12-mm-] wide strip of filling the length of one of the strips of dough so that it's closer to one of the long edges than the other. Fold that side of the dough over the filling, but do not meet the other edge of the dough. Instead, leave a ½-in- [12-mm-] wide border of dough uncovered. If there is more dough, trim to leave roughly this amount. Check to making sure the dough is folded in a relatively straight line.

Brush a thin line of the egg wash along the seam where the pasta encloses the filling. Using your fingers, gently pinch in the dough at 1-in [2.5-cm] lengths. Do not pinch the top and bottom layers of dough together. You want to indicate the borders of the agnolotti.

With a fluted pasta cutter, cut through the centers of the indentations, forming little pillows 1 in [2.5 cm] long. As you cut through the dough, it will roll over itself, with a fold of dough draped over one side where the border of dough was. (This creates a little cavity that will capture the buttery pan sauce, picada, and grated cheese.) The process is fairly simple, once you get the hang of it. Move the agnolotti to the prepared baking sheet and cover with a kitchen towel. Refrigerate until ready to use. (They will hold for several hours, but need to be eaten the same day.)

Continued

To make the walnut picada: In a small, dry frying pan over medium heat, toast the walnuts until fragrant, about 3 minutes. Let cool.

With your hands, crush the walnuts into relatively small, irregular pieces. In a small bowl, combine the crushed walnuts with the lemon zest, parsley, thyme, rosemary, and olive oil and combine with your fingers. Season with flaky sea salt. Let stand at room temperature until ready to use.

Bring a large pot of salted water to a boil over high heat.

Meanwhile, in a large sauté pan over medium-high heat, melt the butter and cook until it begins to brown slightly. Add the shallot confit and cook for about 3 minutes.

Cook the agnolotti in the boiling water, in batches if necessary so as not to crowd the pan, just until tender, 1 to 1½ minutes. With a slotted spoon, transfer the agnolotti to the pan with the butter and confit. Add about ¼ cup [60 ml] of the pasta cooking water and cook over medium-high heat until the sauce reduces slightly and starts to coat the pasta, about 3 minutes. Add the vinegar and lemon juice to the sauce. Remove from the heat.

Transfer the pasta to serving plates and sprinkle with the walnut picada and finish with pepper. Serve immediately, offering Parmesan at the table.

CHAPTER SIX

SOUPS, STEWS & GRAINS

Many a night, there is nothing better to put on the table than a big bowl of something warm and comforting. The recipes in this chapter all fill that urge for me. Like many cooks, I have a love affair with meat- and bone-based broths, and I use them broadly in my cooking. I firmly believe in the health benefits of well-crafted bone broths. But more important, their flavor satisfies the soul; giving comfort on all levels, even if just served simply by themselves. Stocks and broths are versatile staples to have in the kitchen.

Folks who train in our kitchen are often surprised by how many of our pan sauces are simple combinations of wine, aromatics, herbs, and a couple splashes of some kind of broth. I have had to learn not to automatically grab for the chicken broth as a go-to base for almost all soups and even vegetable dishes, as many of our guests simply prefer to avoid meat-based products of any sort. However, I still maintain that a bone-based broth is the best way to bring body and texture to even the simplest dishes, such as a plate of quickly sautéed snap peas or roasted root vegetables. The soups, stews, and grains that are made with bone-based broths are crucial for your repertoire, and are the best way to bring soulful, restorative qualities to your cooking. Most soups and stews will keep, covered, for up to 1 week in the refrigerator.

When it comes to grains, look for the heirloom or locally grown varieties of wheat berries, rye, barley, grits, and oats. These have completely different qualities—they are more earthy and flavorful—than the comparatively dreary commodity-grade grains that are industrially grown and harvested. Many people are now reporting ill health effects, allergies, and disease from eating grains that for many generations were generally considered healthful. Perhaps this is an unintended consequence of Big Ag's effort to produce a highly resistant, very productive species. Luckily there are increasing numbers of thoughtful producers who are bringing traditionally grown and harvested grains to the marketplace, making their health benefits and delicious flavors and textures much more accessible.

VEGETABLE STOCK

MAKES ABOUT 1 GL [3.8 L] / The idea here is to create a rich, satisfying stock that even a meat eater will happily slurp down. Depending on how we plan to use the stock, we vary the ratio of certain ingredients to make either the mushrooms, fennel, or leeks come forward. Mushrooms, kombu (a type of seaweed), and tomatoes bring a meaty umami quality, which contributes to the body and texture of vegetable-based stocks. So I do recommend using small amounts of these, as in this recipe.

¼ cup [60 ml] extra-virgin olive oil

3 yellow onions, quartered

2 carrots, cut into 4-in [10-cm] pieces

2 celery ribs, cut into 4-in [10-cm] pieces

1 fennel bulb, quartered, and tops

1 garlic head, halved through the equator

4 Roma tomatoes, halved

2 oz [55 g] dried shiitake mushrooms

One 4-in [10-cm] square piece of kombu, rinsed

2 leeks (green part only; optional)

1 bunch fresh flat-leaf parsley

3 fresh thyme sprigs

3 dried bay leaves

Kosher salt

In a large, heavy-bottomed stockpot over medium heat, warm the olive oil until hot but not smoking. Add the onions, carrots, celery, fennel bulb and tops, and garlic and sauté until the vegetables just start to soften, about 20 minutes. Add water to cover the vegetables by about 2 in [5 cm]. Bring to a rolling boil over high heat and cook for 5 minutes. Lower the heat and bring to a mellow simmer. Add the tomatoes, mushrooms, kombu, leeks (if using), parsley, thyme, and bay leaves and continue simmering for 1 hour, adding more water as necessary to keep the vegetables covered.

Season with salt and remove the kombu from the pot. Continue to cook, tasting the broth every 15 minutes, until it has the desired body and flavor.

Remove the stock from the heat and let sit, undisturbed, for about 20 minutes. Set a medium-mesh strainer over a container large enough to hold all the liquid, and strain the stock. Discard the solids and allow the stock to cool completely.

Store in an airtight container in the refrigerator for up to 1 week, or in the freezer for up to 3 months. Skim any fat from the surface before using.

CHICKEN STOCK

MAKES ABOUT 1 GL [3.8 L] / Our basic formula for chicken broth calls for a 2:1 ratio of chicken to vegetables. The weight of chicken is about twice the weight of the vegetables. And the amount of onion is roughly equal to the carrot and celery combined. Do not skim off the precious golden chicken fat that rises to the top. This stuff is magic and contains a disproportionate amount of chicken-flavored decadence that will enhance your stock as it cooks. Many a visiting chef has commented on my need to skim my stocks more often. I happily nod my head and then ignore them.

It is hard to apply a precise cooking time to stock. Learn to taste and watch for certain cues. Begin to taste your stock after it has cooked for 1 hour, and then keep tasting every 15 minutes or so. You'll begin to understand how the flavor and body of the stock changes as it cooks. Small quantities of stock, like this recipe, can be ready in 2 hours. There is such a thing as overcooking a stock, which results in a muddy, over-extracted taste. Be sure to season the stock with salt to open up the flavors.

For the home cook, the simplest method is to use a whole chicken, head to toe, cut up into parts. Assuming you have a very high-quality, organic, pasture-raised bird, there is no need to blanch or wash it meticulously beforehand. The head and feet add great body to a stock; do include them in your broth unless they are unavailable. A few extra chicken wings are a good replacement for the head and feet, if you feel like your stock needs extra body and flavor.

One 2½- to 3-lb [1.2- to 1.4-kg] chicken, head and feet intact, cut into pieces
2 yellow onions, halved through the equator
2 carrots, each cut into 4 pieces
2 celery ribs, each cut into 4 pieces
1 garlic head, halved through the equator

1 bunch fresh flat-leaf parsley
2 dried bay leaves
2 fresh thyme sprigs
1 dried guajillo chile
1 Tbsp black peppercorns
Kosher salt

In a large, heavy-bottomed stockpot, cover the chicken pieces with about 2 in [5 cm] water. Bring to a rolling boil over high heat and cook for 5 minutes. Skim any foam or impurities that rise to the top. Lower the heat and bring to a mellow simmer. Add the onions, carrots, celery, garlic, parsley, bay leaves, thyme, chile, and peppercorns and stir to distribute evenly throughout the stock. Continue simmering and, after 1 hour, taste the stock, and continue tasting every 15 minutes to check its progress. Add more water if necessary to keep the chicken and vegetables covered.

After 1½ hours, season with salt. Continue cooking and tasting until the stock has a rich chicken flavor and a slightly viscous body, at least 30 minutes, or up to 4 hours, longer.

Remove the stock from the heat and let sit, undisturbed, for about 20 minutes. Set a medium-mesh strainer over a container large enough to hold all the liquid, and strain the stock. Discard the solids and allow the stock to cool completely.

Store in an airtight container in the refrigerator for up to 1 week, or in the freezer for up to 3 months. Skim any fat from the surface before using.

FISH STOCK

MAKES ABOUT 1 GL [3.8 L] / Good fish stock is not only essential for making lovely fish soups and stews but it's a holistic, soulful way of utilizing fish bones, which comprise a large part of a fish's mass. White-fleshed, less-oily fish such as snapper, halibut, bream, sea bass, and sole are ideal for stock, but cod, salmon, grouper, and tuna could be used for a "fishier" stock. Lobster, shrimp, and crab also work amazingly well, so don't shy away from using a combination of fish and shellfish, especially as a base for Cioppino (page 275). This is useful if you have a variety of bones and shells saved, or can gather them at the fishmonger. The key is to simmer very slowly; this prevents you from pulling out the more aggressive fishy notes or impurities that tend to come with rapid boiling. Be sure to taste your broth to achieve the intensity you desire.

1 lb [455 g] fish head and bones, preferably snapper, bream, or halibut

Extra-virgin olive oil for cooking

1 fennel bulb, quartered, and tops

1 white onion, quartered

1 leek (green parts only), halved lengthwise and rinsed

2 celery ribs, cut into 3-in [7.5-cm] pieces

1 carrot, cut into 3-in [7.5-cm] pieces

1 garlic head, halved through the equator

2 Roma tomatoes, halved

1 Fresno chile, halved

1 bunch fresh flat-leaf parsley

1 dried bay leaf

1 fresh thyme sprig

¼ tsp peppercorns

Sea salt

Split the fish head in half and rinse under running water. Rinse the fish bones thoroughly under running water, washing off any blood or guts that remain attached. Set aside.

In a large, heavy-bottomed stockpot over medium heat, warm enough olive oil to cover the bottom of the pot until hot but not smoking. Add the fennel bulb and tops, onion, leek, celery, carrot, garlic, tomatoes, chile, parsley, bay leaf, thyme, and peppercorns and sautée until the vegetables just start to soften, 5 to 7 minutes. Add the fish head and bones. Add water to cover the fish pieces. Turn the heat to medium-high and bring to a boil, then lower the heat to medium-low. The liquid should be at a slow simmer. Skim any foam or impurities that rise to the top in the first 5 minutes. Season with salt and continue simmering and tasting until the stock has a rich, fishy flavor, 30 to 40 minutes.

Remove the stock from the heat. Set a fine-mesh strainer over a container large enough to hold all the liquid and strain the stock. Press down on the vegetables to extract all of the liquid from them. You can pour the liquid through cheesecloth or a fine-mesh strainer a second time for a clearer broth; I don't. Discard the solids and allow the stock to cool completely.

Store in an airtight container in the refrigerator for up to 1 week, or in the freezer for up to 3 months.

BEEF STOCK

MAKES ABOUT 1 GL [3.8 L] / A well-made beef stock has restorative properties that go far beyond the famed curative powers of chicken stock. Beef bones, especially marrow-rich leg and shank bones, bring an unparalleled tongue-and-stomach-coating richness to a soup. I can be perfectly content with a small bowl of seasoned beef stock, garnished with a few scallions and a couple of cracks of black pepper when my energy is stagnant or my stomach is off-kilter. I like a combination of clean bones and bones with meat, and prefer leg and shank bones to ribs or necks for their high proportion of marrow. We roast the bones first, but only until light brown. We've found that even a small section of charred or slightly burnt bone can throw off the flavor of the stock, so roast carefully. A very strong and delicious beef stock can be made in 5 hours. I have heard people talk about 12-, 16-, and even 24-hour extractions, which sound cool but I have found them unnecessary. Don't be put off by the sweet spices here, as they serve to balance the stock's richness.

5 lb [2.3 kg] beef shanks, with about equal amounts of meat and bone

2 large onions, quartered

2 leeks (green part only; optional)

2 carrots, cut into 4 pieces

2 celery ribs, cut into 4 pieces

3 Roma tomatoes, halved

1 garlic head, halved through the equator

3 fresh thyme sprigs

One bunch fresh flat-leaf parsley (optional)

3 dried bay leaves

One 2-in- [5-cm-] long cinnamon stick

1 star anise

1 whole clove

1 tsp black peppercorns

1 dried guajillo chile

Kosher salt

Preheat the oven to 425°F [220°C].

On a baking sheet, spread out the bones and roast until aromatic and light to medium brown, about 20 minutes. Transfer the roasted bones to a large, heavy-bottomed stockpot and add enough water to cover by about 2 in [5 cm]. Bring to a rolling boil over high heat and cook for 5 to 10 minutes, skimming any foam or impurities that rise to the surface. Lower the heat and bring to a mellow simmer. Add the onions, leeks (if using), carrots, celery, tomatoes, garlic, thyme, parsley (if using), bay leaves, cinnamon stick, star anise, clove, peppercorns, and chile and stir to distribute evenly throughout the stock.

Simmer, stirring occasionally, for 2 hours, and season with salt. Begin to taste the stock, so you can gauge how the flavors are developing. Cook until the desired flavor and body are reached, 3 to 5 hours. I look for a rich, beefy flavor and the mouthfeel and texture of a slightly gelatinous stock. The soup should coat your tongue a bit as you taste it. It should not have a noticeable bone flavor or be super-cloudy. This would mean you have either boiled it too vigorously, or simmered it too long.

Remove the stock from the heat and let sit, undisturbed, for about 20 minutes. Set a medium-mesh strainer over a container large enough to hold all the liquid, and strain the stock. Discard the solids and allow the stock to cool completely.

Store in an airtight container in the refrigerator for up to 1 week, or in the freezer for up to 3 months. Skim any fat from the surface before using.

BEEF BONE BROTH WITH GREENS & POACHED EGG

SERVES 4 / There are times when there's no substitute for the soul-satisfying essence of a dense, gelatinous beef-bone broth. We roast the shank and knee bones before adding them to the stock, but lightly, so as not to give the stock an overly roasted flavor. If possible, get bones that still have some meat on them; otherwise buy a short rib or two to add to the broth.

2 Tbsp extra-virgin olive oil

2 garlic cloves, minced

1 bunch spigarello, chard, or kale, stemmed and roughly chopped

6 cups [1.4 L] Beef Stock (facing page)

Kosher salt

4 eggs

Chunk of Parmesan cheese for grating

Freshly ground black pepper

2 Tbsp snipped fresh chives

In a large sauté pan over medium heat, warm the olive oil until hot but not smoking. Add the garlic and swirl it in the oil just until fragrant, about 1 minute. Stir in the spigarello. Add 2 to 3 Tbsp water to keep the garlic from burning, and cook just until the spigarello begins to soften, 2 to 3 minutes. Set aside.

Skim the fat off the stock. In a medium saucepan over medium-high heat, bring the stock to a boil. Lower the heat so the stock is simmering, taste, and season with salt if necessary. Crack one of the eggs into a small cup or ramekin and gently tip the egg into the simmering stock. Repeat with the remaining eggs. Poach the eggs in the stock just until the whites are set but the yolks are still runny, 3 to 4 minutes.

Divide the sautéed spigarello evenly among four soup bowls. With a slotted spoon, gently set a poached egg on top of the greens in each bowl. Ladle the broth into the bowls. Grate some Parmesan over the top, season with pepper, and sprinkle with the chives. Serve hot.

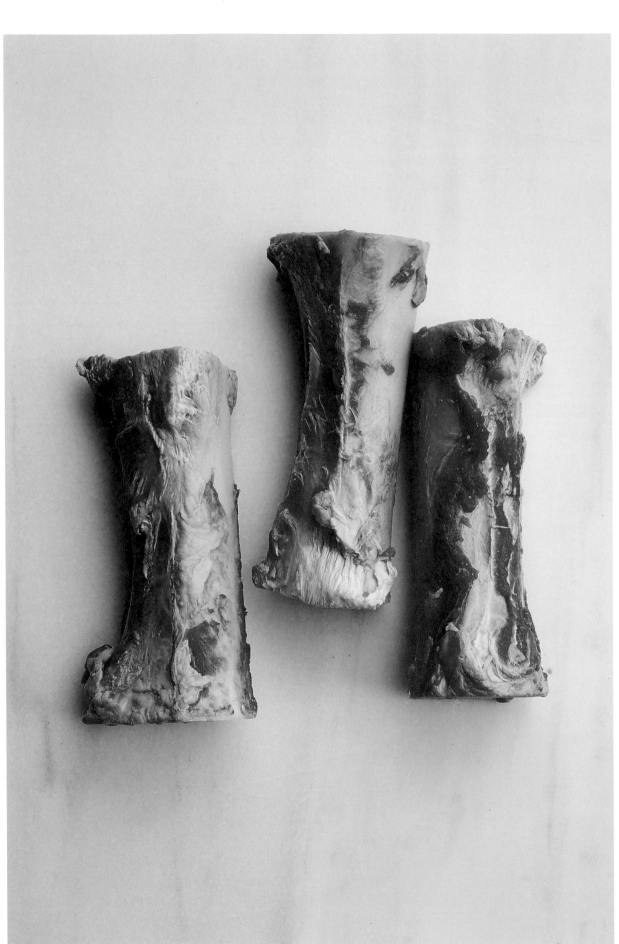

CHICKEN & ESCAROLE SOUP WITH CHARMOULA & LEMON

SERVES 4 TO 6 / It's very difficult to get sick of the kind of soups that have a midweek vibe. I have quite a few customers who make this soup an almost daily event, especially in the winter. We occasionally add small ricotta gnocchi (see page 206) to create our version of chicken and dumplings. This is a good call if you are going to make this soup your dinner or simply crave a more substantial version.

3 Tbsp extra-virgin olive oil

2 carrots, peeled and cut into
¼-in- [6-mm-] thick half-moons

2 ribs celery, cut into ¼-in- [6-mm-] thick slices

1 large yellow onion, diced

2 leeks (white and light green parts only), sliced

1 dried guajillo chile

4 garlic cloves, sliced

2 fresh thyme sprigs

1 bay leaf, bruised

Kosher salt

Freshly ground black pepper

One 2½-lb [1.2-kg] chicken, cut into parts

About 8 cups [2 L] Chicken Stock (page 223),
Vegetable Stock (page 222), or water

2 heads escarole, torn into medium-size pieces

2½ Tbsp [40 g] Tomato Confit (page 60)

¼ cup [50 g] Charmoula (page 50)

1 lemon

In a large enameled or stainless-steel pot over medium heat, warm the olive oil. Add the carrots, celery, onion, leeks, chile, and garlic and sauté until translucent, 10 to 15 minutes. Add the thyme and bay leaf, and season with salt and pepper. Add the chicken and just enough of the stock to cover it. Turn the heat to medium-high and bring to a boil, then lower the heat to maintain a slow simmer, skimming any foam that rises to the top. Cook until the chicken is just about cooked through, about 1 hour. Once the chicken meat is fully cooked and starting to separate from the bone, remove all the chicken parts and set aside to cool. Remove the broth from the heat and set aside. Remove all the meat from the bones, shred into bite-size pieces, and reserve. (The recipe can be made up to this point and refrigerated for up 2 days.)

Warm the reserved broth and add the reserved chicken, the escarole, and tomato confit. Taste again for seasoning. Ladle into serving bowls, drizzle with the charmoula, and squeeze in some lemon juice. Serve immediately.

TOMATO, BEET & CARROT SOUP

SERVES 4 TO 6 / This soup is reminiscent of a classic borscht. It has a deep reddish purple hue and delicious, mineral-laced savory and sweet flavors. I like to garnish the soup with strained yogurt, but you could just as easily drop in a spoonful of homemade Buttermilk Crème Fraîche (page 55) and sprinkle with snipped chives.

3 Tbsp extra-virgin olive oil

1 small yellow onion, chopped

Kosher salt

2 carrots, peeled and chopped

5 red beets, peeled and chopped

4 garlic cloves, sliced

1 tsp tomato paste

½ tsp Harissa (page 52)

1½ cups [360 ml] Beef Stock (page 226)

1½ cups [360 ml] Vegetable Stock (page 222)

1 bay leaf, bruised

½ cup [120 ml] Pomodoro Sauce (page 59)

Freshly ground black pepper

½ cup [60 ml] Spiced Yogurt (page 55)

2 Tbsp snipped fresh chives

Best-quality olive oil for drizzling

In a large soup pot over medium-high heat, warm the olive oil until hot but not smoking. Add the onion and cook just until fragrant, about 2 minutes. Season with salt. Add the carrots and beets and turn the heat to medium-low. Cook, stirring occasionally, until the vegetables are cooked through and slightly caramelized, 20 to 30 minutes. Stir in the garlic and cook just until fragrant, about 2 minutes longer. Stir in the tomato paste and harissa and cook until aromatic and beginning to brown, about 3 minutes. Add the beef stock and vegetable stock and bring to a simmer. Add the bay leaf and simmer until the carrots and beets are very tender, about 20 minutes. Add the pomodoro sauce.

Remove from the heat and, with an immersion blender, purée until relatively smooth. (Alternatively, purée the hot soup, in small batches in a blender or food processor.) Return to medium-high heat and cook until warmed though. (Add more stock if the soup is too thick.) Season with salt and pepper.

Ladle into serving bowls and top with the spiced yogurt. Sprinkle with the chives, drizzle with a little best-quality olive oil, and add a few grinds of black pepper before serving.

HEIRLOOM BEAN STEW WITH BARLEY & GREEN HARISSA

SERVES 4 TO 6 / We buy a blend of unusual heirloom beans that includes tongue of fire, scarlet runner, trout, and orca beans. I love the stunning colors and patterns of the dried beans, and they taste amazing when cooked together in a stew like this one. The barley in this recipe is cooked like a risotto. The texture becomes very creamy, without adding butter or cream. I prefer to use water rather than vegetable stock here as it lets the nutty character of the grain shine through.

BEAN STEW
1 lb [455 g] mixed heirloom beans
3 Tbsp extra-virgin olive oil
1 onion, diced
4 garlic cloves, minced
Kosher salt
Freshly ground black pepper
¼ cup [65 g] Tomato Confit (page 60)
1 dried guajillo chile
1 dried chipotle chile
6 cups [1.4 L] Vegetable Stock (page 222), plus more as needed

1 bay leaf
4 fresh thyme sprigs

2 Tbsp extra-virgin olive oil
2 shallots, minced
¾ cup [170 g] barley
Kosher salt
1 Tbsp red wine vinegar
Freshly ground black pepper
¼ cup [55 g] Green Harissa (page 53)
½ cup [15 g] fresh cilantro leaves

To make the stew: In a large bowl, cover the beans with water by 2 in [5 cm] and soak overnight.

In a large soup pot over medium-high heat, warm the olive oil until hot but not smoking. Add the onion and garlic and cook just until translucent, 3 to 5 minutes. Season with salt and pepper. Take time to cook down the onion to create a substantial base of flavor, about 10 minutes longer. Add the tomato confit, guajillo, and chipotle and continue to cook until the ingredients start to brown, 6 to 8 minutes.

Drain the beans and add them to the pot. Add the stock and bring to a boil. Lower the heat, bringing the liquid to a steady simmer, and add the bay leaf and thyme. Partially cover the pot with a lid or parchment paper, and simmer, stirring occasionally, until the beans swell and start to become tender, about 1 hour. Add more stock if necessary throughout the cooking process to maintain a stewlike consistency. Season with more salt and pepper and turn off the heat. Set aside while you prepare the barley.

In a medium sauté pan over medium-high heat, warm the olive oil until hot but not smoking. Add the shallots and sauté until translucent, 2 minutes. Add the barley and cook just until toasted and aromatic, about 3 minutes.

Slowly pour in enough room-temperature water to just cover the grains, stirring constantly. Bring to a boil, lower the heat, and simmer, stirring often and adding more water, 2 Tbsp at a time, until the barley is tender but still holds its shape, 30 to 40 minutes. Season with salt.

Reheat the bean stew. Add the vinegar and season with salt and pepper.

Divide the barley evenly among individual bowls, making a well in the centers with the back of a spoon. Ladle the warm beans over the barley, top with the harissa, and garnish with cilantro leaves. Serve warm.

CHICKPEA STEW WITH TOMATO, TURMERIC, YOGURT & HARISSA

SERVES 4 TO 6 / This satisfying fall and winter stew would traditionally be served with couscous, but I find it substantial enough to stand on its own or with a slice of grilled bread. It tastes better if it has time to sit while the flavors meld, so make it in advance.

CHICKPEAS
1 lb [455 g] dried chickpeas
1 yellow onion, quartered
1 carrot, peeled and quartered
2 garlic cloves, smashed
1 bay leaf
4 fresh thyme sprigs
Kosher salt

½ tsp cumin seeds
1 tsp coriander seeds
1 tsp fennel seeds
¼ cup [60 ml] extra-virgin olive oil
3 carrots, peeled and cut into half-moons
1 yellow onion, coarsely chopped

3 garlic cloves, minced
Kosher salt
Freshly ground black pepper
1 tsp smoked paprika
¼ tsp ground turmeric
3 fresh thyme sprigs
1 bay leaf
2 Tbsp tomato paste
1 cup [240 ml] dry white wine
4 cups [960 ml] Vegetable Stock (page 222)
1 bunch Tuscan kale, stemmed and cut into 2-in- [5-cm-] wide strips
1 tsp red wine vinegar
⅓ cup [75 ml] Spiced Yogurt (page 55)
¼ cup [55 g] Harissa (page 52)

To make the chickpeas: In a large bowl, cover the chickpeas with water by 2 in [5 cm] and soak overnight. Drain the chickpeas and rinse with cool water.

In a large soup pot over medium-high heat, combine the chickpeas, onion, carrot, garlic, bay leaf, and thyme. Add fresh water to cover by about 2 in [5 cm]. Season with a little salt. Bring to a boil, lower the heat, and simmer until the chickpeas are tender but still hold their shape, about 45 minutes. Discard the bay leaf. Cool the chickpeas in the cooking liquid and then drain, discarding the liquid. Set the chickpeas aside.

In a small, dry frying pan over medium heat, toast the cumin seeds, coriander seeds, and fennel seeds just until fragrant, about 3 minutes. Let cool. With a mortar and pestle or a spice grinder, grind to a powder.

In a clean, large soup pot over medium-high heat, warm the olive oil until hot but not smoking. Add the carrots, onion, and garlic; season with salt and pepper; and cook until the vegetables begin to soften and brown slightly, about 5 minutes. Add the powdered cumin mixture and the paprika, turmeric, thyme, and bay leaf and cook until quite fragrant, about 3 minutes. Stir in the tomato paste, scraping the bottom of the pot frequently so that it does not burn, and cook until fragrant and beginning to brown, about 5 minutes. Add the wine, bring to a boil, and cook, scraping up the browned bits on the bottom of the pan until reduced by more than half, 2 to 3 minutes. Add the stock, discard the bay leaf, and return to a simmer.

In a blender, combine 1 cup [240 ml] of the soup base with 2 cups [350 g] of the cooked chickpeas and purée until smooth. Return the puréed beans to the soup pot. Throw the kale into the stew and cook until softened. Add the remaining cooked chickpeas and gently stir. Remove from the heat and let stand at room temperature for about 20 minutes.

Just before serving, adjust the salt and spike with the vinegar. Serve with a dollop of spiced yogurt and a drizzle of harissa.

WILD RICE WITH CHORIZO, WALNUTS & POMEGRANATE

SERVES 4 TO 6 AS A SIDE DISH / This very flavorful rice dish reminds me of Thanksgiving stuffing. I like it with duck confit or seared duck breast, as well as with smaller birds like quail or squab. Try rolling this out with some collard greens and cannellini beans for a little midweek soul food.

WILD RICE
2 cups [320 g] wild rice
3 Tbsp extra-virgin olive oil
3 shallots, minced
5 garlic cloves minced
Kosher salt
Freshly ground black pepper
2 Tbsp pomegranate molasses
2 Tbsp tomato paste
3 fresh thyme sprigs
1 bay leaf
3 cups [720 ml] water

½ cup [50 g] walnuts
2 Tbsp extra-virgin olive oil
6 oz [170 g] Chorizo (page 296)
½ cup [120 ml] Chicken Stock (page 223)
Kosher salt
Freshly ground black pepper
¼ cup [7 g] roughly chopped fresh flat-leaf parsley
½ cup [80 g] pomegranate seeds
1 Tbsp red wine vinegar

To make the wild rice: In a large bowl, cover the rice with cold water and let sit at room temperature for 12 hours, or up to overnight.

In a large soup pot over medium heat, warm the olive oil until hot but not smoking. Add the shallots and garlic, season with salt and pepper, and cook until translucent, about 5 minutes. Stir in the pomegranate molasses and tomato paste. Drain the rice and add it to the pot along with the thyme and bay leaf. Cook until the rice smells toasty, about 2 minutes. Pour in the 3 cups [720 ml] water and bring to a boil. Season with more salt, lower the heat, and simmer, uncovered, until the liquid is almost gone, about 40 minutes. The grains should be splitting open and beginning to unfurl but not completely softened. Remove from the heat, cover, and allow the rice to steam for 15 minutes. Remove the bay leaf. Fluff the rice with a wooden spoon and set aside.

In a small, dry frying pan over medium heat, toast the walnuts until fragrant, 3 to 5 minutes. Let cool.

In a large frying pan over medium-high heat, warm the olive oil until hot but not smoking. Add the chorizo and cook, without stirring, until browned on one side, 2 to 3 minutes. Use a wooden spoon to break up the browned sausage into thumbnail-size pieces. When the sausage is almost cooked through but still a bit pink, add it to the rice. Add the stock. Return the pot to the stove top and cook over high heat until the stock has almost evaporated.

Season with salt and pepper and garnish with the parsley, pomegranate seeds, and toasted walnuts. Spike the dish with the vinegar and serve warm.

WHEAT BERRIES WITH FENNEL BROTH

SERVES 4 TO 6 AS A SIDE DISH / Wheat berries have an amazing texture when simmered. Here, they capture the beautiful flavor of the aromatic broth. I love the monochromic personality of a humble bowl of these, simply garnished with some of the green fronds from a fennel bulb and a drizzle of finishing olive oil. They pair especially well with fish dishes that demand a substantial side, and they bring a bit more presence to a dish of stewed beans or vegetables than a side of steamed rice.

2 cups [200 g] wheat berries

FENNEL BROTH
¼ cup [60 ml] extra-virgin olive oil
1 large yellow onion, sliced
4 fennel bulbs, roughly chopped (fronds reserved)
4 fresh thyme sprigs
1 bay leaf, bruised
Kosher salt
8 cups [2 L] water

2 Tbsp unsalted butter
1 Tbsp extra-virgin olive oil
Kosher salt
¼ cup [7 g] fennel fronds, finely chopped
Best-quality olive oil

In a medium bowl, cover the wheat berries with cold water and let stand at room temperature for at least 8 hours, or up to 12 hours.

To make the broth: In a large soup pot over medium heat, warm the olive oil until hot but not smoking. Add the onion and cook, stirring frequently, until soft and translucent but not browned, about 5 minutes. Adjust the heat as necessary to avoid browning. Add the chopped fennel bulb, thyme, and bay leaf. Season with salt, turn the heat to low, and cook, stirring every so often, until the fennel is very soft and falling apart.

Add the 8 cups [2 L] water, raise the heat to medium-high, and bring to a simmer. Turn the heat to low and continue simmering until very fragrant, 20 to 30 minutes. Remove the bay leaf. Strain the broth through a fine-mesh sieve, pushing some of the vegetable matter through to yield a thicker broth. Season the broth with salt, and reserve.

In a large soup pot over medium heat, melt the butter in the extra-virgin olive oil. Drain the wheat berries, add them to the pot, and toast in the hot fat for 3 or 4 minutes. Add enough of the fennel broth to cover the wheat berries by 1 in [2.5 cm]. Bring to a boil, lower the heat, and simmer, adding more broth, ¼ cup [60 ml] at time, as the liquid begins to dry out. Cook until the wheat berries are tender and the outer hulls begin to split open, 30 to 45 minutes. Season with salt.

Transfer the wheat berries to a serving platter, garnish with the chopped fennel fronds, and drizzle with best-quality olive oil. Serve immediately.

FARRO WITH BEET & MINT YOGURT

SERVES 4 TO 6 AS A SIDE DISH / Cooking farro slowly while constantly stirring helps pull the starches out of the grain and lends it a creamy texture without the need for copious amounts of butter or cream. The addition of roasted beet purée tints this dish a really cool deep-burgundy red and imparts a sweetness that is offset by the sharp, herbaceous yogurt.

MINT YOGURT
2 Tbsp chopped fresh mint
1 Tbsp chopped fresh flat-leaf parsley
¼ cup [60 ml] Greek-style yogurt
1 lime
1 tsp extra-virgin olive oil
Kosher salt
Freshly ground black pepper

2 red beets
Kosher salt
Freshly ground black pepper
1 Tbsp extra-virgin olive oil
3 shallots, minced
4 garlic cloves, minced
1 cup [160 g] farro
3 sprigs fresh thyme
1 bay leaf
½ cup [120 ml] dry white wine
2 Tbsp Buttermilk Crème Fraîche (page 55)
Best-quality olive oil for drizzling

To make the mint yogurt: In a mortar and pestle, crush the mint and parsley until it looks quite pulpy and wet. Gradually stir in the yogurt. Add a little water to make a loose sauce. With a Microplane, grate the zest from the lime directly into the yogurt. Squeeze 1 tsp of lime juice into the sauce. Stir in the olive oil, and season with salt and pepper. (Store in an airtight container in the refrigerator for up to 2 days.)

Preheat the oven to 425°F [220°C].

Put the beets in a small ovenproof pan, and add about ¼ in [6 mm] water. Cover tightly with aluminum foil or a lid, and roast until the beets can be easily pierced with the tip of a knife, 30 to 40 minutes. Remove from the oven and let cool in the pan. When cool enough to handle, slip the skins off the beets, and cut the beets into quarters.

In a blender, process the beets with ½ cup [120 ml] water to make a smooth purée with the consistency of tomato sauce. (Add more water if necessary.) Season with salt and pepper.

Fill a teakettle with 2 qt [2 L] water and bring to a boil over high heat. Remove from the heat and set aside where it will stay warm.

In a large, heavy pot over medium heat, warm the extra-virgin olive oil until hot but not smoking. Add the shallots and garlic and cook until translucent but not browned, about 3 minutes. Add the farro and thyme and cook until the farro is toasted and warmed through, 3 to 4 minutes. Season with salt. Add the bay leaf and wine and cook until the wine has reduced by more than half, 2 to 3 minutes. Add just enough of the warm water from the teakettle to barely cover the farro. Bring to a very slow but steady simmer. Cook, stirring often, and adding warm water as necessary to keep the farro barely covered, until the grains begin to soften, 30 to 40 minutes. Remove the bay leaf. At this point, begin to stir more aggressively, and continue adding water a few spoonsful at a time to maintain a moist but thick consistency. When cooked, I like this to be wet enough to spread out flat on the serving plate, but not so soupy that the liquid runs out of the grains. In other words, you want a fully incorporated, emulsified mass that holds its shape but is very soft and creamy.

Stir in the crème fraîche right before spooning the farro out onto a large serving plate. Top with a spoonful of the minted yogurt and drizzle on some best-quality olive oil. Serve immediately.

FARRO PICCOLO COOKED IN POMODORO

SERVES 4 TO 6 AS A SIDE DISH / A well-executed spaghetti pomodoro is one of my favorite things to eat. Here, we riff on that simple idea of tomato, olive oil, and herbs, but we pair it with farro piccolo, a lesser known, smaller cousin to farro that dates back some ten thousand years in Italy. Anson Mills sells a good version. It's harvested in late summer, which coincides nicely with the time when you might have tons of freshly canned tomato sauce around. The lighter texture and faster cooking time of the farro piccolo make it a good match for this simple sauce. Load on the herbs and fruity olive oil at the end to give the dish plenty of character.

4 cups [960 ml] Vegetable Stock (page 222)

3 Tbsp extra-virgin olive oil

1 small yellow onion, finely chopped

1 carrot, peeled and finely chopped

1 celery rib, finely chopped

4 garlic cloves, minced

2 cups [340 g] farro piccolo

½ cup [120 ml] dry white wine

1 cup [240 ml] Pomodoro Sauce (page 59)

½ cup [15 g] fresh basil leaves, torn into irregular pieces

1 Tbsp dried oregano

Flaky sea salt

Best-quality olive oil for finishing

Chunk of Parmesan cheese for grating

In a medium saucepan over medium heat, warm the stock.

In a heavy-bottomed medium pot over medium heat, warm the extra-virgin olive oil until hot but not smoking. Add the onion, carrot, celery, and garlic and cook until tender but not browned, about 5 minutes. Stir in the farro piccolo and cook until toasted and warmed through, 3 to 4 minutes. Lower the heat if the onion and garlic take on too much color. Stir in the wine and cook until just about evaporated, scraping the browned bits from the bottom of the pot with a wooden spoon. Stir in the pomodoro sauce. Add just enough of the warm stock to cover the farro piccolo. Toss in a few pieces of basil leaves and the oregano. Bring to a very slow but steady simmer. Cook, stirring often and adding small amounts of warm stock as necessary to keep the farro piccolo barely covered, until the mixture has the consistency of a very wet stew, 15 to 20 minutes, depending on the size and age of the farro. When it's done, the farro piccolo should be tender but still hold its shape. Season with salt. Stir in some best-quality olive oil and the rest of the basil.

Transfer to a serving platter and grate the Parmesan over the top. Serve hot.

RUSTIC CORN GRITS WITH MUSHROOM SUGO & POACHED EGG

SERVES 4 AS A MAIN COURSE / Look for coarse-ground, new-crop grits, either white or yellow. What matters more is your ability to find field-ripened, coarsely ground grits, which are vastly superior to commodity cornmeal. The robust corn flavor of these grits is so intense that it really needs little embellishment. Substitute any cultivated variety of mushroom you like for the wild mushrooms here. But if you do happen upon some good-looking wild fungi, by all means take advantage and use them.

GRITS

1 cup [170 g] old-fashioned or coarse-ground corn grits

2½ cups [600 ml] water

Kosher salt

2 Tbsp unsalted butter

Freshly ground black pepper

MUSHROOM SUGO

5 Tbsp [80 ml] extra-virgin olive oil, plus more as needed

1 lb [455 g] assorted mushrooms, such as shiitake, oyster, cremini, and hen of the woods, chopped or torn into halves or quarters, depending on size (smaller ones can be left whole)

Kosher salt

Freshly ground black pepper

3 shallots, minced

4 garlic cloves, sliced

2 Tbsp tomato paste

4 fresh thyme sprigs

1 bay leaf

½ cup [120 ml] dry white wine

2 cups [480 ml] Chicken Stock (page 223)

¼ cup [7 g] chopped fresh flat-leaf parsley

4 eggs

Flaky sea salt

Freshly ground black pepper

Best-quality olive oil for drizzling

To make the grits: In a large, heavy-bottomed saucepan, soak the grits in the water overnight. Do not drain.

Place the saucepan over medium heat, bring the grits to a simmer, and cook, stirring constantly with a wooden spoon, until the grits are suspended evenly in the water, about 5 minutes. Turn the heat to low, cover the pan, and continue cooking, stirring the grits every 10 minutes to keep them from sticking to the bottom of the pan, until tender and creamy but still a bit al dente, about 50 minutes. Season with kosher salt after the first 25 minutes. (If the grits become too thick, thin with a bit of hot water.) Stir in the butter and season with salt and pepper. Keep warm until ready to serve.

To make the mushroom sugo: Heat a large sauté pan over medium-high heat. Drizzle in about 2½ Tbsp of the olive oil, gently swirling the pan so that the oil is evenly distributed. Add about half of the mushrooms, enough to cover the bottom of the pan. Cook the mushrooms, without stirring, until well seared on the bottom. With a spatula, flip the mushrooms and continue cooking until well seared on the other side. Once the mushrooms are well caramelized, season with kosher salt and pepper and transfer to a plate. Repeat with the remaining mushrooms and another 2½ Tbsp olive oil, and set aside.

Continued

In the same pan, sauté the shallots and garlic, adding a bit more olive oil if needed, until translucent but not browned, about 3 minutes. Stir in the tomato paste and cook until it begins to brown around the edges. Add the thyme and bay leaf. Add the wine and cook, stirring with a wooden spoon to scrape up any browned bits stuck to the bottom of the pan, until the wine has reduced by about half. Add the stock, bring to a simmer, and return the mushrooms to the pan. Simmer very gently until the sauce has reduced slightly and the mushroom flavor is pervasive, 10 to 15 minutes. Remove the bay leaf and add the parsley.

Bring a large sauté pan filled with salted water to a simmer over medium heat.

Just before serving, crack the eggs into ramekins or small cups. Slip the eggs into the simmering water and cook until the whites are just set but the yolks are very runny, 4 to 6 minutes.

Spoon a fourth of the grits into each of four shallow bowls. Divide the mushroom sugo evenly among the bowls, and top each serving with a poached egg. Season with sea salt and pepper and drizzle a little best-quality olive oil on top. Serve immediately.

CHAPTER SEVEN
FISH

Anyone with a mild interest in fish and marine habitats knows that the world's fisheries are in need of increased human awareness. Like many chefs, I've made it a priority to source seafood responsibly and in line with greater environmental concerns, without sacrificing the enjoyment and celebration of the ocean's bounty. As much as our hearts are in the right place, I've learned that it is difficult to keep up with the ever-changing stream of data about the fishing industry and its greater impact.

As is the case with meat, we should start by questioning the sheer quantity of seafood we consume, particularly the large marine species that we generally prefer and place higher value on, such as tuna, salmon, bass, and cod. I'm not suggesting that we stop eating these fish, only that we consider how to balance our consumption of them with more sustainable, well-managed species.

At Gjelina, we follow a couple of rules of thumb: First, we stick close to the bottom of the food chain. Smaller, rapidly reproducing fish such as sardines, anchovies, squid, and the smaller varieties of mackerel, as well as shellfish such as clams, mussels, oysters, scallops, and prawns, are generally found in good numbers and are absolutely delicious. Since they primarily feed on plankton and other tiny marine life, as opposed to other fish, they tend to have low levels of mercury. They also have a short life cycle, so they simply spend less time in the water. Coincidentally, I prefer these little suckers to the larger species just in terms of sheer tastiness. When I find these at the fish market, I almost always go for them, and have featured many of these creatures on the menu at Gjelina since day one. Fishermen are rewarded for bigger, more expensive fish, which makes going after a vessel full of sardines decidedly less glamorous and less lucrative. However, as awareness and value systems change regarding marine resources, hopefully the market will demand more of these sustainable types of fish and create more value for the people going after them. Bivalves such as mussels, clams, and oysters are great choices, as they are being successfully farmed in their natural habitats with minimal negative impact on the environment.

Our second rule at Gjelina is to choose locally harvested fish when possible. We pick up spot prawns and uni from nearby Santa Barbara and the amazing Monterey Bay fishery just north of there. Sardines, Dungeness crab, mackerel, Pacific black cod, and California king salmon are just a few of the species we can get from relatively close by. But the fact is, we have a difficult time getting enough fish to satisfy our demand solely from nearby waters. We end up buying seafood from all of North America—from the East Coast as well as the West, from Baja all the way up to Alaska, and from the fisheries around Hawaii. When we purchase from outside our area, we try to get a sense for how well that species or the fishery of origin is being managed, and get as much information as we can get about bycatch (what has been caught along with the fish or shellfish we are buying) and any other issues.

It's an imperfect system that requires constant management. Many fish are seasonal, so if we have any hopes of acting responsibly, it's important to know when to expect certain species to arrive at the marketplace. It's a good way to ensure you are getting high-quality fish and are buying what is abundant.

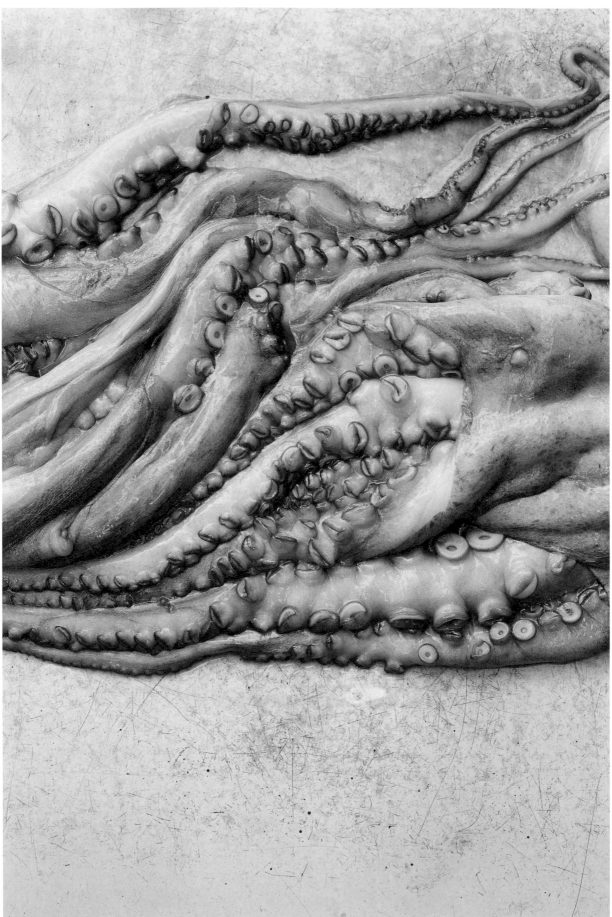

OYSTERS

Oysters are unquestionably best eaten raw—just moments after they are opened. Freshness is everything with oysters, and the best are delicious on their own or with just a squeeze of lemon. I do, however, love garnishes that accentuate the buttery brininess of the shellfish without overwhelming them, such as horse-radish or some quickly pickled Fresno chile and fennel, and ¼ tsp of these does the trick.

Oysters should always be very tightly closed, and feel relatively heavy and dense for their size. Holding the oyster securely in one hand, using a doubled-up kitchen towel, insert the tip of an oyster knife into the hinge of the shell with your other hand. Twist the blade to pop open the shell, holding the oyster level so the "liquor" doesn't spill out. Run the blade around the lid of the shell to sever the abductor muscle. Lift away the top shell. Run the tip of the blade under the oyster meat to release it from the bottom shell. Once opened, I generally like to see that the meat fills the shell nicely, with an abundant amount of that beautiful oyster liquor, which I beg you not to pour off.

RED ONION & BLACK PEPPER MIGNONETTE

MAKE ½ CUP [120 ML] / When the proportions of onion, vinegar, and coarsely ground black pepper are properly struck, this makes a surprisingly delicious, and dead-simple, garnish for raw oysters.

¼ cup [60 ml] red wine vinegar
¼ tsp kosher salt
1 tsp sugar

¼ cup [30 g] minced red onion
1 tsp coarsely ground black pepper
(Use the coarsest setting on your pepper mill.)

In a small bowl, whisk together the vinegar, salt, and sugar until the salt and sugar dissolve. Stir in the onion and then, at the very last moment before serving, add the pepper.

FENNEL, CHILE & ORANGE SAUCE

MAKES ¾ CUP [180 ML] / I love to use multiple parts of the same plant in a single dish. Here, fresh fennel bulb is lightly sautéed before going into a white vinegar–orange brine. We accent it with some of the bulb's feathery fronds and toasted fennel seeds.

¼ tsp fennel seeds

¼ cup [60 ml] white wine vinegar

¼ cup [60 ml] fresh orange juice, plus zest of 1 orange

1 tsp sugar

2 tsp extra-virgin olive oil

½ fennel bulb, cut into small cubes,
plus 1 Tbsp chopped fennel fronds

1 medium-hot green or red chile,
preferably Fresno, seeded and minced

Kosher salt

Freshly ground black pepper

In a small, dry frying pan over medium heat, toast the fennel seeds just until fragrant, about 3 minutes. Let cool. With a mortar and pestle or a spice grinder, grind to a powder. Set aside.

In a small bowl, whisk the vinegar, orange juice, and sugar until the sugar has dissolved. Add the olive oil, fennel cubes and chopped fronds, chile, and orange zest. Season with salt and pepper before serving.

TOMATO, HORSERADISH & LIME COCKTAIL SAUCE

MAKES ABOUT 1 CUP [240 ML] / This is my riff on a classic cocktail sauce, though there's very little similarity other than the combination of tomato and horseradish. I think this hits the spot when you want a garnish with more presence than simply lemon juice or a mignonette.

½ cup [130 g] Tomato Confit (page 60), chopped to a pulp

1 Tbsp minced shallot

One 1-in [2.5-cm] piece fresh horseradish,
peeled and finely grated

1 Tbsp fresh lime juice

1 Tbsp plus 1 tsp olive oil

2 Tbsp red wine vinegar

2 Tbsp Worcestershire sauce

1 Tbsp chopped fennel fronds

¼ cup [60 ml] water, as needed (optional)

Kosher salt

Freshly ground black pepper

In a small bowl, combine the tomato confit, shallot, horseradish, lime juice, olive oil, vinegar, Worcestershire sauce, and chopped fennel fronds and mix well. If the sauce seems too thick, loosen it with water, adding 1 Tbsp at a time. Season with salt and pepper. Let sit at room temperature for 2 hours before serving so the flavors can develop and meld.

SPICY GINGER, JALAPEÑO & LIME SAUCE

MAKES ABOUT 1 CUP [240 ML] / One of my favorites, this spicy, sweet, and savory combo has a Latin vibe.

2 jalapeño chiles, partially seeded and minced

2 Tbsp minced shallot

1 tsp grated peeled fresh ginger

½ cup [120 ml] fresh lime juice

2 tsp honey

1 garlic clove

Kosher salt

Freshly ground black pepper

In a small, nonreactive bowl, combine the jalapeños, shallot, ginger, lime juice, and honey. Using a Microplane grater, grate the garlic into the bowl. Season with salt and pepper. Let sit at room temperature for 1 to 3 hours before serving so the flavors can develop and meld.

FRESH CHILE HOT SAUCE

MAKES 3 CUP [720 ML] / If you take your oysters spicy, this sauce is for you. It has a thinner body than other sauces in this chapter, similar to Tabasco but with a more fruity, lively flavor. Use whatever combination of hot peppers you can find, or use just one type if you prefer. The point is to allow the chiles to steep in the vinegar, which cools the searing heat just enough to make it palatable. I put this on everything from eggs to rice and beans.

2 jalapeño chiles, cut into ¾-in [2-cm] rounds

2 medium-hot green or red chiles, preferably Fresno, cut into ¾-in [2-cm] rounds

2 habanero chiles, halved crosswise

1 poblano chile, halved crosswise

2 serrano chiles, halved crosswise

4 baby Thai chiles, halved lengthwise

1 shallot, sliced

3 garlic cloves, sliced

Zest of ½ orange

3 cups [720 ml] white wine vinegar

Pinch of kosher salt

In a large jar with a lid, combine all the ingredients, making sure that there is enough vinegar to cover the solids by about 1 in [2.5 cm]. Let sit at room temperature for 2 days.

In a blender, purée until just a few small pieces of chile remain. It should not be a perfectly smooth purée. Use immediately, or cover the jar and store in the refrigerator for up to 3 weeks.

CRUDO

We often serve our *crudo,* or raw, fish dishes in conjunction with or immediately preceding oysters, and the same general rules to selecting the fish apply. Freshness is always a primary consideration. We steer away from bluefin tuna, Atlantic salmon, Alaska halibut, and the other, more obvious choices. Some of the more oily varieties, such as Spanish mackerel, bonito, sardines, shima aji, and king mackerel, perform well with strongly flavored garnishes, and deliver more bang for your buck in terms of flavor. That said, I also love a little fluke, snapper, or Pacific halibut, as they are extremely delicate and easy to like, even for our guests who are a little timid when it comes to raw seafood. Filleting and slicing fish for crudo requires more advanced knife work, but any properly sharpened chef's knife will do.

KANPACHI WITH SESAME & CHILE OIL

SERVES 4 / Kanpachi, or amberjack (also often misidentified as yellowtail), is a buttery, delicious fish and it's perfect raw when superfresh. I like to cut thicker, ¼-in [6-mm] slabs for this preparation (pictured opposite) and grill them lightly with a butane torch. This cooks just the top layer of flesh, but loosens up the oil in the flesh, making it extra buttery. This technique is not hard to do, but it looks complicated. You could just as easily not grill this, but then slice the fish a bit thinner.

1 Tbsp sesame seeds

1 dried espelette or guajillo chile

3 Tbsp extra-virgin olive oil

One 1-lb [455-g] kanpachi or Hawaiian Kona Kampachi fillet

½ lemon

Flaky sea salt

1 Tbsp thinly sliced fresh chives

In a small, dry frying pan over medium heat, toast the sesame seeds until fragrant, about 3 minutes. Set aside and let cool.

In the same pan over medium heat, toast the chile until fragrant, with a few brown spots, about 3 minutes. Let cool. In a spice grinder or mortar and pestle, process the chile to a fine powder.

In a small bowl, combine the sesame seeds, ground chile, and olive oil. Let stand at least 1 hour so that the oil takes on some of the heat from the chiles. (This condiment can be made up to 1 day in advance and stored in an airtight container at room temperature until ready to use.)

Slice the kanpachi fillet into two pieces by cutting along either side of the pin bones. Remove the skin. Cut each piece against the grain into ¼-in- [6-mm-] thick slices. As you work, lay the slices on a platter in several straight lines.

Squeeze a few drops of lemon juice onto each slice of fish. Crumble a few flakes of sea salt over each piece. Stir the chile–olive oil mixture and drizzle over the top of the kanpachi. Garnish with a line of chives down the center of each row of kanpachi. Serve immediately.

SNAPPER WITH CITRUS CHILE PASTE, CILANTRO FLOWERS & OLIVE OIL

SERVES 4 / Anyone who has a garden has seen their herbs bolt and go to flower. The leaves are generally bitter at this stage, but I have found that cilantro, in particular, yields a tasty flower. Use if you can find it, and if not, substitute fresh cilantro leaves.

Snapper tends to be lean, with beautiful, almost translucent flesh. Our citrus-chile combination (pictured opposite) riffs on *yuzu koshu*, a Japanese citrus and chile paste, but made with locally available chile and citrus zest.

CITRUS CHILE PASTE
5 medium-hot green or red chiles,
preferably Fresno, partially seeded and minced
Kosher salt
Zest of 1 orange
Zest of 1 lemon, plus juice of ½ lemon
1 tsp extra-virgin olive oil

1 lb [455 g] snapper or Tai snapper fillets, skin removed
Best-quality olive oil for drizzling
Flaky sea salt
2 Tbsp fresh cilantro flowers or leaves

To make the chile paste: With a mortar and pestle, combine the chiles with a healthy pinch of kosher salt and grind until the chiles begin to release some of their liquid. Add both citrus zests and continue to smash to make a rough purée. Squeeze in a little of the lemon juice to loosen the purée slightly, then stir in the extra-virgin olive oil. Transfer to a glass jar and let sit at room temperature so the flavors can meld and develop, at least 2 hours or up to 6 hours.

Slice the snapper on a steep bias to get thin, even slices and arrange on a serving plate. Drizzle with best-quality olive oil. Put a bit of the citrus chile paste on each slice, along with some of the liquid from the paste. Sprinkle a few flakes of sea salt on each slice, and garnish with the cilantro flowers. Serve immediately.

SALMON WITH HORSERADISH, AIOLI, GREEN ONIONS & LEMON

SERVES 4 / We only use wild salmon when they can be found at their peak, and we try to get the ones that swim around the Sacramento–San Joaquin Delta. Ocean trout and arctic char are also good choices. Don't be shy with the horseradish when using the fresh root instead of the jarred prepared type. I love its nose-stinging quality with the fatty salmon.

We cut the salmon into 1-lb [455-g] blocks and freeze them overnight, tightly wrapped with plastic or sealed with a vacuum sealer to kill any potentially harmful bacteria from their contact with freshwater. I'm not sure how scientifically sound this method is, but I was shown this technique by a sushi chef I worked with and have used it ever since with good results. Ideally the salmon blocks are not held frozen for more than 2 days. Transfer to the refrigerator to defrost slowly 6 hours prior to using them.

2 green onions (white and green parts), thinly sliced
One 1-lb [455-g] salmon fillet, skin on
2 Tbsp Basic Aioli (page 56)
Flaky sea salt

Freshly ground black pepper
½ lemon
One 1-in [2.5-cm] piece fresh horseradish,
peeled and finely grated

Continued

Place the green onions in a bowl of cold water and rinse thoroughly. Let sit at room temperature for 3 to 5 minutes. Pat dry with paper towels.

Turn the salmon fillet skin-side down on your work surface and slice 1 in [2.5 cm] off the top of the fillet by making a horizontal slice all the way through, yielding two pieces of about equal thickness, one with skin attached. One at a time, slice the pieces of fish on a slight bias to get even slices.

Arrange the salmon slices on a serving plate. Top each slice with a dab of aioli, a few flakes of sea salt, and some pepper. Squeeze a few drops of lemon juice on top, grate the horseradish over the fish, and sprinkle with the green onions. Serve immediately.

MACKEREL WITH JALAPEÑO VINEGAR, ROASTED GARLIC, TOASTED SESAME & GREEN ONIONS

SERVES 4 TO 6 AS AN APPETIZER / Jalapeño vinegar has a more delicate flavor than the name suggests, and it can be used almost as generously as you would use ponzu. The roasted garlic definitely punches through the dish, but it does wonders for a more robust fish, such as mackerel or sardine.

JALAPEÑO VINEGAR
¼ cup [60 ml] rice wine vinegar
2 Tbsp fresh lemon juice
2 Tbsp fresh orange juice
1 Tbsp sugar
½ tsp kosher salt
1 jalapeño chile, seeded and roughly chopped
¼ cup [60 ml] water

ROASTED GARLIC PURÉE
1 garlic head

1 tsp extra-virgin olive oil
½ tsp fresh lemon juice
Kosher salt

2 skin-on Spanish mackerel fillets
(about 1 lb [455 g] total weight)
2 tsp sesame seeds
Best-quality olive oil for drizzling
Flaky sea salt
3 green onions, cut into thin strips

To make the jalapeño vinegar: In a small saucepan over medium heat, combine the vinegar, lemon juice, orange juice, sugar, and kosher salt and stir until the sugar and salt dissolve. Remove from the heat and add the jalapeño and water. Transfer to a blender, and process on high speed until the jalapeño is liquefied. Strain through a fine-mesh sieve into a small bowl and reserve. (The vinegar can be made up to 1 day in advance. Store in an airtight glass jar in the refrigerator until ready to use.)

To make the garlic purée: Preheat the oven to 375°F [190°C].

Wrap the garlic tightly in aluminum foil and roast until soft to the touch, about 1½ hours. Allow to cool. Unwrap the garlic and remove the papery skin.

In a small bowl, use a fork to mash the peeled garlic with the extra-virgin olive oil and lemon juice to make a chunky paste. Season with kosher salt. (The roasted garlic purée can be made up to 1 day in advance. Store in an airtight container in the refrigerator until ready to use.)

Turn the mackerel fillet skin-side up on your work surface and, working from the corner of the fillet, use your fingers to peel the topmost layer of skin back, leaving some of the brilliantly colored underlayer of skin behind. Holding the fillet down with one hand, gently pull off the outer layer of skin completely. You can also do this with a knife, but be careful not to break or damage the fish while doing so. This is a bit tricky but very possible once you get the hang of it. You can also just ask your fish guy to skin the fillets for you. Slice the mackerel on a steep bias to get thin, even slices and arrange on a serving plate. (You can prepare the fish 1 hour or so in advance. Cover with plastic wrap until ready to serve.)

In a small, dry frying pan over medium heat, toast the sesame seeds just until fragrant and beginning to brown, about 3 minutes. Set aside and let cool.

Top each fish piece with a dab of the garlic purée and plenty of the jalapeño vinegar. Drizzle with best-quality olive oil, sprinkle with sea salt, garnish with the green onions, and finish with a light sprinkle of sesame seeds. Serve immediately.

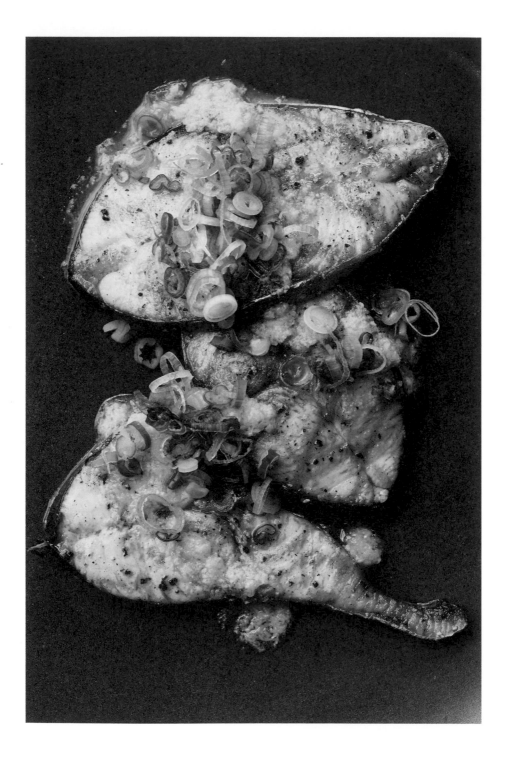

GRILLED MACKEREL WITH GINGER, GARLIC, LIME & GREEN ONION

SERVES 4 TO 6 / Mackerel might be my favorite fish to eat and it is so versatile to prepare. We serve it raw, smoked, pickled, sautéed, and grilled and I find that no one way is better than any other. This recipe, in which mackerel is grilled on the bone, is suited to fillets cut from a 5- to 10-lb [2.3- to 4.5-kg] fish often sold as king or Atlantic mackerel, or *sawara* in Japanese markets. The small bones in this cut are easily removed with tweezers after cooking or picked out as you eat. Leave the fish on the bone; it will stay succulent through grilling.

2 green onions

One 2-in [5-cm] piece fresh ginger, peeled and grated

2 garlic cloves, grated

Juice of 2 limes

2 Tbsp white wine vinegar

1 tsp honey

2 Tbsp olive oil, plus more for drizzling

Kosher salt

Freshly ground black pepper

Six 4- to 6-oz [115- to 170-g] mackerel fillets, 1 in [2.5 cm] thick

Cut the green onions into thin slices, rinse them, and spread them in a thin layer on a kitchen towel to dry.

Prepare a hot fire in a charcoal grill (or preheat a gas grill to high or heat a grill pan over high heat).

In a small bowl, combine the ginger, garlic, lime juice, vinegar, honey, and olive oil. Season with salt and pepper. Set aside.

Drizzle the mackerel with olive oil and season generously with salt and pepper. Place on the hottest part of the grill (or in a grill pan) and cook until deeply seared, 2 to 3 minutes. Flip the fillets, turning them 90 degrees so the grill marks run in the opposite direction. Cook for 2 minutes longer. Check for doneness by checking the flesh closest to the bone; it should be a touch under-done as it will continue cooking off the heat.

Transfer to a serving platter, drizzle with the ginger-garlic mixture, and sprinkle the green onions over all. Serve warm.

WHOLE GRILLED SEA BREAM WITH GREEN TOMATOES, BASIL & MINT

SERVES 4 TO 6 / Sea bream is a lesser known fish that looks like a grayish cousin to a red snapper, with a similar flavor profile. We often find small ones that weigh just about a pound [half a kilo], an ideal size for serving whole. There's something about picking apart a beautiful fish from the bone that makes me and a lot of other people happy. Drenched with a sauce made from green zebra tomatoes cooked down with shallots, herbs, and wine, this dish is immensely enticing to anyone who loves fish. You can use any tomato for this sauce, but ripe green zebra tomatoes with the aggressive amount of green herbs, is stunning. Pair this with a simple green, an arugula and radicchio Treviso salad (see page 88) or perhaps a grain or roasted potatoes, and you are set.

Four 1-lb [455-g] whole sea bream, scaled and gutted

Olive oil for drizzling, plus 3 Tbsp

Kosher salt

Freshly ground black pepper

¼ cup [55 g] Shallot Confit (page 64), sliced

8 cloves Garlic Confit (page 64), sliced

24 small green zebra tomatoes, cut into ¼-in- [6-mm-] thick rounds

1 medium-hot green or red chile, preferably Fresno, seeded and thinly sliced

2 cups [480 ml] dry white wine

2 Tbsp fresh lime juice

⅔ cup [20 g] fresh mint leaves

⅔ cup [20 g] fresh cilantro leaves

⅔ cup [20 g] fresh basil leaves

Flaky sea salt

Prepare a hot fire in a charcoal grill (or preheat a gas grill to high).

With a sharp knife, score the fish two or three times on each side by making diagonal cuts just into the flesh. Drizzle both sides of the fish with olive oil and season with salt and pepper.

Cook the fish on the hottest part of the grill until seared a deep golden brown on the bottom, about 5 minutes. Resist the urge to move it as it cooks, in order to preserve the skin (arguably the best part). If the grill flares up you can use a spray bottle of water to calm the flame. Rotate the fish 90 degrees to create crosshatched grill marks and cook until the skin is thoroughly browned, 3 to 4 minutes longer. Turn the fish and cook on the other side until it releases easily from the grill, about 5 minutes. Rotate the fish 90 degrees to create crosshatched grill marks and cook until the skin is thoroughly browned, 3 to 4 minutes longer.

Check for doneness by looking into the belly side, where you can see the spine. If the flesh is cooked and the juices are bubbling near the bone, the fish is done. If it's still pink, move the fish to the cooler side of the grill and allow it to cook another 3 minutes. Transfer the fish to a large serving plate and allow to rest.

In a medium sauté pan over high heat, warm the 3 Tbsp olive oil until hot but not smoking. Add the shallot confit and garlic confit and sauté until fragrant, about 2 minutes. Add the tomatoes and chile and season with salt. Cook until the mixture starts to brown, 2 to 3 minutes. Add the wine, bring to a simmer, and lower the heat to maintain a simmer, swirling the aromatics and tomatoes, until a slightly thickened but still runny sauce develops, 3 to 4 minutes. Season with salt and add the lime juice, mint, cilantro, and basil.

Remove from the heat, drizzle with more olive oil, and stir until the herbs are just wilted. Pour the sauce right over the fish and sprinkle sea salt on top. Serve immediately.

SARDINES BAKED IN TOMATO-PEPPER SAUCE

SERVES 4 / I'm not sure if there is a more deliciously versatile fish than sardines. It's certainly hard to find a more economical one. When they are in season, sardines tend to be available in large numbers and are very cheap, thanks to their working-class identity, short shelf life, and relatively small, bony stature. About one pound [half a kilo] of very fresh sardines will not make much of a dent in your wallet and will give you quite a few fish to play with. At Gjelina, we like to grill or bake what comes in the first day, and then pickle or smoke the leftovers. I'm a sucker for pickled sardines on toast or a cracker with tomato or avocado or both, and a couple of leaves of arugula.

This recipe is fun because you get this ocean-infused tomato-pepper sauce, which you can lap up with the fish and some grilled bread. The puréed red peppers, a tiny bit of sugar, and a little hit of sherry vinegar give this dish a sweet-and-sour profile that perfectly frames the oily fish. A green salad like the Spicy Herb Salad with Ginger-Lime Dressing (page 90) works well alongside.

3 Tbsp extra-virgin olive oil, plus more for drizzling	Kosher salt
3 cloves Garlic Confit (page 64)	Freshly ground black pepper
2 Roasted or Grilled Red Peppers (page 77), cut into ¼-in [6-mm] strips	¼ cup [7 g] fresh flat-leaf parsley leaves
1 Tbsp sugar	8 sardines, gutted and rinsed
1 tsp sherry vinegar	Lemon wedges for serving
1½ cups [360 ml] Pomodoro Sauce (page 59)	2 thick slices Grilled or Toasted Bread (page 77)
	Best-quality olive oil for drizzling

Preheat the oven to 450°F [230°C].

In a small saucepan over medium-high heat, warm the extra-virgin olive oil. Add the garlic confit and let it sweat for 1 minute. Add the roasted peppers, sauté for 1 minute, and stir in the sugar and vinegar. Add the pomodoro sauce, bring to a simmer, and continue simmering until the mixture is the consistency of a slightly thick tomato sauce, about 10 minutes. Season with salt and pepper. Add the parsley.

Pour the sauce into a baking pan wide enough to hold all the sardines when laid on their sides. Season the fish with salt and pepper and drizzle with extra-virgin olive oil. Add the fish to the pan, nestling them into the sauce. The sauce should come about halfway up the sides of the fish. Drizzle with a little more extra-virgin olive oil.

Bake until the sauce is bubbling and starting to brown around the edges and the fish is cooked through but still very moist, about 10 minutes.

Serve out of the baking pan with lemon wedges on the side and slabs of grilled bread, drizzled with best-quality olive oil.

STRIPED BASS STEW WITH KOHLRABI, FENNEL, SAFFRON & PIMENTON AIOLI

SERVES 4 TO 6 / Though we like to keep things local, we make an exception for striped bass. Ours comes from New England waters, where they are doing a great job of managing this species, which was once quite threatened. Ask your fishmonger to fillet the fish, and be sure you get the leftover head and bones. Striped bass bones make for a beautiful broth, and the meat has enough oil to remain moist when poached in it. Getting into the rhythm of using the whole fish feels good and brings a depth to the dish that is not possible if you use only the fillets.

One 2-lb [910-g] whole striped bass, filleted, head and bones reserved

6 Tbsp [90 ml] extra-virgin olive oil

1 yellow onion, quartered

2 celery ribs, cut into large chunks

2 fennel bulbs, cut into ½-in [12-mm] wedges

Kosher salt

3 Roma tomatoes, quartered

1 dried bay leaf

4 fresh thyme sprigs

1 bunch fresh flat-leaf parsley, plus
¼ cup [7 g] fresh flat-leaf parsley leaves

1 tsp black peppercorns

2 cups [480 ml] dry white wine

4 cups [960 ml] Fish Stock (page 224)

1 tsp smoked paprika

¼ cup [40 g] Pimenton Aioli (page 57)

½ lemon

Freshly ground black pepper

1 lb [455 g] kohlrabi, peeled and cut into ½-in [12-mm] wedges

1 medium-hot green or red chile, preferably Fresno, thinly sliced

¼ cup [65 g] Tomato Confit (page 60)

Pinch of saffron

1 lemon, quartered

4 to 6 slices Grilled or Toasted Bread (page 77)

Rinse the fish bones and head with cold water, making sure to remove any blood. Remove the skin from the fillets and cut the meat into 1-in [2.5-cm] cubes. Cover and refrigerate the meat until ready to use.

In a large stockpot over medium-high heat, warm 3 Tbsp of the olive oil until hot but not smoking. Add the onion, celery, and half the fennel and season with salt. Cook until the vegetables are soft but not browned, 3 to 4 minutes. Add the tomatoes, bay leaf, thyme, bunch of parsley, and peppercorns and cook until aromatic, about 2 minutes. Add the wine and stock and slip in the fish bones and head. Add cold water to cover. Bring to a boil, lower the heat, and simmer, tasting as you go, until the broth has a delicate, briny flavor, 1 to 1½ hours.

Remove from the heat when you feel you have a nicely balanced broth. Let cool for 15 minutes. Line a colander with cheesecloth and strain the broth, pressing the liquid out of the vegetables. Taste and season with salt. (The broth is best made the morning of the day that you will serve the fish, but it can be made up to 2 days in advance. Store in an airtight container in the refrigerator until ready to use.)

In a small bowl, stir the smoked paprika into the aioli and squeeze in the juice of the lemon half, stirring to combine.

Preheat the oven to 425°F [220°C].

Season the fish cubes with salt and pepper and set aside.

In a high-sided, ovenproof sauté pan over medium-high heat, warm the remaining 3 Tbsp olive oil until hot but not smoking. Add the kohlrabi and remaining fennel and cook until deep golden brown on the bottom, about 10 minutes. Season with salt and pepper, turn the vegetables, and cook until beginning to soften, 2 to 3 minutes longer. Add the fish broth, chile, tomato confit, and saffron and bring to a simmer. Add the seasoned fish cubes and cook in the oven until the fish is firm to the touch, with a slight give in the center, about 8 minutes.

Ladle the stew into bowls, and garnish with the smoked paprika aioli and parsley leaves. Serve with lemon wedges, grilled bread, and any remaining aioli on the side.

CIOPPINO

SERVES 4 TO 6 / Cioppino is the ultimate expression of the bounty of the sea and something I can eat nearly every day, especially during the months when Dungeness crabs are abundant. I've tasted extravagant versions of this fisherman's stew made with spiny lobster tail and sea urchin. But you can and should add whatever seafood is available to you; keep in mind that small crustaceans such as prawns, mussels, and clams are ideal, and cubed fish such as rock cod, salmon, ling cod, or sea bass are great. When I come upon very fresh squid, I drop a couple of them in at the last moment before serving. Most important, start with a very nice fish stock and amazing seafood and you will be fine.

2 Dungeness crabs

Extra-virgin olive oil for cooking

1 shallot, peeled and sliced into thin rings

3 garlic cloves

4 salt-packed anchovies, halved lengthwise, boned, and rinsed

¼ cup [65 g] Tomato Confit (page 60)

Pinch of crushed red pepper flakes

2 Tbsp Harissa (page 52)

1 lb [455 g] small or medium clams, rinsed

1 lb [455 g] mussels, rinsed and beards removed

6 fresh prawns or large shrimp, head and shell on

8 oz [230 g] rock cod or monkfish tail, skin removed and cut into 1-in [2.5-cm] cubes

½ cup [120 ml] white wine

¼ cup [40 g] Pomodoro Sauce (page 59)

Flaky sea salt

2 qt [2 L] Fish Stock (page 224)

½ bunch parsley, chopped

2 green onions, chopped

Freshly ground black pepper

2 lemons, quartered

Best-quality olive oil for drizzling

4 slices Grilled or Toasted Bread (page 77)

In a large stockpot over medium-heat, bring 2 in [5 cm] water to a boil. Add the crabs and cover the pot. Turn the heat to medium and steam the crabs until fully cooked, 10 to 12 minutes. When done, the legs will break easily from the bodies at the thickest part. Transfer the crabs to a platter and let rest until cool enough to handle, about 10 minutes.

Working over a small bowl, remove the top shell from a crab's body by pulling on the shell from the back. Release all the liquid from inside the crab into the bowl. Be sure to capture all of the delicious bits of viscera that resemble scrambled eggs. Remove the legs and chop at the joint into upper and lower leg sections. Crack the shells at several intervals to make them easy to break later, or break and pick out all the meat. Repeat with the second crab and set aside.

In a 7- to 8-qt [6.6- to 7.5-L] stockpot or Dutch oven over medium-high heat, warm enough extra-virgin olive oil to coat the bottom of the pan generously. Add the shallot and garlic and cook until translucent, 2 to 3 minutes. Stir in the anchovies, breaking them up with a wooden spoon. Add the tomato confit, crushed red pepper flakes, and harissa and cook for 1 to 2 minutes. Add the clams and mussels, then the prawns and cod, stirring to coat. Pour in the wine and pomodoro sauce and turn the heat to high. Bring to a boil, season with salt, and add enough of the stock to cover the ingredients by 2 in [5 cm]. Bring the liquid to a simmer and cook the mixture until the clams and mussels open and the prawns and fish are opaque, 3 to 5 minutes.

Remove from the heat, and add the parsley and green onions. Season with salt and black pepper. Add the lemons, divide into bowls, and drizzle each with best-quality olive oil. Serve warm with grilled bread.

SQUID WITH LENTILS & SALSA VERDE

SERVES 4 / In the fall and winter, we like to pair grilled squid with lentils or shelling beans.

1½ lb [680 g] cleaned squid tentacles and tubes

Zest of 1 lemon

Zest of 1 orange

Zest of 1 lime

¼ cup [60 ml] extra-virgin olive oil, plus 2 Tbsp

2 Tbsp chopped fresh flat-leaf parsley

¼ tsp crushed red pepper flakes

2 cups [400 g] black (beluga) lentils

2 sprigs thyme

1 dried bay leaf

Kosher salt

¼ cup [60 g] Soffrito (page 46)

1 Roasted or Grilled Red Pepper (page 77), cut into ¼-in [6-mm] strips

1 cup [240 ml] Chicken Stock (page 223)

1 tsp red wine vinegar

¼ cup [50 g] Parsley Salsa Verde (page 51)

With a sharp knife, make an incision at the tip of each squid tube straight down the side so that the tubes can be laid flat. Scrape out any cartilage or inner membrane with the edge of the knife. Use the knife to score the tubes in a crosshatch pattern so the marinade will adhere, taking care not to cut through the flesh.

In a large bowl, combine the lemon zest, orange zest, lime zest, ¼ cup [60 ml] olive oil, parsley, and crushed red pepper flakes. Add the squid, toss to coat, cover, and refrigerate for at least 1 hour, or up to 4 hours.

Place the lentils in a large saucepan and add enough water to cover by 1 in [2.5 cm]. Bring to a boil over medium-high heat. Lower the heat, toss in the thyme and bay leaf, and simmer until the lentils become tender and most of the liquid has been absorbed, about 25 minutes. You may have to add more water if the level of the liquid is getting low and the lentils are not finished cooking yet. Remove the bay leaf. Season with salt and spread out the lentils on a baking sheet to cool.

Prepare a hot fire in a charcoal grill (preheat a gas grill to high or heat a cast-iron grill pan over high heat).

In a medium frying pan over medium heat, warm the remaining 2 Tbsp olive oil until hot but not smoking. Stir in the soffrito, roasted red pepper strips, and lentils. Cook briefly to combine, about 3 minutes. Add the stock and cook over high heat until the stock has reduced by about two-thirds, about 3 minutes. The mixture should be saucy but not soupy. Season with salt and the red wine vinegar.

Divide the lentils evenly among four serving plates.

Remove the squid pieces from the marinade, season with salt, and cook on the hot grill just until done, about 1 minute.

Arrange the grilled squid over the lentils. Spoon the salsa verde on top. Serve immediately.

GRILLED OCTOPUS WITH BRAISED BLACK-EYED PEAS

SERVES 4 TO 6 / Octopus simmered just until tender and then charred on a very hot grill is, in my opinion, the best way to handle this creature. I love the charred skin with the tender, but still firm, meat, which becomes almost steaklike. The marinade, which we end up brushing on as the octopus cooks, is a purée of dried chiles and tomato sweetened with honey and spiked with vinegar. To round out the Latin American theme, we serve this with an herb called *huacatay*, which tastes like a marriage of mint and cilantro but with its own distinct flavor. We fashion it into a pesto, which we spoon over a bed of black-eyed peas and over the charred octopus.

When shopping for octopus, do not buy the preboiled variety often sold at Japanese markets. Better to get it raw, or seek out the high-quality previously frozen product. Ask the fishmonger to clean the octopus for you, as that can be a lengthy process. You want to end up with four to six tentacles, depending on the size. They will shrink considerably, so be aware of that when deciding on quantity.

If using dried beans, soak them in room-temperature water overnight for about 12 hours. Dried beans also take longer to cook.

3 Tbsp extra-virgin olive oil

1 yellow onion, quartered

4 garlic cloves

4 Roma tomatoes, quartered

Kosher salt

2 Tbsp dried oregano, preferably Sicilian

1 bay leaf

One 750-ml bottle dry white wine

2 lb [910 g] octopus tentacles, cleaned

BRAISED BLACK-EYED PEAS

3 Tbsp extra-virgin olive oil

1 yellow onion, finely chopped

4 garlic cloves, sliced

1 bay leaf

2 fresh thyme sprigs

1 lb [910 g] fresh or dried black-eyed peas

Kosher salt

GUAJILLO BBQ SAUCE

3 Tbsp extra-virgin olive oil

4 dried guajillo chiles

3 garlic cloves, sliced

¼ cup [65 g] Tomato Confit (page 60)

2 cups [480 ml] water

3 Tbsp honey

¼ cup [60 ml] red wine vinegar

Kosher salt

HUACATAY PESTO

¼ cup [7 g] chopped fresh huacatay leaves, or a mix of mint and cilantro

1 cup [30 g] chopped fresh flat-leaf parsley

½ cup [120 ml] olive oil

Kosher salt

Olive oil for drizzling

Kosher salt

Freshly ground black pepper

Continued

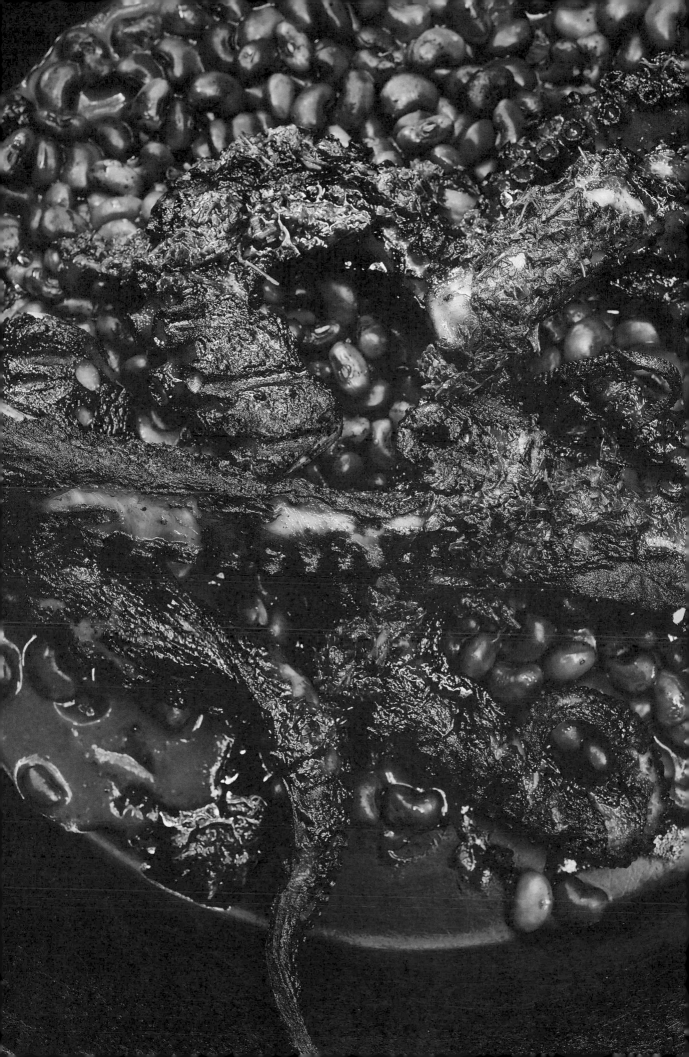

Preheat the oven to 350°F [180°C].

In a large, heavy-bottomed ovenproof pot over medium-high heat, warm the olive oil until hot but not smoking. Add the onion and garlic and cook until soft, about 3 minutes. Add the tomatoes and season with salt. Cook for about 5 minutes longer. Add the oregano and bay leaf and pour in the wine. Bring to a simmer and lower the heat to cook at a slow simmer. Slip the octopus into the hot liquid. There should be just enough to keep the octopus submerged, but not swimming in a soup. Add a little water if you need to. Return to a simmer.

Cover and cook in the oven until the octopus is very tender and beginning to soften, about 1½ hours. If you apply some pressure with your index finger and thumb on either side of the base of one of the larger tentacles, the flesh should feel firm, but like it's starting to yield. It should not be rubbery. If the octopus is still too firm, continue cooking until tender, about 20 minutes longer. I like it soft but not mushy. The bouncy texture is part of the fun. Remove from the oven and allow to cool in the cooking liquid for 30 minutes. Transfer the octopus to a baking sheet. (You can use the braising liquid in a fish stew.)

To make the black-eyed peas: In a large sauté pan over medium heat, warm the olive oil until hot but not smoking. Add the chopped onion and garlic and cook until translucent, 3 to 5 minutes. Add the bay leaf and thyme. Add the peas and water to cover. Season with salt. Simmer the peas until tender and creamy, 15 to 20 minutes. Add more water as necessary to keep the peas covered until cooked through and becoming creamy. Remove the bay leaf. Remove the black-eyed peas from the heat and let them cool in their cooking liquid.

To make the BBQ sauce: In a small saucepan over high heat, combine the olive oil, chiles, garlic, and tomato confit and cook until starting to soften and become fragrant, 3 to 5 minutes. Add the water and bring to a boil. Lower the heat slightly, cover, and simmer vigorously for 30 minutes. Uncover and continue to cook until the chiles have softened and all but about ¼ cup [60 ml] of the liquid has evaporated. Remove from the heat and let cool.

In a food processor or blender, process the chile mixture to a coarse paste. Add the honey and vinegar and pulse to combine. Taste and season with salt. The mixture should have the consistency of a BBQ sauce, but a bit more runny than store-bought stuff. The flavor should be earthy and spicy, with subtle sweet and acid notes. (The sauce can be made up to 1 day in advance and stored, tightly covered, in the refrigerator.)

To make the pesto: With a mortar and pestle, break down the huacatay and parsley into a paste, and slowly drizzle in the olive oil to loosen slightly. Season with salt. (The pesto can be made 3 or 4 hours in advance and set aside on the counter, covered with plastic wrap until ready to use.)

Reheat the peas over low heat while you grill the octopus.

Prepare a hot fire in a charcoal grill (or preheat a gas grill to high). Drizzle olive oil on the cooled octopus and season with salt and pepper. Place on the hottest part of the grill and cook, without moving, until beginning to char on the bottom, about 3 minutes. If the octopus sticks to the grill when you try to move it, continue to cook until it releases easily. Turn and paint the charred side with the BBQ sauce. Cook for another 3 minutes, turn, and paint with more BBQ sauce. The idea is to get a nice char on all sides while painting generously with the sauce on all sides. Once charred, remove from the grill.

Ladle the warm peas onto a serving platter. Top with the grilled octopus and the huacatay pesto. Serve warm.

MUSSELS WITH CHORIZO & TOMATO CONFIT

SERVES 4 TO 6 / This can be pulled together in a matter of minutes, provided you have the ingredients on hand. I like the little black mussels that turn up at the fish market in huge volume in the fall and winter; they are amazingly fresh and inexpensive. Take time to make your own loose chorizo if you can; otherwise, go with a good-quality, store-bought loose or cased fresh chorizo or another pork sausage. These will work as long as you buy from a reliable source.

5 oz [140 g] Chorizo (page 296)

½ cup [130 g] Tomato Confit (page 60)

2 Tbsp Shallot Confit (page 64)

6 cloves Garlic Confit (page 64), chopped

3 lb [1.4 kg] black mussels, rinsed and beards removed

¾ cup [180 ml] dry white wine

Kosher salt

¼ tsp crushed red pepper flakes

¼ cup [7 g] chopped fresh flat-leaf parsley

Grilled or Toasted Bread (page 77) for serving

In a large sauté pan over medium-high heat, cook the chorizo, breaking it apart with a wooden spoon, until it begins to brown, about 3 minutes. Add the tomato confit, shallot confit, and garlic confit and continue cooking until the chorizo is browned and has rendered most of its fat, another 2 to 3 minutes.

Add the mussels to the pan and toss quickly to combine. Add the wine and stir with a wooden spoon, scraping up any browned bits from the bottom of the pan. Season lightly with salt and the crushed red pepper flakes. Partially cover the pan, allowing some steam to escape, and cook until the mussels open, 2 to 3 minutes. Check any unopened mussels. If they are relatively lightweight, they are probably dead and should be discarded. Otherwise, cook for 1 or 2 minutes longer to see if they open. Add the parsley and season with additional salt if necessary.

Transfer the mussels and chorizo to serving bowls and serve with grilled bread.

RAZOR CLAMS SEARED IN CAST IRON WITH PARSLEY BUTTER

SERVES 4 AS AN APPETIZER / This was inspired by a dish found all over northern Spain—razor clams cooked on a plancha, a type of griddle used over very high heat. The sweet meat of these amazing bivalves is unparalleled and is enhanced when cooked over very high heat for just a minute or two. A large cast-iron frying pan holds heat well enough to create a result very similar to the Spanish planchas.

You want to end up with a plate full of beautiful razors so fresh that they were still living when they hit the pan. The trick is not to open these too far in advance. We pop them open when the order hits the kitchen, so the customer gets to experience their incredible sweetness. Parsley is good with just about any seafood, especially when you want a little added flavor and richness, as long as you don't use so much that it competes with the main ingredient.

12 large razor clams

4 Tbsp [55 g] unsalted butter, at room temperature

Zest of 1 lemon, 1 Tbsp fresh lemon juice, plus lemon wedges for serving

2 Tbsp roughly chopped fresh flat-leaf parsley, plus parsley leaves for garnish

1 garlic clove

Flaky sea salt

Freshly ground black pepper

3 Tbsp extra-virgin olive oil

Kosher salt

In a large bowl of cold water, soak the razor clams for 10 minutes.

Heat a large cast-iron frying pan over very high heat until quite hot, about 10 minutes.

Meanwhile, in a small bowl, combine the butter, lemon zest, lemon juice, and chopped parsley. Using a Microplane, grate the garlic into the bowl. Stir, and season with sea salt and pepper. Let stand at room temperature until ready to use.

Remove the clams from the water and shuck them with a clam knife by inserting the knife up under the shell but above the meat to dislodge the flesh from the upper shell. Work your way around all sides of the clam, gathering all the meat on the bottom shell and separating it from the shell. Place the meat on a work surface and clean, using kitchen scissors, by removing the tip of the siphon, the gills, and digestive tract (all the dark parts of the meat). Drizzle the shucked clams with the olive oil and season with kosher salt and pepper.

Cook the clams in the hot pan, gently pressing on them with a spatula to make sure they lie flat. Sear them aggressively until browned, about 2 minutes. Transfer to a medium bowl. Add a large spoonful of the herbed butter and toss gently to distribute the butter.

Transfer the clams to a serving platter, along with any remaining liquor from the pan. Scatter the parsley leaves over the clams. Serve with lemon wedges and small forks.

ROASTED PRAWNS WITH GARLIC, PARSLEY, CRUSHED RED PEPPER FLAKES & LEMON

SERVES 4 AS AN APPETIZER / We cook this in our 850°F [455°C] wood-burning oven, and what happens to a delicate piece of seafood like a fresh prawn in an oven that hot is magic. Leaving the shell on insulates the meat and helps prevent it from overcooking.

I have found two good ways to reproduce this dish at home. The first is to heat a cast-iron frying pan in the oven on its hottest setting for 1 hour and then roast the prawns on it. The other, more amusing, way is to let the pan get scorching hot over live fire. I do this sometimes when I'm camping to cook proteins that like intense high heat, such as bay scallops and squid. We are lucky enough to get amazing live prawns from Santa Barbara, but any good-quality head-on shrimp works well. I like to keep the heads on because I really think the shrimp taste better that way, but I also just love sucking the sweet, flavorful juice from them after they cook. Serve these on their own, or with Romesco (page 58). Cold beer is essential.

12 fresh prawns, head and shell on
¼ cup [60 ml] extra-virgin olive oil
Flaky sea salt
Freshly ground black pepper

8 cloves Garlic Confit (page 64), chopped, with some of the oil
2 Tbsp roughly chopped fresh flat-leaf parsley
1 tsp crushed red pepper flakes
1 lemon, quartered

Preheat the oven to 500°F [260°C]. Put a large, dry cast-iron frying pan in the oven and heat until very hot, about 1 hour. Alternatively, heat the pan over a hot fire in a charcoal grill or over a gas grill on high.

With a paring knife, cut a slit down the back of the prawn shells and rinse the prawns well under cold water. Pat dry.

In a medium bowl, combine the prawns and olive oil and season with salt and pepper. Add the garlic confit, parsley, and crushed red pepper flakes and toss to combine. At the last minute, squeeze the juice from the lemon quarters into the bowl, and drop them into the mix.

Unload the prawns and their aromatic juices into the hot pan and quickly close the oven door or cover the grill. Roast the prawns, undisturbed, just until they are cooked through, 3 to 4 minutes.

Transfer the prawns and the roasted lemon wedges to a serving platter. Serve immediately.

CHAPTER EIGHT
MEAT

In an ideal world, we would buy only whole animals raised in the region where we live, according to the highest standards of animal husbandry with regard to feed and access to space, and our cooks would put every centimeter of those animals to use. In reality, we have limited storage space and it is only occasionally that we have whole animals or large pieces of meat aging at Gjelina. We do buy primal cuts of beef, pork, and lamb along with the occasional whole pig, lamb, or goat and those get broken down and cooked as soon as they arrive. We get a steady flow of lovely rabbits, chickens, and ducks from our suppliers. Fortunately, there are increasing numbers of larger-scale meat producers that are raising the bar, providing meat from pasture-raised animals, free of hormones and antibiotics, so they are good options for us, too.

Buying better-quality meats does mean paying more, so we are always trying to develop recipes that utilize less-expensive cuts, including shoulders, ribs, legs, tongues, hearts, and livers. This brings diners at Gjelina into the conversation about using the whole animal and discovering delicious uses for less-common parts. But I also love the occasional giant bone-in rib-eye or juicy pork chop as much as the next guy.

We also love pâtés, sausages, terrines, and rillettes at Gjelina. Charcuterie is one of my favorite ways to consume meat, and we feature it widely on our menu. Pâtés and terrines are generally served alongside grilled bread, pickles, and condiments. We use many of our sausages loose—without bothering to stuff them in casings—sautéing them in pasta sauces, egg dishes, shellfish dishes, and pizza toppings. When we serve sausages at the center of the plate, we case them and grill or smoke them.

The recipes here lend themselves well to making large batches, some of which can easily be portioned off and frozen for later use. Pâtés and terrines can be capped with cooled rendered fat or clarified butter and stored for up to two weeks in the refrigerator. These recipes demand considerable effort, it's true, but you'll be rewarded with leftovers that have many exciting uses.

Eating meat is a luxury, and we often treat it as an accessory to the vegetables that really take center stage at Gjelina. Many dishes containing meat often use it more as a seasoning component, such as adding cured meat or freshly made sausage to pizzas and pastas, or enhancing charred Brussels sprouts with a salty hit of bacon.

We do love roasting, grilling, braising, smoking, and confit-ing large chunks of meat (and anything else we can think of), but we encourage our guests to order these items sparingly and to share them with the table. Yes, we are as turned on as any omnivore by a mammoth bone-in porterhouse searing over a wood-fired grill, but we really want to encourage folks to see that as a celebratory gesture and not an everyday practice.

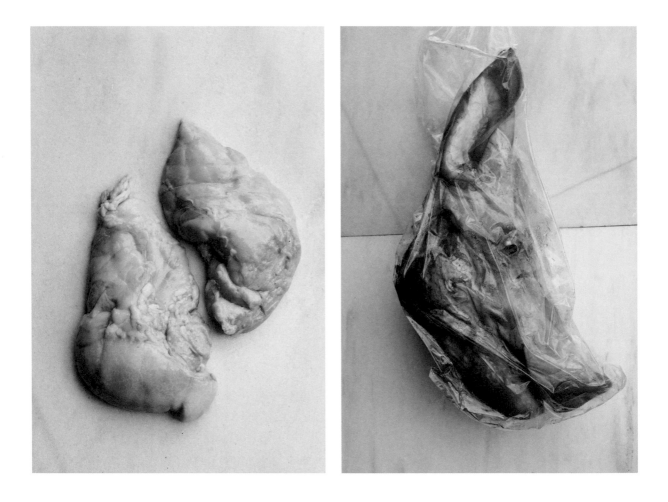

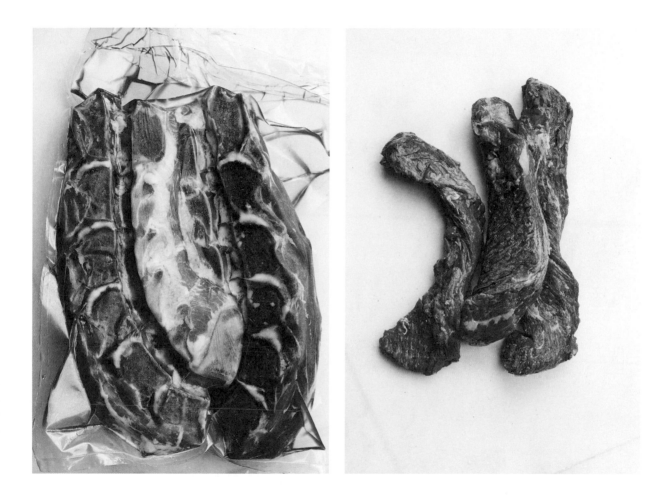

RUSTIC CHICKEN & DUCK LIVER PÂTÉ

MAKES 3½ LB [1.6 KG] / Rich in iron and with a silky texture, this pâté is spectacular and relatively easy to make. It's been on the menu at Gjelina since day one. We sometimes serve it on its own next to a pile of pickles and toast. We also use it as a filling for agnolotti, and as a filling in sandwiches to riff on the idea of a banh mi. I love it smeared on grilled bread alongside a bitter-sharp leafy salad. New employees at Gjelina often claim to not like liver, but they inevitably convert once they get properly acquainted with its flavor.

2 lb [910 g] organic chicken livers, cleaned

1 lb [455 g] organic duck livers, cleaned

Kosher salt

¼ tsp pink curing salt

Olive oil as needed

½ yellow onion, minced

2 garlic cloves, minced

1 tsp fresh thyme leaves

1 Tbsp Dijon mustard

½ cup [120 ml] Madeira

¾ cup [170 g] cold unsalted butter, cut into ½-in [12-mm] cubes

2 Tbsp balsamic vinegar

2 Tbsp sherry vinegar

1 tsp red wine vinegar

Freshly ground black pepper

½ cup [15 g] chopped fresh flat-leaf parsley

½ cup [150 g] rendered fat or clarified butter, cooled and solidified (optional)

Line a standard 4-by-12⅔-in [10-by-32-cm] terrine mold or loaf pan (with a 1½-qt [1.4-L] capacity) with plastic wrap, leaving 4 in [10 cm] of overhang on the sides.

In a large bowl, season the chicken livers and duck livers with 3 tsp kosher salt and the pink curing salt and let stand a few minutes. (This helps to allow the curing salt to take effect and disperse evenly throughout the pâté.)

In a large sauté pan over medium-high heat, add enough olive oil to coat the bottom of the pan, and warm until hot but not smoking. Add the seasoned livers and cook, in batches if necessary so as not to crowd the pan, until well-browned but still pink in the center, 3 to 5 minutes. Transfer the livers to a plate and let cool for 10 to 15 minutes. They don't have to be room temperature, but you do not want to add them to the food processor while they are still hot.

Return the sauté pan to medium-high heat, add a little more olive oil to the pan, and add the onion, garlic, and thyme. Cook until the onion is translucent, about 5 minutes. Stir in the mustard. Add the Madeira and cook, scraping up the browned bits from the bottom of the pan with a wooden spoon, until the liquid is reduced to 3 Tbsp. Remove from the heat and let cool for 10 minutes.

In a food processor, combine the seared livers with the mustard, butter, balsamic vinegar, sherry vinegar, and red wine vinegar. Process until relatively smooth and textured to your liking, about 10 seconds. Season with salt and pepper. Add the parsley and pulse just until combined. Taste and add more salt and pepper if necessary.

Transfer the liver mixture to a metal bowl and set the bowl inside a larger one filled with ice water. Stir the mixture with a spatula until cool, about 10 minutes.

Transfer the cooled pâté to the prepared pan a portion at a time to prevent air pockets from forming, smoothing the mixture with the back of a rubber spatula after each addition. When the pan is full, tap it against the work surface to release any remaining air pockets, then smooth the top and fold the plastic wrap over the surface to cover completely. Refrigerate for at least 8 hours. (If you plan on storing it for longer, cap the terrine with the rendered fat and rewrap tightly with the plastic. When capped, the pâté can be stored in the refrigerator for up to 2 weeks.)

When ready to serve, pull the pâté from the mold by grabbing the plastic wrap at both sides and lifting up. Unwrap the amount that you plan to use and rewrap the remainder tightly to help avoid oxidation. The outside will start to oxidize somewhat once it is unmolded, but the inside should remain very rosy pink.

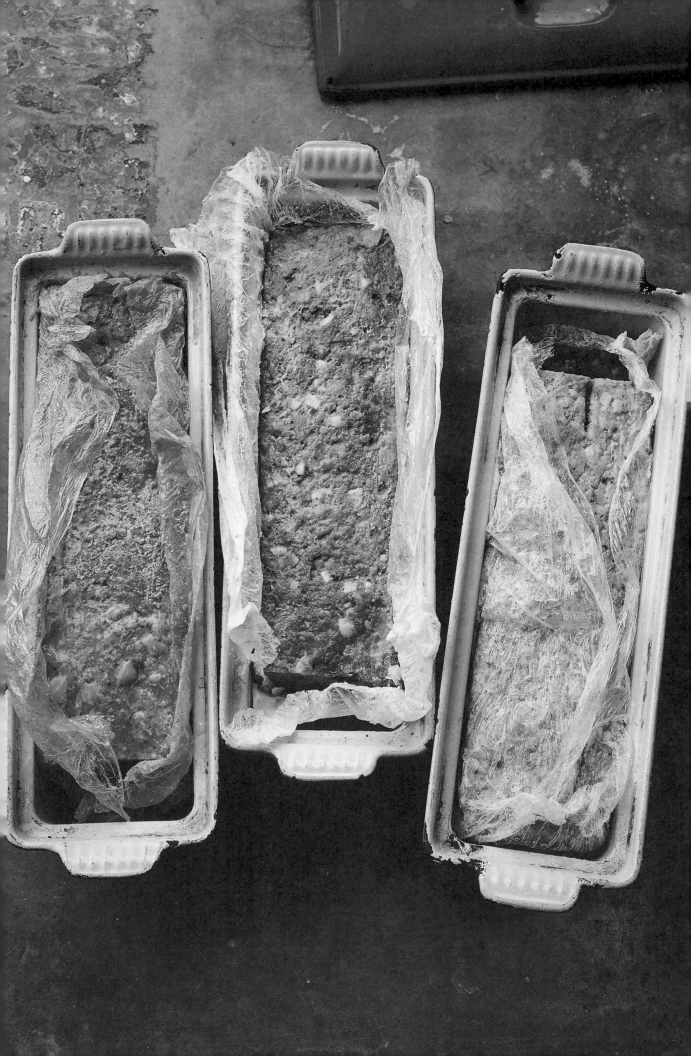

PORK SHOULDER & DUCK LIVER PÂTÉ WITH PAPRIKA & GARLIC

MAKES 4 LB [1.8 KG] / This quintessential country-style terrine hits a deliciously porky note. We like to tuck a few pieces of duck liver in the center of the terrine. Just make sure not to overcook it, so the livers show a slightly rosy pink hue when you slice the terrine.

2 lb [910 g] boneless pork shoulder

8 oz [230 g] pork fatback

8 oz [230 g] duck livers, cleaned

3½ tsp kosher salt

¼ tsp pink curing salt

6 garlic cloves, minced

2 Tbsp smoked paprika

1 tsp freshly ground black pepper

1 Tbsp yellow mustard seeds

2 tsp Dijon mustard, plus more for serving

1 Tbsp chopped fresh oregano

1 egg

¼ cup [60 ml] heavy cream

⅓ cup [75 ml] dry red wine

Caul fat or olive oil for lining or greasing the terrine mold

½ cup [150 g] rendered fat or clarified butter, cooled and solidified (optional)

Pickles for serving

Cut 4 oz [115 g] of the pork shoulder into ½-in [12-mm] cubes. Cut half the pork fatback into ¼-in [6-mm] cubes. In a medium bowl, combine the cubes of pork shoulder and fatback and refrigerate until ready to use.

Cut the remaining 1¾ lb [795 g] pork shoulder and the remaining fatback into large chunks. Cut half the duck livers into large chunks. Combine in a large metal bowl, and set the bowl in a larger bowl filled with ice water. Add the kosher salt, pink curing salt, garlic, paprika, pepper, mustard seeds, mustard, and oregano. With your hands, mix well to combine. Spread out the meat mixture on a baking sheet, cover with plastic wrap, and refrigerate until very cold, at least 2 hours or up to overnight. You can put the pan in the freezer to speed the chilling, but do not let the meat freeze.

Refrigerate the large blade, die, tray, and other components of your meat grinder for at least 2 hours before using. Set a clean large metal bowl in another ice-water bath.

With the meat grinder fitted with the chilled blade, grind the chilled seasoned meat into the metal bowl. Remove a third of the ground meat and run it through the meat grinder a second time. Using your hands, mix the ground meat thoroughly to incorporate the finer ground meat. Mix in the reserved chilled pork shoulder and fatback cubes.

In a small bowl, whisk together the egg, cream, and red wine. Add to the ground meat mixture and mix vigorously with one hand until the meat begins to offer some resistance.

Line a standard 4-by-12⅔-in [10-by-32-cm] terrine mold or loaf pan (with a 1½-qt [1.4-L] capacity) with caul fat.

Pack half of the chilled meat mixture into the prepared pan, pressing down and into the corners to make an even layer. Lay the remaining duck livers down the center of the meat in a single layer. Top with the remaining meat mixture, tapping the terrine against the work surface to release any air pockets and make sure the mixture is fully compacted. Cover with plastic wrap and refrigerate until a thermometer inserted into the center of the terrine registers less than 42°F [5°C], 60 to 90 minutes.

Preheat the oven to 300°F [150°C].

Fill a medium saucepan with water and bring to a simmer over high heat.

Put the chilled terrine in a roasting pan and fill the roasting pan with enough simmering water to reach one-third of the way up the sides of the terrine. Bake until a thermometer inserted into the center of the terrine registers 137°F [58°C], about 1 hour. Remove from the oven and, using oven mitts, immediately transfer the terrine to an ice-water bath to cool completely. (We use coated ceramic terrine molds that can be shocked in ice water without breaking or cracking. If you have a more delicate mold, then allow it to cool standing on the counter for 10 minutes before setting it in the ice-water bath.) Refrigerate the pâté for at least 24 hours before serving. (If you plan on storing it for longer, cap the terrine with the rendered fat and wrap tightly with plastic. When capped, the pâté can be stored in the refrigerator for up to 2 weeks.)

When ready to serve, remove the pâté from the refrigerator, unwrap, and scrape off any fat from the top to expose the meat. Run a knife along all sides of the terrine and invert onto a cutting board to unmold. If it sticks to the mold, leave it out to temper for 20 minutes and try again. If it still resists, you can either wait another 20 minutes or place in a shallow pan of warm water to get it to release from the bottom of the mold. My terrine mold can handle a firm tap on the counter; if your mold is equally sturdy, you may do the same to loosen the terrine. Once unmolded, slice to the desired thickness, depending on use. I like 1-in [2.5-cm] slabs for a charcuterie plate, but would slice it ¼ in [6 mm] thick and shingle on a baguette for a sandwich. The pâté improves in flavor as it comes to room temperature, so take out early if time permits. Serve with pickles and mustard.

CHORIZO

MAKES ABOUT 4 LB [1.8 KG] / We can always find a use for fresh chorizo, and so will you. We fry it in olive oil and use it as a pizza topping and to flavor steamed mussels, and we cook it with lentils and escarole. You could also form it into patties and serve it with fried eggs at breakfast.

1 Tbsp coriander seeds

1½ tsp cumin seeds

2 dried guajillo chiles, stems removed

3½ lb [1.6 kg] pork shoulder, cut into 1-in [2.5-cm] cubes

8 oz [230 g] pork fatback, cut into 1-in [2.5-cm] cubes

2 Tbsp dried oregano, preferably Sicilian

4 Tbsp smoked paprika

4 garlic cloves

1 tsp crushed red pepper flakes

1 Tbsp plus 1 tsp kosher salt

In a small, dry frying pan over medium heat, toast the coriander seeds and cumin seeds until fragrant, about 3 minutes. Set aside to cool. In the same pan, toast the chiles until blistered and fragrant, about 3 minutes. Let cool. With a mortar and pestle or in a spice grinder, pulverize the toasted seeds and chiles to a powder.

Set a large metal bowl in a larger bowl filled with ice water. In the metal bowl, combine the pork shoulder, fatback, ground toasted spices, oregano, paprika, garlic, crushed red pepper flakes, and salt. With your hands, mix well. Remove the bowl from the ice-water bath, cover with plastic wrap, and refrigerate until very cold, at least 12 hours or up to 2 days.

Refrigerate the large blade, die, tray, and other components of your meat grinder for at least 2 hours before using. Set a clean large metal bowl in another ice-water bath.

With the meat grinder fitted with the chilled blade, grind the chilled seasoned meat into the prepared bowl. Remove a third of the ground meat and run it through the meat grinder a second time. Using your hands, mix the ground meat thoroughly to incorporate the finer ground meat.

Divide all the meat, or whatever you're not using the same day, into 8-oz [230-g] portions and wrap in plastic wrap. Chill all the sausage thoroughly before using. Freeze what you don't plan to use within 2 days for up to 1 month and defrost in the refrigerator for 6 hours before using.

LAMB SAUSAGE

MAKES ABOUT 4 LB [1.8 KG] / We usually don't bother to stuff this sausage into casings, and instead keep it loose to crumble on pizza. This is handy to have around for pasta and egg dishes. You can also form the meat into small patties and serve them as a breakfast sausage, or even in a North African–inspired sandwich made with toasted baguette or flatbread. Traditional merguez sausage has similar spices but is made without pork fat. You can substitute lamb fat for the pork if you like, but we find that pork fat makes a more moist sausage that still expresses the lamb's character. Play with the spice levels and jack up the heat or fennel or cumin, depending on what suits you.

1 Tbsp fennel seeds

1 Tbsp coriander seeds

1½ tsp cumin seeds

3 lb [1.4 kg] lamb shoulder, cut into 1-in [2.5-cm] cubes

1 lb [455 g] pork fatback or beef fat, cut into 1-in [2.5-cm] cubes

Pinch of fennel pollen

2 Tbsp smoked paprika

2 medium-hot green or red chiles, preferably Fresno, minced

5 garlic cloves, minced

1 shallot, minced

Pinch of crushed red pepper flakes

¼ cup [7 g] chopped fresh cilantro

1 Tbsp plus 1 tsp kosher salt

In a small, dry frying pan over medium heat, toast the fennel seeds, coriander seeds, and cumin seeds just until fragrant, about 3 minutes. Let cool. With a mortar and pestle or in a spice grinder, grind to a powder.

Set a large metal bowl in a larger bowl filled with ice water. In the metal bowl, combine the lamb shoulder, fatback, ground seeds, fennel pollen, paprika, chiles, garlic, shallot, crushed red pepper flakes, cilantro, and salt. Remove the bowl from the ice-water bath, cover with plastic wrap, and refrigerate until very cold, at least 12 hours or up to 2 days.

Refrigerate the large blade, die, tray, and other components of your meat grinder for at least 2 hours before using. Set a clean large metal bowl in another ice-water bath.

With the meat grinder fitted with the chilled blade, grind the chilled seasoned meat into the prepared bowl. Remove a third of the ground meat and run it through the meat grinder a second time. Using your hands, mix the ground meat thoroughly to incorporate the finer ground meat.

Divide all the meat, or whatever you're not using immediately, into 8-oz [230-g] portions and wrap in plastic wrap. Chill all the sausage thoroughly before using. Freeze what you don't plan to use within 2 days for up to 1 month and defrost in the refrigerator for 6 hours before using.

BLOOD SAUSAGE

MAKES TWELVE 5-OZ [140-G] SAUSAGES / Many cultures use fresh pork blood or beef blood to add a smooth, custardy texture to sausage. Examples include boudin noir, black pudding, moronga, and blutwurst. Our variation is inspired by the paprika-spiked Spanish version, morcilla. We add minced jalapeño for heat and sear slices in a hot pan to serve doused in chimichurri. If you are not familiar with blood sausage, you may be surprised to discover that the flavors are actually quite subtle, especially given its expressive violet hue. Ask your butcher if they can source pork blood.

3 Tbsp extra-virgin olive oil, plus more for frying

5 garlic cloves

1 yellow onion, chopped

2 jalapeño chiles, minced

Kosher salt

1 Tbsp dried oregano, preferably Sicilian

2 Tbsp smoked paprika

2 lb [910 g] pork belly, cut into 1-in [2.5-cm] cubes

¼ cup [7 g] chopped fresh flat-leaf parsley

2 tsp freshly ground black pepper

¼ tsp pink curing salt

1½ lb [680 g] fresh pork blood

8⅓ ft [2.5 m] hog casing

Chimichurri (page 51) and Grilled or Toasted Bread (page 77) for serving

In a medium frying pan over medium heat, warm the 3 Tbsp olive oil until hot but not smoking. Add the garlic, onion, and jalapeños and cook until tender and slightly caramelized, about 10 minutes. Season with ½ tsp kosher salt. Remove from the heat and stir in the oregano and paprika. Spread out the onion mixture on a plate and refrigerate until well chilled, about 2 hours.

Set a large metal bowl in a larger bowl filled with ice water. In the metal bowl, combine the pork belly, parsley, pepper, chilled onion mixture, 1 Tbsp plus ½ tsp kosher salt, and the pink curing salt. Remove the bowl from the ice-water bath, cover with plastic wrap, and refrigerate until very cold, at least 12 hours or up to 2 days.

Refrigerate the large blade, die, tray, and other components of your meat grinder for at least 2 hours before using. Set a clean large metal bowl in another ice-water bath.

With the meat grinder fitted with the chilled blade, grind the chilled seasoned meat into the prepared bowl. Remove a third of the ground meat and run it through the meat grinder a second time. Using your hands, mix the ground meat thoroughly to incorporate the finer ground meat. Return the mix to the refrigerator and chill thoroughly, about 2 hours.

Pour the pork blood into the chilled meat mixture and blend with one hand. The mixture should have the consistency of a lumpy pancake batter.

Rinse the casing in several changes of cold water. Thread the entire length of the casing onto the nozzle of a sausage stuffer and begin to stuff with the chilled sausage mixture. Avoid air pockets by applying steady, constant pressure while cranking the machine and guiding the extruded meat into a coil as it comes out. Sprinkle a little water on the work surface so the sausage slides easily into a coil shape. Once the casing is full, cut the casing and lift it vertically, compacting the sausage, before tying off the end. Pinch and twist to form twelve sausages.

Fill a large frying pan with water and heat the water to 160°F [71°C], leaving room for the sausage. Poach the blood sausages in batches until they feel as firm as a sponge, about 10 minutes. Immediately plunge the hot sausages in a bowl of ice water to chill. When thoroughly chilled, pat the sausages dry with paper towels. Put them on a baking sheet and refrigerate, uncovered, for at least 4 hours or up to overnight. This allows the sausages to dry completely and the flavors to develop. Freeze what you don't plan to use within 2 days for up to 1 month and defrost in the refrigerator for 6 hours before using.

To cook, slice the sausage ½ in [12 mm] thick. In a frying pan over medium heat, add a little olive oil and cook the sausage slices until crisp on both sides, basting them in their own fat until warmed through, about 5 minutes. Garnish with chimichurri and serve with grilled bread.

PORK & FENNEL SAUSAGE WITH FAVA & CHERRY TOMATOES

MAKES TWELVE 5-OZ [140-G] SAUSAGES / The classic pork-and-fennel sausage, made right, is hard to beat. Keeping all the meat, fat, bowls, and grinder attachments very cold while grinding is the best way to ensure a silky texture; adding coarsely ground spices and hand-chopping some of the meat and fat gives the sausage a rustic, gutsy texture. In order to achieve the snappy quality favored by sausage connoisseurs, we hang the sausages in a cool, dry place for 2 to 3 days to dry out the casings. Drying also keeps the casings from splitting when they hit a hot grill. Never pierce the casing prior to cooking; the priceless, fatty juices will run out. To me this is sacrilege akin to pressing a burger on the grill.

PORK & FENNEL SAUSAGE
1 Tbsp fennel seeds
½ tsp black peppercorns
1¼ lb [570 g] pork shoulder, cut into 1-in [2.5-cm] cubes
8 oz [230 g] pork fatback, cut into 1-in [2.5-cm] cubes
2 garlic cloves, minced
1 shallot, minced
½ tsp freshly ground black pepper
2 Tbsp chopped fennel fronds
Large pinch of fennel pollen (optional)
2 tsp kosher salt
¼ cup [60 ml] ice water
6 ft [1.8 m] hog casing

Extra-virgin olive oil for brushing, plus 2 Tbsp
Kosher salt
Freshly ground black pepper
½ cup [225 g] fresh fava beans, shelled
1 large fennel bulb, cut into 8 wedges, and fronds
1 cup [115 g] cherry tomatoes
1 cup [240 ml] white wine
½ cup [120 ml] Chicken Stock (page 223)
2 tsp dried oregano
Pinch of crushed red pepper flakes
½ bunch parsley
1 Tbsp white wine vinegar

To make the sausage: In a small, dry frying pan over medium heat, toast the fennel seeds and peppercorns just until fragrant and beginning to brown, about 3 minutes. Let cool. With a mortar and pestle or in a spice grinder, pulverize to a fine powder.

Set a large metal bowl in a larger bowl filled with ice water. In the metal bowl, combine the pork shoulder, fatback, garlic, shallot, ground toasted spices, black pepper, fennel fronds, fennel pollen (if using), and kosher salt. With your hands, mix well. Remove the bowl from the ice-water bath, cover with plastic wrap, and refrigerate until very cold, at least 12 hours or up to 2 days.

Refrigerate the large blade, die, tray, and other components of your meat grinder for at least 2 hours before using. Set a clean large metal bowl in another ice-water bath.

With the meat grinder fitted with the chilled blade, grind the chilled seasoned meat into the prepared bowl. Remove a third of the ground meat and run it through the meat grinder a second time.

Continued

Add the ¼ cup [60 ml] ice water to the ground meat mixture in a steady stream and mix vigorously with one hand until the meat begins to offer some resistance and bind with itself, about 1½ minutes. The idea is to create a creamy texture and engage the proteins so your sausage isn't crumbly. Return to the refrigerator to chill thoroughly.

Rinse the casing in several changes of cold water. Thread the entire length of the casing onto the nozzle of a sausage stuffer and begin to stuff with the chilled sausage mixture. Avoid air pockets by applying steady, constant pressure while cranking the machine and guiding the extruded meat into a coil as it comes out. Sprinkle a little water on the work surface so the sausage slides easily into a coil shape. Once the casing is full, tie off the end. Pinch and twist to form twelve sausages.

Pat the sausages dry with paper towels. Put them on a baking sheet and refrigerate, uncovered, for at least 4 hours or up to overnight. This allows the sausages to dry completely and the flavors to develop. Freeze what you don't plan to use within 2 days for up to 1 month and defrost in the refrigerator for 6 hours before using.

To cook the sausages, brush with olive oil and season with salt and pepper. In a frying pan over medium heat, cook, in batches if necessary to avoid crowding the pan, until just cooked through, about 6 minutes. You can also cook them on a medium-hot grill, searing for 4 to 5 minutes on the first side and 3 to 4 minutes on the second side. Rest for 5 minutes before cutting into them.

If working with medium to large fava beans, prepare an ice-water bath by filling a large bowl with ice water. Blanch the beans in lightly salted boiling water for about 15 seconds and plunge them into the ice-water bath. Remove them from the bath and peel them once they are cool. If working with young, tender fava beans, leave them whole.

Place a large frying pan over high heat and warm the 2 Tbsp olive oil until hot, but not smoking. Add the fennel bulb to the pan, using tongs to place so the cut sides are against the pan bottom to get a good sear. Cook until the fennel is caramelized, about 3 minutes. Flip the fennel, lower the heat to medium-high, and cook on the other side until caramelized, another 3 minutes. Add the cherry tomatoes and cook until they start to burst in the hot oil. Add the wine and stock and bring to a boil. Cook until reduced by half, about 4 minutes. Add the fava beans, oregano, and crushed red pepper flakes and season with salt and pepper. Once the beans are tender and the liquid has almost evaporated, add the parsley and vinegar.

Transfer to a serving platter and top with the sausages. Serve warm.

MEATBALLS BRAISED IN RED WINE & TOMATO

MAKES 25 TO 28 MEATBALLS; SERVES 4 TO 6 AS A MAIN COURSE / The key to this recipe is to balance the pork, fat, bread cubes, and egg so these meatballs are nearly but not quite falling apart. If you can grind your own meat, grind the aromatics, seasoning, and bread with it so there is less mixing, which makes for more-tender meatballs. If you buy your meat already ground, mix gently, carefully folding the ingredients together. Simmered in a bit of good tomato sauce and red wine, these meatballs make a satisfying plate when served with a couple of slices of grilled bread and a few fresh greens.

1½ lb [680 g] boneless pork shoulder,
cut into ¾-in [2-cm] pieces

8 oz [230 g] fatty pork belly, cut into ¾-in [2-cm] pieces

Kosher salt

Freshly ground black pepper

1 carrot, peeled and finely chopped

1 yellow onion, finely chopped

4 garlic cloves, chopped

2 Tbsp chopped fresh flat-leaf parsley,
plus more for garnish

2 tsp fresh thyme leaves

1 Tbsp paprika

½ tsp freshly grated nutmeg

4 oz [115 g] day-old bread, crust removed,
cut into 1-in [2.5-cm] cubes

1 egg

2 Tbsp heavy cream

3 Tbsp freshly grated Pecorino Romano cheese

2 Tbsp extra-virgin olive oil, plus more as needed

½ tsp sugar

1 cup [240 ml] red wine

8 cups [2 L] Pomodoro Sauce (page 59)

1 tsp dried oregano, preferably Sicilian

Chunk of Parmesan cheese for grating

Best-quality olive oil for drizzling

Grilled or Toasted Bread (page 77) for serving

In a large bowl, season the pork shoulder and pork belly pieces with 1 Tbsp salt and 1 Tbsp pepper. Add the carrot, half the onion, half the garlic, and all of the parsley, thyme, paprika, nutmeg, and bread cubes and mix together. Cover with plastic wrap and refrigerate until very cold, about 2 hours.

Refrigerate the medium blade, die, tray, and other components of your meat grinder for about 2 hours before using.

With the meat grinder fitted with the chilled blade, grind the chilled meat mixture into a large bowl.

In a small bowl, whisk the egg and cream to combine. Drizzle over the meat, add the Pecorino, and mix gently to combine. Shape the mixture into balls the size of golf balls.

In a large Dutch oven over medium-high heat, warm the extra-virgin olive oil until hot but not smoking. Cook the meatballs, in batches, until well browned all over, about 10 minutes. Take your time with this step. It adds great character to the meatballs if the browning is done with care. Transfer the browned meatballs to a platter.

Continued

Add the remaining onion and garlic to the Dutch oven and cook just until translucent, about 5 minutes. Add more extra-virgin olive oil if the pan is dry. Season with salt and pepper and add the sugar. Add the wine to the pan, bring to a boil, and cook, scraping up the browned bits from the bottom of the pan with a wooden spoon, until slightly thickened, about 4 minutes.

Add the pomodoro sauce and oregano to the pan and bring to a simmer. Lower the heat and simmer, stirring occasionally, until the sauce is slightly thickened, about 15 minutes

Add the meatballs to the sauce and simmer over medium-low heat, stirring occasionally, until the meat is cooked through, about 12 minutes. Simmer slowly so the meatballs don't overcook and toughen. They should be amazingly tender.

Transfer to a serving platter, grate Parmesan over the top, garnish with parsley, and drizzle with best-quality olive oil. Serve hot, with grilled bread.

If you don't want to grind the pork shoulder and pork belly, substitute 2 lb [910 g] ground pork. Pulse the bread cubes briefly in a food processor. In a large bowl, gently mix the bread crumbs into the ground meat along with 1 Tbsp salt, 1 Tbsp pepper, the carrot, half the onion, half the garlic, and all of the parsley, thyme, paprika, and nutmeg. Proceed as directed.

PAN-SEARED CALF LIVER WITH LEEKS & RED WINE

SERVES 2 OR 3 / This is my take on the classic liver and onions, which has been a standard of economy-minded cooks for generations. Many of us approach this dish with wariness, having been victims of less-than-stellar interpretations. But when liver is well seared and cooked just to medium pink, it has a lovably silky texture and rich but mild beefy flavor. Use the cooking pan to build a delicious little sauce to cut through the richness of the liver and balance the minerality.

1 lb [455 g] calf liver, cut into
three ¾-in- [2-cm-] thick slices
2 Tbsp grapeseed oil
2 Tbsp extra-virgin olive oil
1 leek (white part only), cut into ¼-in [6-mm] rounds
Kosher salt

Freshly ground black pepper
1 fresh thyme sprig, leaves only
½ cup [120 ml] red wine
¼ cup [60 ml] Beef Stock (page 226)
1 Tbsp aged balsamic vinegar
2 Tbsp coarsely chopped fresh flat-leaf parsley

With a sharp knife, score the liver slices at ¼-in [6-mm] intervals, taking care not to cut too deeply into the meat. Rotate the slices and score again to make a crisscross pattern on the surface.

In a large frying pan over high heat, warm the grapeseed oil until hot but not smoking. Add the liver slices and cook until well seared, 2 to 3 minutes. Flip the liver and cook on the other side until well seared, about 2 minutes longer. Transfer the liver to a serving platter.

Turn the heat to medium and add the olive oil and leek to the pan. Cook until softened and beginning to brown, about 5 minutes. Season with salt and pepper and add the thyme. Add the wine and stock and bring to a boil, scraping up any browned bits on the bottom of the pan with a wooden spoon. Cook until the liquids thicken enough to coat the back of the spoon, 5 to 7 minutes. Drizzle in the vinegar, taste, and season with more salt and pepper if necessary. Add the parsley and stir.

Pour the sauce over the seared liver slices and serve hot.

CHARRED BLADE STEAK WITH GREEN PEPPERCORN & SHERRY PAN SAUCE

SERVES 4 TO 6 / Blade steak is a marbled, textured cut from the rib end of the chuck. The rib end of the chuck tends to be much more tender and is suitable for a quick pan sear, as in this recipe, as opposed to a long braise.

Four 6- to 8-oz [170- to 225-g] blade steaks (rib end)	½ cup [110 g] sliced Shallot Confit (page 64)
Kosher salt	1½ cups [360 ml] Madeira
Freshly ground black pepper	2 cups [480 ml] Chicken Stock (page 223)
3 to 4 Tbsp extra-virgin olive oil	2 Tbsp Buttermilk Crème Fraîche (page 55)
¼ cup [35 g] Dijon mustard	1 tsp balsamic vinegar
¼ cup [45 g] brined green peppercorns	1 Tbsp chopped fresh flat-leaf parsley

Place the steaks between two sheets of plastic wrap on a sturdy work surface. With a meat mallet or a heavy frying pan, pound the steaks evenly until about ½ in [12 mm] thick (but no thinner). Season generously with salt and pepper.

Heat a cast-iron skillet over high heat until very hot. Add 2 Tbsp of the olive oil and one of the steaks. Cook, undisturbed, until deeply browned and caramelized, about 4 minutes. Flip the steak and cook just until medium-rare, about 2 minutes longer. The meat should feel soft, but not bounce back when pressed with your finger. Transfer to a cutting board to rest and repeat with the remaining steaks, adding more of the olive oil as needed.

When all the steaks are cooked, turn the heat to medium, and add a little more oil to the pan. Add the mustard, peppercorns, and shallot confit and cook until fragrant and beginning to brown, about 2 minutes. Add the Madeira and stock and bring to a boil, scraping up any browned bits on the bottom of the pan with a wooden spoon. Cook until the liquids thicken enough to coat the back of the spoon, 5 to 7 minutes. Whisk in the crème fraîche, vinegar, and parsley.

Transfer the steaks to a platter and pour the sauce over them. Serve hot.

STEAKS WITH SMOKY TOMATO BUTTER & CIPOLLINI

SERVES 4 / I would not suggest pairing this steak with mashed potatoes; the combo would be too rich. You are better off serving it with greens that have a bitter bite—grilled radicchio or broccoli rabe, or dressed raw dandelion greens.

Flatiron steaks are cut from the shoulder, which is a tough part of the cow. It is also deliciously beefy, but for the best results you have to work the meat. We pound it with a heavy sauté pan or a meat mallet. The idea is to tenderize without pounding it too thin, no less than ½ in [12 mm] thick. Cooking this cut past medium-rare is a mistake, because it just gets tough and loses its iron-rich character. Note the direction of the grain, as it is not always clear after cooking. And be sure to slice against the grain after a thorough resting period. The Smoky Tomato Butter is pretty damn tasty and well worth making to slather on the steak or even a piece of toast.

Four 1-lb [455-g] flatiron or shoulder steaks
Kosher salt
Freshly ground black pepper
¼ cup [60 ml] extra-virgin olive oil
½ cup [150 g] Smoky Tomato Butter (page 59), at room temperature

8 cipollini onions, peeled
¼ cup [60 ml] Madeira
¼ cup [60 ml] Chicken Stock (page 223)
½ tsp sherry vinegar
4 lemon wedges for serving

Preheat the oven to 350°F [180°C].

Place the steaks between two pieces of plastic wrap on a sturdy work surface. With a meat mallet or a heavy frying pan, pound the steaks evenly until about ½ in [12 mm] thick (but no thinner). Season generously with salt and pepper.

Heat a cast-iron skillet over high heat until very hot. Add the olive oil and two of the steaks. Cook, undisturbed, until deeply browned and caramelized, about 4 minutes. Flip the steaks and cook just until medium-rare, 2 to 4 minutes longer. The meat should feel soft, but bounce back when pressed with your finger. Transfer to a cutting board to rest and repeat with the two remaining steaks. Slather the steaks with the tomato butter while they rest and you make the onions.

Set the hot cast-iron skillet over medium-high heat and add the onions, letting them brown, about 8 minutes. Add the Madeira and cook down until syrupy, about 2 minutes. Add the stock and vinegar and swirl the pan to blend and coat the onions with the sauce, about 1 minute. The onions should be tender and hot all the way through when pierced with the tip of a knife. Turn off the heat.

Slice the steaks against the grain on a bias and fan out the slices on a platter. Spoon a bit of the tomato butter that ran off while they rested over the steaks. Spoon the onions and sauce around the steaks. Garnish with the lemon wedges to serve.

SLOW-COOKED LAMB SHOULDER WITH ORANGE, YOGURT & HERBS

SERVES 4 / Pairing rich meats with a generous quantity of bright herbs cuts the fatty flavor. This is a radical idea for someone like me, who was trained to use herbs as garnishes rather than as a main flavor in a dish. This particular recipe was inspired by the Persian lamb stews I've had in L.A., made with copious amounts of herbs cooked with the meat. This tender, flavorful meat is great with crispy shallots (see page 66) and brown rice or served over couscous. You can also use lamb neck in this recipe, if you can get your hands on it. Lamb neck is layered with muscle and fat, not unlike pork belly, and this braising method suits it beautifully.

One 4-lb [1.8-kg] bone-in lamb shoulder roast
Kosher salt
Freshly ground black pepper

FLAGEOLET BEANS
3 Tbsp extra-virgin olive oil
1 onion, halved
1 garlic head, halved lengthwise
1 bay leaf
1 thyme sprig
Kosher salt
Freshly ground black pepper
1 lb [455 g] flageolet beans, soaked in water to cover overnight
6 cups [1.4 L] Vegetable Stock (page 222), plus more as needed
Soffrito (page 46)

¼ cup [60 ml] extra-virgin olive oil, plus more as needed
1 yellow onion, coarsely chopped
1 carrot, peeled and coarsely chopped
1 celery rib, coarsely chopped
Kosher salt
Freshly ground black pepper
1 garlic head, halved through the equator
1 bay leaf
4 fresh thyme sprigs
1 cup [240 ml] dry white wine
1 cup [240 ml] Chicken Stock (page 223)
1¼ cups [300 ml] fresh orange juice
2 cups [50 g] packed chopped mixed fresh herbs such as tarragon, dill, basil, mint, chives, and parsley
¼ cup plus 1 Tbsp [75 ml] Greek-style yogurt

Season the lamb with salt and pepper and allow to sit at room temperature for about 1 hour.

To make the beans: In a large soup pot over medium-high heat, warm the olive oil until hot, but not smoking. Add the onion, garlic, bay leaf, and thyme and cook until fragrant, 3 to 5 minutes. Season with salt and pepper. Drain the beans and add them to the pot. Add the stock and bring to a boil. Lower the heat, bringing the liquid to a steady simmer. Partially cover the pot with a lid or parchment paper, and simmer, stirring occasionally, until the beans swell and start to become tender, about 1 hour. Add more stock if necessary throughout the cooking process to maintain a stewlike consistency. Season with more salt and pepper, stir in the soffrito, cover, and turn off the heat.

Preheat the oven to 350°F [180°C].

Continued

In a large Dutch oven with a 12-qt [11.4-L] capacity over medium-high heat, warm the olive oil until hot but not smoking. Add the seasoned lamb, fatty-side down, and sear until the fat turns a deep chestnut brown, about 5 minutes. Carefully flip the lamb to the other side and continue to sear until well browned, about 5 minutes longer. Sear the edges of the meat as well by standing it up in the pan. Once you have a dark sear on all sides, transfer to a plate and set aside.

Add the onion, carrot, and celery to the hot pan. If the lamb soaked up all the olive oil, add another 2 to 3 Tbsp. Lightly season with salt and pepper. Cook the vegetables until caramelized, scraping up the browned bits on the bottom of the pan with a wooden spoon, about 5 minutes. Add the garlic, bay leaf, and thyme; turn the heat to low; and cook for another 3 minutes. Add the wine, stock, and 1 cup [240 ml] of the orange juice. Nestle the lamb into the vegetables, cover, and cook in the oven until the meat is fork-tender, 2½ to 3 hours. Transfer the lamb to a cutting board and let rest.

Strain the braising liquid through a fine-mesh strainer into a small saucepan. Skim off any excess fat. Add the remaining ¼ cup [60 ml] orange juice and cook over medium-high heat until the liquid is reduced by about 60 percent and is thick enough to coat the back of a spoon, about 10 minutes.

Remove the sauce from the heat and, while still hot, stir in the mixed herbs until wilted. Let the sauce cool slightly, and then vigorously whisk in the yogurt. (If the sauce is too hot, it may break when you add the yogurt.) Season with salt and pepper.

Ladle the beans into bowls. Slice the lamb and place the slices over the beans, then pour the herb sauce over the lamb. Serve hot.

GUAJILLO-GLAZED LAMB RIBS

SERVES 4 TO 6 / Although lamb ribs are small, they're fatty, so they have an intense lamb flavor that's hard to get from a rack or loin. Here we cook them slowly in the oven until very tender, and then move them to the grill for a char while brushing them with a tasty, sweet-hot glaze made from guajillo and chipotle chiles. These are best eaten by hand, so pair them with unfussy sides such as sautéed green beans (see page 140) and grilled summer squash (see page 181). If you prefer pork spare ribs or baby back ribs, this glaze is very tasty on them, too.

8 lb [3.6 kg] lamb ribs
Kosher salt
Freshly ground black pepper
¼ cup [60 ml] Chicken Stock (page 223)

GUAJILLO SAUCE
3 Tbsp extra-virgin olive oil
½ yellow onion, sliced
3 garlic cloves, sliced

Kosher salt
3 Tbsp dark brown sugar
¼ cup [65 g] Tomato Confit (page 60)
4 dried guajillo chiles, seeded
½ dried chipotle chile
1 cup [240 ml] Chicken stock (page 223)
3 Tbsp red wine vinegar
Freshly ground black pepper

3 Tbsp extra-virgin olive oil

Season the ribs with plenty of salt and pepper and allow to sit at room temperature for at least 30 minutes, or up to 2 hours.

Preheat the oven to 350°F [180°C].

Pour the stock into a small roasting pan. Put the seasoned ribs in the pan, cover tightly with aluminum foil, and roast until the meat pulls easily away from the bones, about 3 hours. Transfer the ribs to a rack to cool slightly before grilling. (You can do this 1 or 2 days ahead of time and store, well wrapped, in the refrigerator.)

To make the sauce: In a small saucepan over medium-high heat, warm the olive oil until just about to smoke. Add the onion and garlic and cook until softened but not browned, 2 to 3 minutes. Season with salt. Add the brown sugar and tomato confit and cook until the sugar dissolves and begins to caramelize, about 3 minutes longer. Add the guajillos and chipotle and toast in the other warm aromatics for 2 minutes. Add the stock, bring to a boil, and lower the heat to maintain a steady simmer. Cover and continue simmering for 10 to 15 minutes, or until the chiles soften. Set aside and let cool.

Transfer the contents of the saucepan to a blender and purée until smooth. Add the vinegar and season with salt and pepper and pulse to combine. (Store in an airtight container in the refrigerator for up to 2 days.)

Prepare a hot fire in a charcoal grill (or preheat a gas grill to high).

Brush the ribs with the olive oil. Grill the ribs until starting to brown on the bottom, about 3 minutes. Brush with a thin layer of the guajillo sauce and flip the ribs. Repeat this step several times until the ribs are well shellacked with the sauce, forming a beautifully caramelized crust, 8 to 10 minutes total.

Transfer to a serving plate. Serve hot with any remaining sauce alongside.

BRAISED RABBIT WITH BLACK TRUMPET MUSHROOMS & PAPRIKA

SERVES 4 / A farmer friend of ours gives us beautiful rabbits, and this dish is the best I know for cooking a whole rabbit or two. You can use almost any mushroom in this recipe, but we favor smaller varieties like black trumpet, nameko, pioppini, or clamshell, as their size and delicate texture are perfect for this dish. Because rabbits have a lot of messy little bones, we remove the legs as well as the back loins for cooking. We gently braise the legs, and add the delicate loins toward the end, so they don't overcook. I like this served over rice, farro, or buttered pasta, with sautéed turnip or dandelion greens.

Two 2½-lb [1.2-kg] rabbits, divided into hind legs, forelegs, and loins

Kosher salt

Freshly ground black pepper

All-purpose flour for dredging

¼ cup [60 ml] extra-virgin olive oil, plus 3 Tbsp

1 yellow onion, chopped

1 carrot, peeled and chopped

1 celery rib, chopped

4 garlic cloves, sliced

3 fresh thyme sprigs, plus 1 tsp fresh thyme leaves

1 Tbsp tomato paste

2 cups [480 ml] dry white wine

1½ cups [360 ml] Chicken Stock (page 223)

6 oz [170 g] black trumpet mushrooms

½ tsp smoked paprika

1 tsp Dijon mustard

3 Tbsp Buttermilk Crème Fraîche (page 55)

Preheat the oven to 350°F [180°C]. Spread out the rabbit pieces on a baking sheet in one layer and season with salt and pepper. Put some flour in a shallow bowl.

In a large cast-iron frying pan over medium-high heat, warm the ¼ cup [60 ml] olive oil until hot but not smoking. Dredge the seasoned rabbit pieces in the flour, shaking off any excess, and carefully lower them into the hot pan. Brown the rabbit pieces in batches to avoid crowding the pan, about 3 minutes. Transfer the browned foreleg and hind leg pieces to a large baking dish. Transfer the loins to a plate and set aside. Add the onion, carrot, celery, garlic, and thyme sprigs to the pan and cook until beginning to brown, 6 to 8 minutes. Season with salt. Add the tomato paste and cook until lightly browned, 3 to 4 minutes. Add the wine and stock to the pan, bring to a boil, and cook, scraping the browned bits from the bottom of the pan with a wooden spoon, until slightly reduced, about 5 minutes. Add enough of the braising liquid to the baking dish to cover the rabbit pieces by 1 in [2.5 cm]. Cover tightly with aluminum foil and bake until the meat is tender and starting to separate from the bone, 1 to 1½ hours. Remove from the oven and drop in the browned loins, pressing them into the braising liquid, then return to the oven. Cook for an additional 6 to 8 minutes, or until the loins are just cooked through. It won't take long.

Transfer the rabbit pieces to a serving platter and cover loosely with foil to keep warm. Strain the pan juices into a bowl, and discard the solids.

In a large frying pan over medium-high heat, warm the remaining 3 Tbsp olive oil until hot but not smoking. Add the mushrooms and cook until well seared on one side, about 4 minutes. Flip the mushrooms and season with salt and pepper. Add the strained pan juices and whisk in the paprika, mustard, thyme leaves, and crème fraîche. Turn the heat to medium and cook until the liquids coat the back of a spoon, 5 to 7 minutes.

Pour the sauce over the rabbit pieces on the serving platter. Serve hot.

ROASTED HALF CHICKEN WITH SMOKY BRAISED KALE

SERVES 4 TO 6 / I have been serving this chicken, prepared in exactly this way, for quite some time now and it's remarkably well received year after year. Some Gjelina customers order this and only this, despite having more than sixty items at any time to choose from; it's one of those classic dishes that neighborhood regulars seek. We bone the leg, brine the chicken for a few hours, and then cook the legs to order in a cast-iron skillet instead of roasting them with the breasts. This cuts down on the cooking time and allows the leg and breast to finish at the same time. It may seem like a lot of work to bone the leg, but it is actually not difficult and a cool technique to nail down. Buy a whole chicken, find a good tutorial online, and try your hand. Or you can ask your butcher to cut up your chicken into airline breasts and two deboned halves with legs attached. The best way to ensure a good result with this recipe is to get your hands on a pasture-raised chicken that was walking around its yard, pecking at bugs and worms and snacking on leftover farm bits. Make sure you pat the skin dry after removing the chicken from the brine. That will help ensure a crisp-skinned bird.

BRINE
2 cups [240 ml] room-temperature water,
plus 2 cups [240 ml] ice water
¼ cup [50 g] kosher salt
¼ cup [55 g] sugar
1 lemon, cut into thin rounds
4 fresh thyme sprigs
1 dried bay leaf
1 dried guajillo chile

Two 2½-lb [1.2-kg] whole chickens, halved and deboned, with airline breasts detached

BRAISED KALE
3 Tbsp extra-virgin olive oil
1 yellow onion, cut into small dice

4 garlic cloves, sliced
1 Tbsp tomato paste
2 Tbsp Tomato Confit (page 60)
¼ tsp smoked paprika
Kosher salt
Freshly ground black pepper
2 cups [480 ml] Chicken Stock (page 223)
2 Tbsp red wine vinegar
3 bunches Tuscan kale, thick stems thinly sliced, leaves cut into 1-in- [2.5-cm-] wide strips

Kosher salt
Freshly ground black pepper
3 to 4 Tbsp extra-virgin olive oil
2 Tbsp red wine vinegar

To make the brine: In a medium saucepan over high heat, combine the room-temperature water, salt, sugar, lemon rounds, thyme, bay leaf, and chile. Bring to a boil, remove from the heat, and let steep for 30 minutes. Add the ice water and let cool completely.

Put the chicken parts in a plastic or glass container, cover them with the brine, and refrigerate for 4 to 6 hours.

To make the kale: In a large, deep-sided sauté pan over medium-high heat, warm the olive oil until hot but not smoking. Add the onion and garlic and cook until the onion is translucent, about 5 minutes. Add the tomato paste, tomato confit, and smoked paprika and cook until very fragrant and beginning to brown, about 5 minutes. Season with salt and pepper. Add the stock and vinegar, and bring to a boil. Add the kale, lower the heat, and simmer until the kale is tender, about 20 minutes. Season again with salt and pepper, but not too aggressively because the sauce will reduce some more later. Set aside.

Continued

Preheat the oven to 500°F [260°C].

Remove the chicken halves from the brine and pat dry with paper towels. Season both sides of each half with a dash of salt and a generous amount of pepper.

Heat two large ovenproof frying pans over high heat until very hot. Add enough of the olive oil to coat the pans and place the chickens in the pans, skin-side down. Turn the heat to medium-high and cook, basting the chickens with the remaining olive oil and any fat and juices rendered from the birds, until the skin is well seared, about 3 minutes. I particularly like to get some of the hot oil inside the leg cavity. Without flipping the chicken, move the pans to the hot oven and roast until crisp and golden, about 10 minutes.

Remove the pans from the oven and baste the chicken with the rendered chicken fat and pan juices. Peek into the leg cavities. If the meat is still very reddish pink, continue cooking on top of the stove for about 5 minutes. If the meat is slightly pink, then you know the chicken will be done in a couple of minutes.

Remove the chickens from the pans and discard some, but not all, of the rendered fat. Add the braised kale to the pans with enough of its cooking juices to keep it moist. Return the chickens to the pans, skin-side up, and nestle them into the greens a bit. Return the pans to the oven and roast until the chickens are done, 2 to 5 minutes longer. Season the greens with salt and pepper and stir in the red wine vinegar.

Spread out the kale in a shallow serving bowl or deep plate, pour the pan juices over it, and top with the roasted chickens. Serve hot.

CHAPTER NINE
DESSERT

For the most part, I've found high-concept restaurant desserts fail to satisfy after an epic meal. Multiple purées, tuiles, quenelles of strange gelatos, and dehydrated crumbles all look cool, but generally don't hit that soulful note I am after. Even the words "pastry chef" tend to carry pretense that suggests an elevated style. In our kitchen, the word "baker" is more applicable to the style of desserts we want to serve, desserts your grandmother or mother might have baked if you were lucky. It says something about our desserts that our most popular is, essentially, a pudding. Our desserts typically have limited components and often employ some degree of a savory-sweet balance.

We try to stray away from fussy preparations and stick with beautiful, seasonal ingredients that are the centerpiece of the dish. Similarly, we don't want a cloyingly sweet treatment, which is the downfall of so many desserts. At Gjelina, a perfect flavor balance is what makes our final course shine. Whether sweet and savory, fresh and baked, or a singing combination of herb and fruit, our desserts satisfy without overwhelming.

As with the other chapters, picking the right ingredients will make the final dish even better. Looking for local, organic fruits that are in season will ensure that pies, sorbets, and other treats will have the most flavor possible. Farmers' markets and produce stands will be more likely to have only what is in season, and will also be knowledgeable about the best varieties of produce. Keep in mind that you can make substitutions among the fruits, such as blueberries for huckleberries in the Blackberry, Huckleberry & Ginger Pie, to insure that you are making the most flavorful dessert.

Understated, seasonal, but satisfying—this is what we aim for.

FOUR FRUIT SORBETS

During the warmer months, there's nothing better than sorbet to finish a meal. We always serve a sorbet (or several) as our nondairy dessert option in the summer months.

Making your own is a great way to use any kind of fruit at the peak of ripeness. The flavor combinations are less critical for me than the high quality of the fruit and the texture of the final product. The key is to have enough sugar in the sorbet to properly sweeten it, but not too much as to create a cloying result that overtakes the fruit as the main flavor. (The sugar also helps to maintain a soft texture.) The typical errors I come across are too much sugar and an overspun, icy product that has more of the texture of Italian ice than sorbet. A well-executed sorbet should have a creamy texture and tart-sweet taste. It is not unusual to serve sorbet alongside other gelatos in the same bowl so that they can play off each other.

The base recipe for our sorbets includes a very small amount of vodka (or in one case, rosé wine) for a smoother texture. You cannot taste it, and you may omit it altogether, though the sorbet may become a little icier once stored in the freezer. If the sorbet becomes icy, do not worry; simply remove from the freezer 10 to 15 minutes prior to serving to soften slightly.

COCONUT SORBET

MAKES 1 QT [960 ML] / We serve our coconut sorbet with mandarin segments, candied mandarin zest, and fresh lime zest.

½ cup [65 g] unsweetened coconut flakes
1 vanilla bean, halved lengthwise
Three 14-oz [420-ml] cans coconut milk

1 cup [240 ml] agave nectar
Juice of 1 lime
Pinch of sea salt

Preheat the oven to 325°F [165°C]. Place a fine-mesh sieve over a medium heatproof bowl.

Spread out the coconut on a baking sheet and toast until lightly browned, about 5 minutes.

Scrape the seeds from the vanilla bean into a medium saucepan. Add the bean pod, toasted coconut, and coconut milk. Stir over low heat for 30 minutes to infuse. Carefully strain through the sieve, pushing all the liquid out of the coconut flakes with the back of a wooden spoon. Discard the pod and the coconut flakes and allow the coconut milk mixture to cool until warm.

Stir the agave nectar, lime juice, and salt into the coconut mixture. Refrigerate until very cold, at least 4 hours or up to 8 hours. Churn according to your ice-cream maker's directions until frozen.

Store in an airtight container in the freezer for up to 2 weeks.

BLACKBERRY-GINGER SORBET

MAKES 1 QT [960 ML] / Blackberries have a tart, tannic quality that combines well with the heat of fresh ginger. This refreshing sorbet brings all the qualities of a *digestif*, minus the alcohol, to the ending of a meal.

1 cup [240 ml] hot water
¼ cup [50 g] peeled and chopped fresh ginger
¾ cup [150 g] sugar
4 pt [455 g] blackberries

Zest and juice of 1 lime
Pinch of sea salt
1 Tbsp vodka

Set a fine-mesh sieve over a medium bowl.

In a small saucepan over medium-low heat, simmer the water, ginger, and sugar until the sugar has dissolved completely, about 3 minutes. Transfer to a blender and purée until smooth. Be careful; it's hot and will expand when blended, so process in small batches. Strain through the sieve and let cool to room temperature, or refrigerate until you are ready to make your sorbet, up to 8 hours.

Combine the blackberries and cooled sugar syrup in a blender and purée until smooth. Strain through the sieve, and stir in the lime zest, lime juice, salt, and vodka. Churn according to your ice-cream maker's directions until frozen.

Store in an airtight container in the freezer for up to 2 weeks.

RASPBERRY ROSÉ SORBET

MAKES 1 QT [960 ML] / This fuchsia sorbet is bright to the eyes and to the taste.

½ cup [120 ml] hot water
¾ cup [150 g] sugar
½ cup [120 ml] rosé wine

4 pt [455 g] raspberries
Zest and juice of 1 lemon
Pinch of sea salt

Set a fine-mesh sieve over a medium bowl.

In a small saucepan over medium-low heat, simmer the water and sugar until the sugar has dissolved completely, about 3 minutes. Remove from the heat and let cool to room temperature, or refrigerate until you are ready to make your sorbet, up to 12 hours.

Once cooled, add the rosé.

Combine the rosé syrup and raspberries in a blender and purée until smooth. Strain through the sieve, and stir in the lemon zest, lemon juice, and salt. Churn according to your ice-cream maker's directions until frozen.

Store in an airtight container in the freezer for up to 2 weeks.

STRAWBERRY & MEYER LEMON SORBET

MAKES 1 QT [960 ML] / Naturally sweet strawberries and gentle Meyer lemon, a less-tart citrus than regular lemon, produce a bright sorbet that contrasts nicely with a barely sweetened dollop of crème fraiche.

½ cup [120 ml] hot water
¾ cup [150 g] sugar
4 pt [455 g] strawberries, hulled

Zest and juice of 1 large Meyer lemon
Pinch of sea salt
1 Tbsp vodka

Set a fine-mesh sieve over a medium bowl.

In a small saucepan over medium-low heat, simmer the water and sugar until the sugar has dissolved completely, about 3 minutes. Remove from the heat and let cool to room temperature, or refrigerate until you are ready to make your sorbet, up to 8 hours.

Combine the strawberries and cooled sugar syrup in a blender and purée until smooth. Strain through the sieve, and stir in the lemon zest, lemon juice, salt, and vodka. Churn according to your ice-cream maker's directions until frozen.

Store in an airtight container in the freezer for up to 2 weeks.

OLIVE OIL GELATO

MAKES ABOUT 1 PT [480 ML] / A scoop of this works well with chocolate shavings, caramel sauce, or more olive oil and a pinch of flaky sea salt. This gelato is also the perfect topping for Strawberry-Rhubarb Polenta Crisp (page 335).

¼ vanilla bean, halved lengthwise

1 cup [240 ml] whole milk

½ cup [120 ml] heavy cream

Pinch of salt

1 egg, plus 1 egg yolk

½ cup [100 g] sugar

½ cup [120 ml] Buttermilk Crème Fraîche (page 55)

2 Tbsp honey

⅓ cup [75 ml] green olive oil, such as Arbequina

Scrape the seeds from the vanilla bean into a small saucepan. Add the bean pod, milk, cream, and salt. Stir over medium-low heat until steaming and bubbles begin to form around the edges. Set aside to cool completely, about 20 minutes. Discard the bean pod.

In a medium bowl, whisk together the egg, egg yolk, and sugar until the mixture is pale yellow and falls in smooth ribbons when lifted with a spoon. Pour the cooled milk and cream into the egg base, whisking constantly. Whisk in the crème fraîche and honey.

Refrigerate the milk mixture for at least 4 hours, or up to overnight. Churn according to your ice-cream maker's directions until frozen. Remove the ice-cream-maker beater and stir in the olive oil by hand.

Store in an airtight container in the freezer for up to 2 weeks.

GINGER GELATO

MAKES ABOUT 1 PT [480 ML] / I like the piercing quality of fresh ginger. I want as much of that to come through this gelato as possible. I am not much for powdered ginger or extracts; they give you the floral qualities but none of the real punch that makes this gelato special. We generally serve this on its own, with one exception: as a garnish for our sticky date cake (see page 344), which we make in the wood oven and serve warm.

¼ vanilla bean, halved lengthwise

½ cup [120 ml] whole milk

1 cup [240 ml] heavy cream

One 4½-oz [130-g] piece fresh ginger, peeled and sliced ¼ in [6 mm] thick

Pinch of kosher salt

1 egg, plus 1 egg yolk

½ cup [100 g] sugar

½ cup [120 ml] Buttermilk Crème Fraîche (page 55)

2 Tbsp honey

Scrape the seeds from the vanilla bean into a small saucepan. Add the bean pod, milk, cream, ginger, and salt. Stir over medium-high heat until steaming and bubbles begin to form around the edges. Turn off the heat and let steep for at least 20 minutes, or up to 2 hours.

In a medium bowl, whisk together the egg, egg yolk, and sugar until the mixture is pale yellow and falls in smooth ribbons when lifted with a spoon. Transfer to a large liquid measuring cup or pitcher, and set a fine-mesh sieve over the top.

Discard the bean pod. Pour the warm milk-ginger mixture into a blender and purée on high speed until smooth, about 10 seconds. Pour the mixture through the fine-mesh sieve into the liquid measuring cup. Gradually pour the strained milk-ginger mixture into the egg base, whisking constantly. Whisk in the crème fraîche and honey.

Refrigerate the mixture for at least 4 hours, or up to overnight. Churn according to your ice-cream maker's directions until frozen.

Store in an airtight container in the freezer for up to 2 weeks.

BUTTERSCOTCH POTS DE CRÈME WITH SALTED CARAMEL

SERVES 8 / This is the single, most talked about item we sell at Gjelina. Since we work tremendously hard on our entire menu, we would love to see some of this attention go to our more recent creations. But our butterscotch pots de crème inspire childlike wonder, giving us reason enough to continue serving them after all these years. The dramatic contrasts in flavor and texture are deeply satisfying—smoky caramel–flavored custard, combined with whipped crème fraîche, thick caramel sauce, and flaky sea salt.

9 egg yolks, at room temperature

1¼ cups [250 g] packed dark brown sugar

4 Tbsp [55 g] unsalted butter

3½ cups [840 ml] heavy cream

1 tsp kosher salt

½ vanilla bean, split lengthwise

SALTED CARAMEL SAUCE

¼ cup [50 g] granulated sugar

2¼ tsp water

¼ tsp kosher salt

⅓ cup [75 ml] heavy cream

WHIPPED CRÈME FRAÎCHE

¼ cup [60 ml] whipping cream

1 Tbsp Buttermilk Crème Fraîche (page 55)

Flaky sea salt for sprinkling

Preheat the oven to 300°F [150°C]. Arrange eight ramekins or custard pots with a ¾-cup [180-ml] capacity in a large, shallow baking pan. Set a fine-mesh sieve over a large liquid measuring cup or pitcher. Place the egg yolks in a large bowl and set aside.

In a medium, heavy-bottomed saucepan over medium heat, cook the brown sugar and butter, without stirring, until the sugar turns a deep amber color and develops a nutty smell, 10 to 15 minutes. Pour the heavy cream into the mixture gradually (and carefully, to avoid hot spatters), whisking constantly. Remove from the heat. Add the kosher salt, and scrape the seeds from the vanilla bean into the mixture. Stir to combine.

Slowly pour the hot butterscotch mixture into the egg yolks, whisking constantly. Strain the custard through the sieve into the measuring cup. Pour into the ramekins, dividing the custard evenly. Pour hot water into the baking pan until it reaches halfway up the outside of the ramekins, and cover the pan with aluminum foil. Bake for 45 minutes. Rotate the pan and continue to bake for 15 minutes more, or just until the custard has set and doesn't jiggle with you shake the pan. Remove the pan from the oven, uncover, and, using tongs, carefully lift the custards from the water bath and set on a cooling rack. (The custards can be made up to 1 week in advance and stored, covered, in the refrigerator. Bring to room temperature before serving.)

To make the caramel sauce: In a small saucepan over medium-high heat, combine the granulated sugar, water, and kosher salt and cook, without stirring, until the mixture turns red-brown in color, about 5 minutes. Gradually add the heavy cream, whisking constantly until the sauce is smooth. Set aside until ready to use.

To make the whipped crème fraîche: In a large bowl, whip the whipping cream with the crème fraîche until soft peaks form.

Serve the pots de crème at room temperature, topped with a dollop of the whipped crème fraîche, a drizzle of the salted caramel sauce, and a sprinkle of sea salt.

YOGURT PANNA COTTA WITH WINTER CITRUS

SERVES 6 TO 8 / Slightly sour Greek yogurt makes the perfect medium for eggless custards, such as panna cotta. Its tang and richness complement just about any seasonal fruit: macerated cherries, roasted apricots and peaches, pears poached in port wine, or even wild huckleberries (which we drizzle with very good balsamic vinegar). Here, we capture winter in California with various bright citrus fruits and their candied peels. If you can't find an oro blanco or a pomelo, use pink grapefruit instead.

2 tsp unflavored gelatin

2 Tbsp cold water, plus 1 cup [240 ml]

½ vanilla bean, halved lengthwise

2 cups [480 ml] heavy cream

Pinch of kosher salt

1½ cups [300 g] sugar

1½ cups [360 ml] Greek-style yogurt

6 mandarin oranges

1 grapefruit

1 oro blanco

1 pomelo

2 lemons, cut into ¼-in [6-mm] rounds and seeded

1 cup [200 g] sliced and seeded kumquats
(¼-in [6-mm] rounds)

Set a fine-mesh sieve over a 10-by-12-in [25-by-30.5-cm] glass or metal baking dish or pan.

In a small bowl, bloom the gelatin in the 2 Tbsp water, about 3 minutes.

Meanwhile, scrape the seeds from the vanilla bean into a small saucepan. Add the bean pod, cream, salt, and ½ cup [100 g] of the sugar. Stir over medium-low heat until steaming and bubbles begin to form around the edges. Discard the bean pod.

Put the yogurt in a medium bowl and slowly whisk in the hot cream. Strain the mixture through the sieve into the baking dish. Refrigerate the panna cotta until set, about 2 hours.

Section one of the oranges by cutting off both ends. Set it on one end, and use a paring knife to cut away the peel and pith in strips, starting at the top and following the curves to the bottom. Then, holding the fruit in one hand, carefully insert the blade of the knife between the flesh and the membrane to cut out the sections without any membrane attached. The sections should come out easily. Repeat with the remaining oranges, the grapefruit, oro blanco, and pomelo and set aside.

In a medium saucepan over medium heat, bring the lemons, kumquats, remaining 1 cup [200 g] sugar, and remaining 1 cup [240 ml] water to a simmer. Continue simmering until the sugar has dissolved, about 10 minutes. Remove from the heat and set aside to cool to room temperature, about 20 minutes.

Use a large spoon to scoop out portions of the panna cotta onto dessert plates. Top with the assorted citrus sections and the candied lemons and kumquats. Drizzle on a bit of the juices from the citruses and the syrup from the candied citrus rounds to serve.

STRAWBERRY-RHUBARB POLENTA CRISP

SERVES 10 TO 12 / Serve this when summer strawberries are at their finest. Their sweet, concentrated juice bubbles up and oozes over the sides of the baking dish.

TOPPING
½ cup plus 3 Tbsp [155 g] unsalted butter, cut into small cubes
1 cup [120 g] all-purpose flour
½ cup [80 g] quick-cooking polenta
⅓ cup [65 g] sugar
1 egg
½ tsp baking powder
Pinch of kosher salt

STRAWBERRY-RHUBARB FILLING
2 qt [1.4 kg] strawberries, hulled and halved
2 large stalks rhubarb, thinly sliced
½ cup [100 g] sugar
2 Tbsp all-purpose flour
Juice of ½ lemon
Pinch of kosher salt

Olive Oil Gelato (page 328) for serving

Preheat the oven to 375°F [190°C].

To make the topping: In a food processor, combine the butter, flour, polenta, sugar, egg, baking powder, and salt. Pulse ten times or until a crumbly dough forms. Refrigerate until you are ready to use. (The topping can be made up to 1 week in advance and stored in an airtight container in the refrigerator.)

To make the filling: In a large bowl, gently combine the strawberries and rhubarb with the sugar, flour, lemon juice, and salt.

Pour the filling into a 10-by-14-in [25-by-35.5-cm] baking dish. Crumble the topping over the top. Bake until the crisp is lightly browned and the filling is bubbling, 30 to 40 minutes. Let cool on a wire rack for 40 minutes.

Put a generous scoop of the warm crisp into each dessert dish and top with the gelato to serve.

BLACKBERRY, HUCKLEBERRY & GINGER PIE

MAKES ONE 9½-IN [24-CM] PIE; SERVES 8 TO 10 / Nicole Rucker was Gjelina's baker, and the secret to her super-flaky pie dough is vinegar. I've been told that it tenderizes the gluten so that you get a flakier, shatteringly crispy crust. Moreover, the shape and soul of a pie has a lot to do with the hands that shaped it and, for whatever reason, Nicole's hands just make the best pies I've ever had. If you cannot find huckleberries for the filling, substitute blueberries. We make our own candied ginger by boiling fresh ginger in simple syrup, but quality products are available at gourmet shops. Finally, glass pie dishes allow you to see that your bottom crust is nicely browned and fully cooked. Underbaking bottom crusts is a common mistake for beginner pie makers.

CRUST
3 Tbsp [45 ml] hot water

⅓ cup [65 g] granulated sugar

1 tsp kosher salt

2 tsp white wine or cider vinegar

2 oz [50 g] ice cubes

3 cups plus 2½ Tbsp [385 g] all-purpose flour

1 cup plus 2½ Tbsp [270 g] unsalted butter

BERRY FILLING
3 cups [430 g] blackberries

3 cups [360 g] huckleberries

¾ cup [150 g] granulated sugar

½ cup [60 g] all-purpose flour

Pinch of salt

2 Tbsp chopped candied ginger

¼ cup [60 ml] heavy cream

1 Tbsp superfine sugar

To make the crust: In a small pitcher, combine the hot water, granulated sugar, salt, and vinegar. Swirl until the sugar dissolves, and then add the ice. Stir until the ice has melted completely and set aside.

In a medium bowl, combine the flour and butter. Toss to coat the butter pieces with flour, then freeze for 10 minutes.

Put the butter and flour in a food processor and pulse until the butter is pea-size. Dump out onto a clean surface.

Using the palms of your hands, smear the butter into the flour, pressing away from your body with the heels of your hands. This action coats the flour in butter; you will see the mixture change color as you do this, from white to a buttery off-white. Work quickly to maintain a cool temperature. If you are nervous and feel that the butter is getting too warm, scrape the whole mess into a bowl and put it in the freezer for 15 minutes before continuing. Keep smearing until all the butter has been smashed and the dough looks shaggy.

Form the dough into a mound and make a well in the center. Pour half the liquid in the pitcher into the well you've made and mix from the center outward with your hands, incorporating the flour slowly with your fingertips. Start to push and press the dough together to form a shaggy mass, sprinkling the remaining liquid over it and squeezing it until it comes together. Divide into two equal disks. Wrap each disk in plastic wrap and refrigerate for at least 2 hours, or up to 2 days.

Roll out each disk of dough to a ¼-in- [6-mm-] thick round, 11 in [28 cm] in diameter. Line the bottom of a 9½-in [24-cm] pie pan with one round, pressing the dough into the pan.

To make the filling: In a large bowl, gently combine the blackberries, huckleberries, granulated sugar, flour, salt, and candied ginger. (If you prepare the filling too soon, your berries will exude their juices, which will result in a soupy pie.)

Fill the crust with the berry filling. Paint the edges of the crust with some of the heavy cream. Lay the second dough round over the top and press the edges together to seal. Fold the edges under to create a nice fat lip around the pie. Paint the entire top crust with the remaining cream and sprinkle with the superfine sugar. Crimp the edges with your fingers or seal with a fork. Cut three or four slits in the top to allow steam to escape. Place the pie in the freezer for 10 minutes.

Preheat the oven to 375°F [190°C].

Bake the pie for 15 minutes. Lower the oven temperature to 325°F [165°C], and bake until the crust is golden brown and thick juice bubbles from the slits, 35 to 45 minutes longer. Transfer to a wire rack and let cool for at least 2 hours before serving.

CHOCOLATE TART

SERVES 12 / I try to keep our chocolate desserts about one thing: Chocolate. It's difficult to improve on the complexity and texture of well-crafted chocolate, so we are constantly striving for honest and straight-forward chocolate desserts that don't distract from that main flavor. This tart has a particularly dense, rich texture and contrasts well with unsweetened crème fraîche. Pistachios are a nice addition, as well as blackberries, blood oranges, cherries, raspberries, or even the juice from the pomegranate seeds. My recommendation would be to keep it simple and just choose one or two of these accents so you keep the focus on the chocolate.

CRUST

1 cup [120 g] all-purpose flour

½ cup [50 g] unsweetened Dutch-process cocoa powder

1 cup [50 g] almond meal

½ cup [110 g] ground pine nuts, pistachios, or pecans

½ tsp fine sea salt

1 cup [225 g] unsalted butter, at room temperature

¾ cup [150 g] granulated sugar

CHOCOLATE FILLING

1 cup [225 g] butter

2½ oz [70 g] chocolate, 73%–77% cacao

1½ Tbsp unsweetened Dutch-process cocoa powder

1 cup [200 g] packed light brown sugar

½ tsp kosher salt

4 eggs

Whipped cream and pomegranate seeds for serving

To make the crust: In a medium bowl, Combine the flour, cocoa powder, almond meal, pine nuts, and sea salt. Set aside.

In the bowl of a stand mixer fitted with the paddle attachment, beat the butter and granulated sugar on medium speed until fluffy, 2 minutes. Turn the mixer speed to low, add the flour mixture, and mix until just combined. Transfer the dough to a sheet of parchment paper. Place another sheet of parchment on top and roll out the dough to a ⅛-in- [4-mm-] thick round, 12 to 13 in [30.5 to 33 cm] in diameter. Refrigerate for at least 2 hours, or up to overnight.

Preheat the oven to 350°F [180°C]. Butter a 10-in [25-cm] tart or springform pan with a removable bottom and 3-in [7.5-cm] sides. Press the dough into the bottom and sides of the pan. Bake for 10 to 15 minutes, until firm to the touch. Don't worry if the crust slouches down the sides of the pan a little as it bakes. Transfer the pan to a wire rack and let cool completely. Lower the oven temperature to 325°F [165°C].

To make the filling: Set a large heatproof bowl over 1 in [2.5 cm] water in a large saucepan over medium heat. Add the butter and chocolate to the bowl and melt, stirring occasionally, until smooth. Whisk in the cocoa powder, and then add the brown sugar and salt. Continue whisking until the sugar is dissolved and the mixture looks shiny and loose. Add the eggs, one at a time, incorporating each one fully before adding the next. The filling should be shiny and smooth.

Pour the filling into the tart shell and bake until it puffs up slightly and the surface is shiny and light, like a brownie, and the center is set and does not jiggle when you shake the pan, about 35 minutes. Remove from the oven and let cool in the pan on a wire rack for 40 minutes. Gently remove the sides of the pan.

Slice and serve with a generous dollop of whipped cream and a sprinkle of pomegranate seeds.

KABOCHA, OLIVE OIL & BITTERSWEET CHOCOLATE CAKE

SERVES 6 TO 8 / This cake goes down equally well as a breakfast pastry, tea cake, or simple dessert. The deep, mineral flavor of the kabocha, and the rustic crumb it produces is swirled with dark bittersweet chocolate. You can skip the olive oil glaze if you prefer to steer it more in the direction of breakfast.

One 1-lb [455-g] piece kabocha squash, seeded

Extra-virgin olive oil for drizzling, plus 1 cup plus 1 Tbsp [255 ml]

1½ cups [180 g] all-purpose flour

1½ tsp baking powder

½ tsp baking soda

1 Tbsp ground cinnamon

2 tsp ground nutmeg

¾ tsp kosher salt

1⅓ cups [265 g] granulated sugar

3 eggs

8 oz [230 g] bittersweet chocolate, finely chopped

3 Tbsp pepitas (raw hulled pumpkin seeds)

OLIVE OIL GLAZE

1¼ cups [150 g] confectioners' sugar, sifted, plus more as needed

2 Tbsp hot water, plus more as needed

3 Tbsp extra-virgin olive oil

2 Tbsp crushed cacao nibs

Preheat the oven to 425°F [220°C]. On a baking sheet, drizzle the squash with olive oil, turn the piece cut-side down, and cook until very soft and beginning to caramelize around the edges, 30 to 45 minutes. Remove from the oven and let cool. Scrape out the squash flesh and transfer to a food processor. Pulse until smooth.

In a large piece of cheesecloth, wrap the puréed squash in a tight bundle. Put in a colander set over a bowl, and let drain at least 4 hours, or up to overnight. Squeeze by twisting the cheesecloth to remove any extra water. Unwrap the drained squash and measure out 1 cup [225 g]. (Transfer any leftovers to an airtight container and store in the refrigerator for up to 5 days, saving it for another use.)

Preheat the oven to 325°F [165°C]. Butter a 9-by-5-in [23-by-12-cm] loaf pan.

Sift the flour, baking powder, baking soda, cinnamon, nutmeg, and salt into a large bowl. In a medium bowl, whisk together the granulated sugar, olive oil, squash purée, and eggs. Make a well in the center of the flour mixture and pour in the squash mixture. Whisk until just combined. Stir the chocolate into the batter.

Pour the batter into the prepared pan and bake until browned on the top and a skewer inserted in the center of the cake comes out clean, 75 to 90 minutes. Let cool in the pan on a wire rack for 20 minutes. Run a knife around the edges and invert the cake from the pan and let cool on the rack for another 20 minutes. Transfer to a serving plate.

In a small, dry frying pan over medium heat, gently toast the pepitas just until fragrant and beginning to brown, about 3 to 5 minutes. Let cool.

To make the glaze: In a small bowl, whisk the confectioners' sugar with the 2 Tbsp hot water until you have a thick glaze. Add more confectioners' sugar or water as needed to create a smooth glaze with the viscosity of honey. Slowly drizzle in the olive oil, whisking constantly.

Pour the glaze over the cake, allowing it to drip over the sides. Sprinkle with the cacao nibs and pepitas and let the glaze set completely before serving, about 1 hour.

WARM DATE CAKE WITH GINGER GELATO

SERVES 12 / This ranks among Gjelina's star desserts. The sticky, date-sweetened cake is ridiculously moist. Adding a bourbon-spiked toffee sauce and a scoop of ginger gelato pushes it right over the top. It's impossible not to like this combination.

DATE CAKE

1 lb [455 g] Khadrawy dates, or another type of fresh soft date, pitted

2 tsp baking soda

2⅓ cups [550 ml] very hot water

1 vanilla bean, halved lengthwise

1½ cups [300 g] granulated sugar

1 egg, plus 1 egg yolk

2¼ cups [270 g] all-purpose flour

2 tsp baking powder

WHISKEY SAUCE

5 Tbsp [70 g] unsalted butter

2 cups [400 g] packed dark brown sugar

1 cup [240 ml] heavy cream

2½ Tbsp bourbon

Ginger Gelato (page 329), for serving

To make the cake: Preheat the oven to 350°F [180°C]. Butter a 10-by-14-in [25-by-35.5-cm] glass or metal baking dish or pan.

In a small bowl, combine the dates and baking soda. Pour the hot water over the dates and mix with a fork until they have mostly dissolved and are pulpy, about 5 minutes.

Scrape the seeds from the vanilla bean into a large bowl. Whisk in the granulated sugar, egg, and egg yolk until the mixture is pale yellow and falls in smooth ribbons when lifted with a spoon. Stir in the date mixture, incorporating it completely.

In a small bowl, sift together the flour and baking powder. Gently fold the flour into the date mixture until just incorporated.

Pour the batter into the prepared baking dish and bake until a skewer inserted in the center comes out clean, 35 to 40 minutes. Leave the cake in the pan for about 40 minutes before serving.

To make the whiskey sauce: In a large, heavy-bottomed saucepan, melt the butter with the brown sugar. As soon as the sugar has dissolved, gradually add the cream, pouring in a steady stream while whisking constantly. Remove from the heat and whisk in the whiskey.

Pierce the cake all over twelve to twenty times with a butter knife or a skewer. Pour half of the sauce over the top of the cake, guiding it into these holes, and set aside the rest. (The cake can be stored at room temperature in the baking dish, covered with plastic wrap, for 1 day and in the refrigerator for up to 3 days. Bring back to room temperature before serving.)

Cut the cake into squares and drizzle with the remaining whiskey sauce. Serve on dessert plates, accompanied by scoops of gelato.

INDEX